Smuggling Armageddon

Also by Rensselaer Lee

The White Labyrinth: Cocaine and Political Power
The Andean Cocaine Industry (with Patrick Clawson)

Smuggling Armageddon

The Nuclear Black Market
in the Former Soviet Union and Europe

Rensselaer W. Lee III

St. Martin's Griffin
New York

SMUGGLING ARMAGEDDON

Copyright © Rensselaer W. Lee, 1998. All rights reserved. Printed in the United States of America. No part of this book may be used or reproduced in any manner whatsoever without written permission except in the case of brief quotations embodied in critical articles or reviews. For information, address St. Martin's Press, 175 Fifth Avenue, New York, N.Y. 10010.
ISBN 0-312-22456-7

Library of Congress Cataloging-in-Publication Data
Lee, Rensselaer W., 1937-
  Smuggling Armageddon : the nuclear black market and the Former Soviet Union and Europe / by Rensselaer W. Lee.
    p. cm.
  Includes bibliographical references (p.) and index.
  ISBN 0-312-21156-2 (cloth) 0-312-22456-7 (pbk)
    1. Nuclear terrorism—Former Soviet republics—Prevention.
2. Nuclear nonproliferation. 3. Illegal arms transfers—Former Soviet republics. 4. Black market—Former Soviet republics.
5. Smuggling—Former Soviet republics. 6. Nuclear terrorism-
-Europe, Central—Prevention. 7. Illegal arms transfers—Europe, Central. 8. Black market—Europe, Central. 9. Smuggling—Europe, Central. I. Title.
HV6433.F6L44 1998
363.3'2—dc21   98-3793
                                                          CIP

Design by Acme Art, Inc.
First published in hardcover in the United States of America in 1998
First St. Martin's Griffin edition: December 1999
10 9 8 7 6 5 4 3 2 1

To Christine, Nicholas, and Thomas

Contents

Acronyms

AOS	Academy of Sciences
BKA	Bundeskriminalamt (German Federal Criminal Police)
BND	Bundesnachrichtendienst (German Federal Intelligence Service)
CIA	Central Intelligence Agency
CSIS	Center for Strategic and International Studies
DM	Deutschmarks
DOD	Department of Defense
DOE	Department of Energy
FBI	Federal Bureau of Investigation
FSK	Federal'naya Sluzhba Kontrrazvedki (Russian) Federal Counterintelligence Service
GAN	Gosatomnadzor
GDP	gross domestic product
GRU	Main Intelligence Directorate (military)
HEU	highly enriched uranium
IAEA	International Atomic Energy Agency
IPPE	Institute of Physics and Power Engineering
ISTC	International Science and Technology Center
KGB	State Security Committee
LKA	Land (State) Criminal Police (Bavaria)
MPC&A	materials protection, control, and accountability
MINATOM	Ministry of Atomic Energy
MVD	Ministry of Internal Affairs

NIS	Newly Independent States
NPT	nonproliferation treaty
NSG	Nuclear Suppliers Group
SVR	Sluzhba Vneshnei Razvedki (Russian Foreign Intelligence Service)
UF_6	uranium hexafloride gas

List of Tables and Figures

TABLES

FIGURES

Preface

I embarked on the study of nuclear materials smuggling in the former Soviet Union after many years of observing another modern illegal enterprise—the international traffic in narcotics. I have often contemplated the striking differences between these ventures. For example, illegal drugs are distributed in mass markets and the retail sales volume is enormous (totaling hundreds of billions of dollars annually, according to some estimates). In contrast, markets for stolen or diverted nuclear materials are narrow, rarefied, and inaccessible to many aspiring merchants. Indeed, Western and Russian authorities are hard pressed to verify actual cases of such wares reaching bona fide customers. The oligarchic structures or cartels that dominate sectors of the narcotics trade seemingly do not characterize the nuclear smuggling business (although the apparent disorganization of the enterprise is deceptive, as this book documents). Drug dealers often exhibit attention-seeking, violent, and politically obtrusive behavior; nuclear smugglers in general prize secrecy and stealth and leave few imprints on their surroundings. Drugs exact a visible, continuing, and tangible toll on the institutions and social fabric of the countries that produce and consume such narcotics, whereas the dimensions and severity of the clandestine movement of nuclear materials are not known with certainty—indeed, controversy surrounds the assessment of whether nuclear smuggling poses a genuine, significant threat to Western societies and to the international order. However, even a low level of risk can be grave and patently unacceptable when the worldwide consequences are as dire as those associated with nuclear explosions and nuclear terrorism.

When conducting the research for this book, I was constantly preoccupied with the significance question. Indeed, the vast majority of recorded smuggling cases transferred only small quantities of fissile or radioactive material of little or no use in weapon production. Furthermore, the number of criminal nuclear transactions in the West has dropped perceptibly since the mid-1990s. Nevertheless, dangers abound in equating the observed reality of the nuclear traffic with the pattern of such traffic as a whole. The principal underlying origins of the trade—collapsing nuclear economies, escalating crime and corruption, and waning central government control over the nuclear sector—remain essentially unchanged in Russia and the other countries that make up the Newly Independent States (NIS). Conceivably, more adroit and sophisticated smugglers are operating surreptitiously in today's nuclear marketplace, managing a shadow traffic in nuclear materials and components that is far more lethal than that detected by the constabularies of Central and Western Europe. Indeed, some of my research findings suggest that the modalities and routes of this shadow market already are established and that prospective buyers include both rogue states and more pro-Western countries that covet nuclear weapons programs. Readers can form their own judgments about the reliability of available supporting evidence.

The apparent failure to prevent nuclear smuggling from the NIS must be evaluated in context. As I demonstrate, U.S. programs to bolster nuclear safeguards and export controls indisputably rank as necessary and worthwhile. Nonetheless, intimidating obstacles confront the suppression of illegal and covert activities at the source—that is, where the object subject to control originates. Again, the parallel with drugs readily comes to mind. U.S. international initiatives to curb illegal drugs in Latin American source countries have failed abysmally by almost any standard. U.S. programs to prevent nuclear smuggling in the NIS are better conceived and more professionally managed (albeit not better funded) than U.S. overseas drug programs, and distinctly different market forces drive the movement of drugs compared to nuclear materials. Nevertheless, Americans cannot expect a 100 percent success rate from U.S. policies to halt serious nuclear leakages in NIS source countries—no matter how ardently such results might be desired. The United States therefore must devise techniques not only to enhance the odds of preventing new nuclear thefts and diversions but also to limit any postproliferation damages. The efficacy of Western counterproliferation programs ultimately will depend primarily on whether NIS countries can resolve their various internal crises, rein in criminal elements, and reassert control over nuclear industry managers.

A number of institutions and individuals supported me during the intensive research and preparation of this volume. The United States Institute of Peace Research awarded a research grant that helped underwrite the cost of extensive fieldwork and interviews—often difficult and frustrating inquiries because of the intrinsic sensitivity of the topic. I owe a particular debt of thanks to members of numerous Russian organizations for their willingness to share their views on the nuclear smuggling problem—most notably the Ministry of Internal Affairs, the State Customs Administration, the Ministry of Atomic Energy (Gosatomnadzor), the Academy of Scientists, the Kurchatov Institute, the Institute of Physics and Power Engineering in Obninsk, and the Elektrostal' Machine Building Plant. Several investigative journalists in Moscow also volunteered useful background information. Elsewhere in Europe, interviews with officials of the German Federal Criminal Police (Bundeskriminalamt), the German Federal Intelligence Service (Bundesnachrichtendienst), and the Italian Nucleo Operativo Ecologico also proved illuminating. John Large of Large and Associates in London offered useful observations on both nuclear environmental issues and the pressures plaguing nuclear industry managers in the NIS.

In the United States, I extend special thanks to James Ford of the National Defense University's Center for Counterproliferation and to Richard Schuller at Pacific Northwest Laboratories for their advice and encouragement at various stages of the project and for their thoughtful comments on the manuscript. Ambassador Thomas Graham of the Lawyers Alliance for World Security furnished useful perspectives on the urgent threats posed by nuclear smuggling and nuclear terrorism. Interviews with Mark Mullen and John Immele at the Department of Energy contributed background information on U.S. programs to ensure nuclear materials security in the NIS. Larry Ellis of the U.S. Customs Service briefed me on the state of our customs cooperation with these countries to interdict movement of radioactive contraband. Helpful comments and ideas were received from William Potter, Amy Sands, Tim McCarthy, and Emily Ewell of the Center for Nonproliferation Studies of the Monterey Institute of International Studies. My gratitude and appreciation go to Paul Woessner of the Ridgway Center of the University of Pittsburgh for his unstinting dedication to collecting open-source materials on the illegal nuclear trade. Chris Crowl of George Washington University also furnished invaluable research support. Sallie Birket Chafer devoted her superlative editorial talents to polishing the manuscript. Finally, I must pay tribute to the patience, moral support, and companionship of my wife, Christine Lee, who made the completion of this arduous project possible.

Introduction

This book addresses a crucial international concern of the 1990s and beyond—the illegal trade in nuclear materials that has erupted in the Newly Independent States (NIS) and Europe since the collapse of the former Soviet Union—and raises the central issue of whether such traffic poses a threat of consequence to international security and stability. Government versions of relevant events suggest that the significance of the trade is minor and receding, but governments cannot necessarily be trusted to share important details on proliferation-sensitive issues. Furthermore, a variety of sources—some unofficial or unpublished—document the possibility that smuggling patterns that are visible to the West actually obscure more dangerous and lethal proliferation in the NIS.

This book does not definitively quantify the significance of illegal trafficking in nuclear materials in the NIS. The ambiguity of available evidence troubles the author and undoubtedly will give the reader pause. Nonetheless, the overall picture is not particularly encouraging—the Russian central government may be too weak to confront those bureaucratic or regional vested interests that condone or collude in illicit proliferation activities. Moreover, smuggling operations are becoming progressively more sophisticated, and Russian stockpiles already may have suffered serious losses of weapons-usable materials. Although much less problematic, even the security of finished tactical nuclear weapons and small nuclear devices cannot be taken entirely for granted in the post-Soviet context.

A number of policy inferences follow from this book. Preventing the leakage of nuclear materials from former Soviet states probably does not constitute a realistic, attainable goal. Of course, containing opportunities for such proliferation from the NIS—

especially improving security in the Russian nuclear complex—should continue as the cornerstone of U.S. nuclear policy vis-à-vis the NIS. Concrete measures can and must be devised to ensure the increasing effectiveness of such policies.

Two structural obstacles will impede these compelling policy imperatives. First, the Russian nuclear control regime probably was particularly vulnerable to theft in the chaotic period immediately following the disintegration of the Soviet Union (roughly from late 1991 through 1994), U.S.-Russian cooperation programs to strengthen materials protection, control, and accountability (MPC&A) at Russian enterprises started slowly and did not produce tangible progress (measured in terms of agreements, pilot projects, and training for nuclear workers) until 1995. Indeed, according to the Department of Energy, by the end of 1996, only five NIS facilities actually were equipped with upgraded MPC&A systems.[1] Nuclear smuggling incidents during the approximately three- to four-year window of vulnerability cannot be identified with certainty. However, traffickers captured in smuggling episodes in Europe in 1994 reported that significant quantities of fissile material may have eluded Russian government control during the early post-Soviet years. The current location of these materials is anyone's guess.

Second, some Russian managerial practices apparently abet theft and other types of nuclear diversion. Although Russian officials claim that most thefts are the work of lowly workers, major heists almost certainly require the participation of responsible engineers or managers. Furthermore, enterprise personnel can employ (and in the author's opinion have exploited) a range of smuggling channels, including corrupt ministry or local government officials, organized crime groups, intelligence operatives, and even visiting Western scientists. Such channels are not easily detected by Western or even Russian law enforcement agencies. In addition, U.S. technical and administrative fixes and other instrumentalities of U.S.-Russian nuclear cooperation are unlikely to disrupt the patterns of corruption and collusion that give rise to nuclear diversion. In broad terms, the illicit nuclear traffic is the result of difficult economic and institutional transitions in the NIS, including the catastrophic effects of downsizing on the well-being and morale of nuclear employees. Western assistance can mitigate some of these repercussions but cannot repair the underlying weaknesses in the economic and organizational infrastructure.

Historically, U.S. interventions to combat criminal activities abroad have not proven particularly successful. A noteworthy example, the vaunted overseas war against drugs, has failed signally to halt or even diminish the flow of cocaine, heroin, and other toxic substances into U.S. markets. Concerned observers can hope that programs to counter criminal nuclear proliferation will be more effective; I certainly affirm my qualified support for the continuation and expansion of current U.S. counterproliferation policies in the NIS. However, some damaging proliferation already may have occurred. If nonnuclear states such as Iran possess militarily significant stocks of fissile materials, U.S. policy also must emphasize discouraging such states from manufacturing and deploying finished nuclear armaments.

Seven chapters comprise this book. Chapters 1 and 2 outline in general terms the scope, setting, and principal characteristics of the illegal nuclear trade. These chapters address topics such as statistical trends in smuggling, configurations of criminal actors, diversion scenarios and pathways, and black-market transactions. Chapter 3 identifies and analyzes the principal economic and environmental factors that facilitate the theft of nuclear materials at NIS enterprises. Chapter 4 describes the overall criminal environment in Russia and its possible influence on nuclear smuggling dynamics. Chapters 5 and 6 detail reported theft and smuggling cases in Central Europe and the NIS, respectively. And chapter 7 assesses the implications of these findings for U.S. policy and offers insights on the future of the NIS nuclear smuggling business.

CHAPTER 1

THE SETTING

DIMENSIONS AND SIGNIFICANCE
OF THE NUCLEAR MATERIALS TRAFFIC

THE END OF THE COLD WAR signaled the end of direct East-West military confrontation in Europe, the opening of the former Soviet Union's borders to the West, and the redefinition of the U.S.-Russia relationship, stressing the ideal of a partnership in world affairs. Unfortunately, the breakup of the Soviet Union—and collateral political weaknesses and economic dislocations in the post-Soviet republics—also spawned an array of new threats to international security and stability. Such threats stem in part from the uncertainties associated with the transition from communism to varying forms of government in the Newly Independent States (NIS). For example, the West has much to fear from a meltdown of NIS governing institutions, the failure of economic reform in these states, and the regionalization and criminalization of control of the Russian nuclear defense complex. Moreover, transnational criminal enterprises emerging from the decayed Soviet empire pose additional grave dangers to Western countries, including trafficking in narcotics, weapons, nuclear materials, body parts, prostitutes, illegal aliens, and counterfeit money—and, ominously, the wholesale transplanting of Russian criminal networks and resources to numerous Western countries.

The soaring illegal trade in strategic nuclear materials and other radioactive isotopes exemplifies a particularly alarming class of transnational criminality associated with the collapse of the Soviet Union. Nuclear crime was uncommon in the Soviet period. Although uranium thefts were recorded at the Elektrostal' Machine Building Plant in 1967 and at the Krasnoyarsk-26 fuel reprocessing facility in 1971, the Soviet criminal code did not include laws against the illegal acquisition, possession, transport, and use of radioactive materials until 1988.[1] Since the disintegration of the Soviet Union, however, Russian and NIS facilities—fuel cycle enterprises, research institutes, submarine bases, and even weapons assembly plants—have reported literally hundreds of thefts of such materials. Principal incentives for such larceny include the deteriorating economic conditions in the nuclear industry and the widespread if often faulty perception that nuclear substances command huge premiums on the international black market. The rise in nuclear smuggling activities also is attributable in part to pervasive criminality and corruption in Russia and to the weakening grip of the Russian central government on elements of the country's far-flung nuclear complex. NIS law enforcement and security officials can intercept only a fraction of the nuclear materials diverted from legitimate enterprises—roughly 30 to 40 percent in Russia, according to an estimate by the Russian Federal Security Service. Much of the remaining material is transported abroad or simply discarded.[2]

Transnational smuggling chains have materialized to peddle stolen materials to customers outside of the NIS, principally (but not exclusively) in the Central European market. Although small compared to the flow of other illegal commodities such as weapons or drugs, global illegal commerce in nuclear materials is hardly inconsequential, as different statistical indicators attest. For instance, relying principally on seizure data, the International Atomic Energy Agency (IAEA) database identifies 132 confirmed incidents of international nuclear smuggling between 1993 and 1996.[3] The German Federal Intelligence Service (Bundesnach-

TABLE 1.1

Trends in Nuclear Crime in Germany

Activity	1992	1993	1994	1995	1996	Totals
FRAUDULENT OFFERS OF NUCLEAR MATERIALS	59	118	85	40	28	330
CASES OF ILLEGAL TRAFFICKING IN NUCLEAR MATERIALS	99	123	182	123	49	576
SEIZURES	18	21	19	19	7	84

Sources: German Federal Criminal Police (BKA); other German government agencies.

richtendienst, or BND) maintains a global database that documents more than 500 cases of seizures, thefts, offers, or threats involving nuclear-related materials from 1992 through 1996. In Germany, the principal Western European entrepôt for nuclear trafficking, the German Federal Criminal Police, the Bundeskriminalamt (Bundeskriminalamt, or BKA), recorded 84 actual seizures and 576 apparently genuine offers to sell nuclear materials between 1992 and 1996. In Poland, a key transit country for illegal nuclear commerce, border authorities detected an astounding 2,045 attempts to import radiation-causing substances between 1991 and 1996, primarily across the country's eastern frontier. In such cases, perpetrators were turned back at the border. The data unfortunately do not discriminate between true smuggling events and innocuous encounters (for example, travelers with radium-dial wristwatches or radioactive surgical implants).[4]

Tables 1.1 and 1.2 highlight BKA, BND, and IAEA data. These data uniformly substantiate a steep decline in nuclear smuggling activities after 1994 or 1995, possibly because smugglers have concluded that marketing stolen nuclear wares is both futile and unprofitable.

TABLE 1.2

Worldwide Nuclear Smuggling Incidents

Source	1992	1993	1994	1995	1996	Total
BND	52	56	124	177	112	521
IAEA*	n/a	43	45	27	17	132

Sources: German Federal Intelligence Service (BNA); International Atomic Energy Agency.

* As of May 1997, IAEA reported only two trafficking incidents for that year.

Qualitative factors are more difficult to measure—for instance, the configuration of the nuclear black market and the sophistication of its actors. Such factors are extremely controversial subjects in the West and in Russia. Visible evidence from seizures and other law enforcement data suggests that the nuclear smuggling business ranks more as a minor international nuisance than a world-class strategic threat.[5] Few nuclear materials that are offered for sale actually can be used in military weapons in the classic sense; bona fide buyers seldom appear in the marketplace; and amateur criminals and small-time traders rather than large underworld organizations dominate the supply chain for nuclear materials. Yet such a view probably is incomplete and misleading. On one hand, the traffic displays considerable upside potential as a specialty business—that is, smugglers can learn from their mistakes and increase the sophistication and lethality of their operations. As a recent report published by the National Defense University in Washington notes:

> Current patterns of nuclear theft and smuggling may be a prelude to more serious episodes, including major covert exports of fissile material, weapons components, and even intact nuclear weapons. The current level of nuclear smuggling opens new criminal trade channels and increases potential opportunities for proliferation of weapons of mass destruction.[6]

Furthermore, unsettled political and economic conditions in the NIS are reflected in diminished security and controls in the NIS nuclear establishments, factors that contribute to the risk of nuclear breakout scenarios.

More ominously some tantalizing evidence suggests that the nuclear smuggling business already may be evolving in new and dangerous directions and that sophisticated mechanisms for diverting sensitive nuclear materials are firmly in place, at least in Russia. A possible hypothesis contends that two vastly different markets for nuclear materials coexist in post-Communist Eurasia: the disorganized, supply-driven, and amateurish traffic pattern that is visible to Western analysts and policymakers, and a shadow market organized by professionals and brokered by criminals or corrupt officials that poses an immediate proliferation danger and a direct challenge to Western security. The shape and scope of the shadow market are difficult to ascertain; the few credible accounts of its functioning nonetheless underscore the fragility of NIS nuclear control systems and the inherent limitations of Western counterproliferation policies and initiatives in these nations.

THE POLICY FRAMEWORK

Proliferation dangers abound in the NIS, where countries undergoing difficult political and economic transitions confront varying degrees of crises of authority and legitimacy. In Russia, central government control over nuclear weapons–usable materials and exports of sensitive nuclear goods appears increasingly problematic.[7] The strains of privatization and defense conversion are exacting a toll on nuclear control regimes in the NIS and are propelling many nuclear-field employees to the brink of economic ruin. Salaries in certain sectors of the Russian nuclear establishment, particularly scientific research and weapons design facilities, fall well below the national average, and payments commonly lag by three to four months. Breakdowns in discipline and moral standards, increasing openness to bribery, and a burgeoning free-market mentality also create an atmosphere conducive to nuclear materials trafficking. Powerful bureaucratic actors such as the Ministry of Atomic Energy (MINATOM) express more interest in generating revenues and protecting the livelihood of employees (MINATOM reportedly employs or supports more than 1 million people) than in promoting counterproliferation goals. As William Potter, Director of the Center for Nonproliferation Studies of the Monterey Institute of International Studies observes, economically hard-pressed governments may "emphasize profits over nonproliferation," turning a blind eye to violations of their own export-control regimes.[8] In general, social and economic conditions in Russia and the NIS favor the growth of global black and gray markets that "could greatly accelerate the rate of proliferation by other states desiring nuclear arms."[9]

Furthermore, the former Soviet countries apparently lack a nuclear security culture or philosophy, an internalized appreciation of the magnitude of the risks associated with proliferation.[10] A Russian analyst, Valeriy Davydov of the Russian-American Press Information, writes, "The Russian government has never paid serious attention to the illegal traffic in radioactive materials or to related issues of public health and nuclear proliferation." Davydov remarks that Western alarm after a significant seizure of plutonium in Munich in mid-1994 produced strong diplomatic pressures that forced Moscow to assume a "more cooperative stance" on counter-smuggling issues.[11] If Moscow's primary concern is saving face with the West, cooperation in improving controls and preventing nuclear leakages likely will be perfunctory at best.

Against this bleak backdrop, serious efforts are under way to bolster the counterproliferation regime in Russia and other former Soviet states. Assisted by the United States and other Western countries, NIS republics are improving safeguards at enterprises that house sensitive nuclear materials, strengthening export-control legislation, training law enforcement officials, and upgrading customs posts along NIS borders. (The United States is spending approximately $140 million to $150 million on such projects in fiscal year 1998.) As of January 1998, the U.S. Department of Energy

TABLE 1.3

Locations of MPC&A Cooperation
(as of January 1998)

DEFENSE-RELATED SITES
URANIUM AND PLUTONIUM CITIES

1   Chelyabinsk-65/Ozersk, Mayak Production Association

2   Tomsk-7/Seversk, Siberian Chemical Combine

3   Krasnoyarsk-26/Zheleznogorsk, Mining and Chemical Combine

4   Krasnoyarsk-45/Zelenogorsk, Uranium Isotope Separation Plant

5   Sverdlovsk-44/Novouralsk, Urals Electrochemical Integrated Plant

NUCLEAR WEAPONS COMPLEXES

6   Arzamas-16/Sarov, All-Russian Scientific Research Institute of
     Experimental Physics (VNIIEF)

7   Chelyabinsk-70/Snezhinsk, All-Russian Scientific Research Institute
     of Technical Physics (VNIITF)

8   Avangard Plant

9   Sverdlovsk-45/Lesnoy

10   Penza-19/Zarechnyy

11   Zlatoust-36/Trekhgornyy

MARITIME FUEL

12   Navy Site 49

13   Navy 2nd Northern Fleet Storage Site

14   Navy Site 34

15   PM-63 Refueling Ship

16   PM-12 Refueling Ship

17   PM-74 Refueling Ship

Locations of MPC&A Cooperation
(as of January 1998) (cont.)

18	Sevmash Shipyard
19	Icebreaker Fleet
20	Kurchatov Institute
	Navy Regulatory Project
	Navy Training Project

CIVILIAN AND REGULATORY-RELATED SITES
LARGE FUEL FACILITIES

21	Elektrostal Production Association Machine Building Plant (POMZ)
22	Novosibirsk Chemical Concentrates Plant
23	Podolsk, Scientific Production Association Luch
24	Dmitrovgrad, Scientific Research Institute of Atomic Reactors (NIIAR)
25	Obninsk, Institute of Physics and Power Engineering (IPPE)
26	Bochvar All-Russian Scientific Research Institute of Inorganic Materials (VNIINM)

REACTOR-TYPE FACILITIES

27	Dubna, Joint Institute of Nuclear Research (JINR)
28	Scientific Research and Design Institute of Power Technology (RDIPE)
29	Moscow Institute of Theoretical and Experimental Physics (ITEP)
30	Moscow State Engineering Physics Institute (MEPhI)
31	Karpov Institute of Physical Chemistry
32	Beloyarsk Nuclear Power Plant (BNPP)

Locations of MPC&A Cooperation
(as of January 1998) (cont.)

33	Sverdlovsk Branch of Scientific Research and Design Institute of Power Technology (SK-NIKIET)
34	Khlopin Radium Institute
35	Tomsk Polytechnical University (TPU)
36	Petersburg Nuclear Physics Institute (PNPI)
37	Krylov Shipbuilding Institute
38	Lytkarino Research Institute of Scientific Instruments
39	Norilsk
40	Baltiysky Zavod

NIS AND BALTIC SECTOR

41	Aktau, BN-350 Breeder Reactor
42	Almaty, Research Reactor
43	Institute of Atomic Energy, Kurchatov
44	Ulba Fuel Fabrication Plant, Ust-Kamenogorsk
45	Kharkiv Institute for Physics and Technology (KPIT)
46	Kiev Institute of Nuclear Research (KINR)
47	Sevastopol Naval Institute
48	South Ukraine Nuclear Power Plant (SUNPP)
49	Sosny Institute of Nuclear Power Engineering, Minsk
50	Tbilisi, Institute of Physics
51	Tashkent, Institute of Nuclear Physics
52	Ignalina Nuclear Power Plant (INPP)
53	Salaspils Institute of Nuclear Physics

Source: U.S. Department of Energy. *MPC&A Program Strategic Plan*. Washington, D.C. January 1998, p. 11.

(DOE) and its national laboratories were slated to implement new systems for materials protection, control, and accountability (MPC&A) at 53 civilian nuclear facilities in Russia and other former Soviet states. Table 1.3 lists these installations by category. Also, DOE is cooperating with the Russian State Atomic Inspection Agency (Gosatomnadzor) to develop state systems for accounting and control over nuclear materials in that country. "Our multifaceted cooperation has resulted in impressive successes in the past 2 years," claims a 1997 DOE pamphlet describing the MPC&A program. The degree of access to NIS nuclear complexes that the United States has secured under the MPC&A program is an important accomplishment in itself.[12]

The regulatory framework governing legal and illegal transfers of nuclear material also demonstrates progress in the NIS. In 1996 Russia revised its criminal law on nuclear offenses, imposing especially harsh penalties when nuclear insiders perpetrate such misdeeds and when the theft entails conspiracy and planning. The Russian licensing system for nuclear exports establishes an array of degrees and control procedures; lists categories of fissile, radioactive, and dual-use materials; and increasingly compares more favorably to systems of Western states. (Kazakhstan, Belarus, and Tadjikistan have introduced comprehensive export control laws, and Ukraine and Georgia are contemplating enacting such legislation.)[13] In 1995 the Russian State Customs Administration set up a special operational unit charged with intercepting nuclear contraband at the frontiers and at internal customs posts. However, only 25 percent of the customs checkpoints along Russia's 40,000-mile border are equipped with working radiation monitors—a daunting shortcoming from the standpoint of export control.[14]

A modest U.S. project focuses on strengthening the antitrafficking arsenal of NIS authorities—that is, their capabilities within their respective national territories to intercept stolen or illegally acquired materials and to apprehend the smugglers. For example, the Department of Defense (DOD) and the Federal Bureau of Investigation (FBI) jointly conduct counterproliferation training seminars for NIS law enforcement officers; two such seminars were held in Budapest in the summer of 1997. The U.S. Customs Service, with Department of Energy support, is now training officers in the Baltics and Eastern Europe to identify nuclear-related materials, equipment, and technology. Also, Customs administers the transfer of radioactive monitoring devices to the NIS. By late 1996 nuclear-capable X-ray vans were deployed in Belarus, the Ukraine, and the Baltic states. In addition, in 1995 the United States shipped to Kazakhstan 100 hand-held radiation detectors and $700,000 worth of laboratory equipment for analyzing nuclear material samples. (The Russian deployment, however, is still on hold because of a U.S.-Russian dispute over auditing requirements for U.S.-made equipment.) Legal assistance, training programs, technical support, and law enforcement still rank as relatively low priorities in the U.S. counterproliferation efforts in the NIS, receiving approximately $10 million in funding in fiscal year 1998, compared to $137 million allocated to the MPC&A program.[15]

Furthermore, the nuclear materials security issue is gaining a more prominent place on the agenda of international concern. A May 1995 Clinton-Yeltsin joint statement on nonproliferation affirmed an American-Russian commitment "to strengthen national and international regimes of control, accounting, and physical protection of nuclear materials and to prevent illegal traffic in nuclear materials."[16] At a Moscow summit meeting of the heads of state of the Group of Eight countries (United States, Japan, Canada, Germany, Britain, France, Italy, and Russia) in April 1996, participants agreed on a common "Program for Preventing and Combating Illicit Trafficking in Nuclear Material."[17] The program defined trafficking as a "global proliferation risk and a potential danger to public health and safety." Fundamental program tasks address the safe and secure storage of sensitive nuclear materials, international law enforcement and intelligence cooperation to intercept diverted materials, and joint endeavors to suppress illicit demand for nuclear substances and to deter potential traffickers. At the conference, Russian President Boris Yeltsin proposed establishing an "international nuclear counter terrorism center" and examining the possibility of an international convention against nuclear smuggling—a tangible manifestation of the Russian government's apparent commitment to the counterproliferation objective.[18]

Such signs of cooperation and progress naturally are encouraging. Nevertheless, conditions in the NIS still pose a clear threat to nuclear safety and stability worldwide. Losses of even small amounts of the estimated 600 to 700 tons of fissile materials stored outside of nuclear weapons in the NIS could have catastrophic consequences.[19] The real proliferation danger in the transitional states derives from systemic decay: waning economic prospects in the military-industrial complex (including the nuclear sector), a weakening political control structure, an increasingly corrupt bureaucracy, and broadening penetration of the economy by organized crime formations. Such an environment enhances the likelihood of exports of fissile materials and even weaponry to countries or subnational groups with goals inimical to those of the United States. Nuclear leakages can be curtailed to some extent by infusions of Western technical assistance, NIS security and export control measures, improved East-West dialogue and atmospherics, and what the DOE calls "the spirit of mutual understanding partnership and respect between U.S. and Russian nuclear specialists."[20] Nevertheless, existing safeguards and controls can be circumvented easily—particularly if senior nuclear managers, corrupt officials, and professional underworld criminals are collaborating. The success of counterproliferation policies ultimately hinges on progress in stabilizing NIS economies and in developing effective governing institutions and criminal-justice systems in the new states—a process that could take years.

SUPPOSE THE NEWS IS BAD?

Of course, the true dimensions of the current nuclear trafficking threat are not known with certainty. Only a handful of diversion incidents that involved weapons-usable materials were recorded in the 1990s. However, these reports do not convey the entire story, because governments release few details about nuclear theft and smuggling episodes and government information channels themselves may be impaired. For example, over the years the Russian government has issued statements declaring that "not a single gram of plutonium is moving from storage" and that no diversions of nuclear warheads or weapons-grade fissile materials have occurred in Russia.[21] Yet as this book documents, plutonium smuggled to Munich in August 1994 was backtracked to a Russian facility near Moscow, and two nuclear warheads were stolen from a weapons assembly plant in the Urals in 1993. (Fortunately, the warheads were later recovered.) Furthermore, according to one credible Russian observer, criminal groups have commandeered the isotope separation services of Russian nuclear plants to expedite exports of enriched reactor-grade and weapons-grade uranium to various end-user countries in the Middle East and South Asia. This scenario (discussed in chapter 6) is especially unsettling and highlights serious possible weaknesses, if not an outright breakdown, in the Russian nuclear control system.

Arguments and evidence herein suggest that U.S. policymakers must seriously consider the possibility of worst-case criminal nuclear proliferation. If the proverbial genie (in the guise of militarily significant quantities of fissile materials) has already escaped from the bottle, policy requirements and strategies must correspondingly evolve to accommodate a postproliferation nuclear environment. Of course, current U.S. initiatives in the NIS, such as improving safeguards and export controls, still must be prominent as symbols of the U.S. and international resolve to combat nuclear smuggling. However, the overriding counterproliferation objective would be to discourage threshold states from building or deploying nuclear weapons—or to motivate them to exercise such restraint—using diplomacy, economic sanctions, or preemptive military action as the primary policy tools.

CHAPTER 2

THE VISIBLE FACE OF THE NUCLEAR BLACK MARKET

IN ITS MOST VISIBLE MANIFESTATIONS, nuclear smuggling poses little threat to Western security, although some admittedly dangerous environmental effects cannot be dismissed. Nonetheless, most nuclear materials offered for sale can be categorized as militarily inconsequential, and the rudimentary and disorganized traffic is characterized by scam artists, weak links to customers, few brokering activities, loose or ad hoc criminal networks (sometimes more entrapped by aggressive law enforcement officers than committed to the trade), and nonprofessional East-to-West criminal pathways. This chapter analyzes these relatively nonmenacing characteristics of the visible nuclear black market.[1]

RADIOACTIVE JUNK FOR SALE

Most stolen nuclear material marketed in the West qualifies as radioactive junk—materials that might pose environmental hazards but are useless in constructing fission weapons. Only a small number of the reported interceptions in the West and the diversions from NIS facilities entailed "more than minuscule

TABLE 2.1

Seizures of Nuclear Materials by German Authorities in 1995

BINOCULARS CONTAINING TRITIUM
COBALT-60[*]
CADMIUM-109[*]
CESIUM-137
DEPLETED URANIUM
KRYPTON-85[*]
NATURAL URANIUM
SMOKE DETECTORS CONTAINING PLUTONIUM[†]
SODIUM-22[*]
URANIUM ORE
URANIUM POWDER

Source: The German Federal Criminal Police (BKA).

[*] Radioactive sources for education and testing devices.

[†] Microgram quantities of plutonium.

quantities" of weapons-usable uranium or plutonium.[2] Approximately 12 such cases can be confirmed in the 1990s—6 in the West, 5 in Russia, and 1 in the Ukraine. Moreover, most experts affirm that the first weapon of choice for terrorists would be lethal chemical agents, which are easier to handle, deploy, and activate than radiological weapons. Consequently, the current strategic significance of the illegal flow of radioactive contraband can be ranked as modest at best.

For example, in 1995 the typical nuclear cargo confiscated by the German BKA comprised natural uranium, depleted uranium, industrial-use isotopes (for example, cesium-137, strontium-90, and cobalt-60), or components of Russian-manufactured smoke detectors that contain mere micrograms of plutonium. Table 2.1 summarizes this potpourri of nuclear materials. According to Interpol, from 1989 to mid-1995 natural uranium and radioactive cesium compounds accounted for half of all trafficking thefts and seizures in Europe and Russia. Of course, various nonfissile materials, such as cesium-137 and cobalt-60, can be cataloged as intrinsically hazardous components of destructive weapons when harnessed to a conventional explosive. In one widely publicized incident, Chechen leader Shamil Basayev threatened the population of Moscow with such a radiological weapon in November 1995. Nonetheless, such cases are uncommon. To date, terrorist attacks have employed conventional explosives or poison gas rather than the deliberate dispersal of toxic radioactive materials (as evidenced by the World Trade Center bombing in 1993, the 1995 nerve gas attack on the Tokyo subway, and the 1995 bombing of the Oklahoma City federal office building).

SCAM ARTISTS AND BROKEN PROMISES

The players in the nuclear black market (such as it is) include disproportionate and significant numbers of scam artists, hucksters, and swindlers. The following examples typify current nuclear smuggling patterns.

According to the German BKA, outright fraud underpins some 25 to 50 percent of commercial offers of nuclear materials—that is, sellers do not possess or fail to deliver the promised goods. Quoted prices for black-market nuclear wares often are outlandishly high. Black-market prices for low-quality or worthless goods can outstrip the actual market value by a multiplier of hundreds or thousands. For example, the Interpol Stockholm office notes a case of smugglers offering natural uranium for $700,000 per kilogram, compared to an international price of $50 or $60 per kilogram on the legitimate market.[3] In Russia, brokers for 1.7 kilograms of low-enriched uranium (stolen from the Elektrostal' Machine Building

Plant) demanded $600,000—200 times the Russian state price for such material.[4]

Nuclear hucksters in the early 1990s commonly perpetrated the so-called red mercury scam, peddling a mysterious substance touted as an essential ingredient in stealth technology, missile guidance systems, and nuclear weapons manufacturing. Asking prices for red mercury ranged from $100,000 to $300,000 per kilogram. In some cases, the red mercury was irradiated or shipped in containers with radioactive symbols, probably to impress potential buyers with the strategic value of the dangerous material. Yet samples seized by police usually tested as nothing more than mercury oxide, mercuric iodide, or mercury mixed with red dye—scarcely materials in demand by weapons makers. A 1996 DOE report concluded, "No material has been identified or sample analyzed that matches the claimed properties of red mercury—in short, red mercury is a mythical, nonexistent material."[5]

ELUSIVE CUSTOMERS

Few established links exist between sellers and customers in black-market nuclear commerce. Indeed, authorities in Russia and Central Europe are hard put to identify legitimate buyers of stolen nuclear substances who are not linked to undercover police and intelligence operations.

For example, according to the Russian Ministry of Internal Affairs (MVD), from January 1992 through December 1995, only 8 (or less than 3 percent) of the 278 radioactive thefts recorded in Russia produced actual sales. Moreover, all of these sales represented transactions between various middlemen and brokers. Second, and similarly, the German BKA environmental crime chief Peter Kroemer reported that his organization could not cite a single case in Germany of money actually changing hands for nuclear contraband.[6] Third, in a few documented Russian and Western reports, weapons-usable materials were intercepted. However, subsequent investigations could not actually identify bona fide customers for the merchandise. In most instances, vendors were arrested while trying to unearth an interested broker or buyer. Fourth, promising buyers frequently prove to be undercover police. For example, in 1994 three of four high-profile nuclear smuggling operations in the European cities of Munich, Landshut, and Prague were engineered by undercover police posing as middlemen buyers. Fifth, only thin connections link the black market to Middle Eastern buyers. For example, police engaged in a counterfeiting investigation in Tengen-Weichs stumbled across a cache of plutonium while searching the garage of a German businessman. Although documents seized during that search suggest that the businessman, Adolf Jaekle, attempted to contact Iraqi buyers, no evidence supports an actual business deal with the Iraqis.[7]

UNPROFITABLE BROKERING

Professional criminal organizations and players are not very interested in the relatively low profits generated by procuring and brokering radioactive substances. At least, this view is widely propounded officially.

In testimony before the Senate Permanent Subcommittee on Investigations in March 1996, Central Intelligence Agency (CIA) director John Deutch summarized the best available research by emphasizing: "Organized crime is a powerful and pervasive force in Russia today. We have no evidence, however, that large organized crime groups with established international connections are involved in the trafficking of radioactive materials."[8] According to European police officials, transnational criminal organizations active in Europe—such as the four main Italian crime groups, the Turkish-Kurdish heroin clans, and the Colombian cartels—play no discernible role in the nuclear material traffic. In Russia, spokesmen for the MVD and the Federal Security Service routinely assert that nuclear trafficking does not fall within the sphere of interest of major organized crime groups. "There is no nuclear mafia," the head of Russian Interpol told this author. "We can speak only of individual persons and individual crimes where thefts of nuclear materials are concerned." Similarly, an MVD press briefing in October 1995 contended that nuclear trafficking networks develop spontaneously and that no preestablished system for moving or brokering stolen materials is entrenched in Russia.[9]

If the professional underworld shies away from most radioactive commerce, the principal reason lies not in gang taboos or patriotic self-restraint but rather in simple economics. Core organized crime businesses—narcotics, extortion, bank fraud, and raw materials smuggling—produce secure and tidy profits. Locating buyers for stolen radioactive isotopes can take weeks or months (with no guarantee of success), and the radioactive materials must be managed during such market surveys. In many instances, aspiring nuclear criminals have assessed radioactive deals and then rejected them as unprofitable and cost-ineffective. In one disturbing example, according to a source in the Russian Federal Security Service, in mid-1993 in the Central Volga region, a Volgograd businessman anxious to cancel a debt to a gangster reputedly made a unique offer to Poodle, a *vor-v-zakonye* (thief-in-the-law, or crime boss). Poodle evaluated the proposed in-kind payment of 2.5 kilograms of highly enriched uranium (HEU) and a quantity of tritium by dispatching several henchmen to the Baltic states. Negative responses to inquiries about the demand for such substances prompted Poodle to refuse the nuclear material as payment. (The account does not record the fate of the businessman.)[10]

LOOSE CRIMINAL NETWORKS
AND GOVERNMENT ENTRAPMENT

Nuclear commerce apparently takes place in loosely structured associations with extremely varied memberships. Such ad hoc networks usually coalesce around specific thefts or criminal opportunities, including the blandishments of diligent undercover law enforcement agents. Several examples serve to illustrate the character of nuclear black marketeers and associated marketing processes.

Networks typically comprise combinations of active and former nuclear workers, opportunistic businessmen, and, sometimes, petty criminals. In some cases (such as the Munich plutonium caper), participants have no criminal background. In others, according to data from European police sources, histories of key players included drug dealing, car theft, counterfeiting, weapons trafficking, and various smuggling routines. A German businessman arrested with 6.15 grams of plutonium in Tengen-Wiechs, Germany, in May 1994 claimed a prior record of dealing in counterfeit currency. A Czech heroin dealer arrested in Prague in early 1995 also was suspected of delivering an HEU sample to a prospective buyer in Germany. A Turkish smuggler implicated in a major uranium smuggling case in Istanbul in the spring of 1994 had been convicted for smuggling historic artifacts and antiquities.[11] In Russia professional metals traders frequently broker radioactive materials as a sideline. Scientists sometimes support this nascent dealer network by furnishing assay or certification services for stolen nuclear material. In addition, crews of couriers and guards transport radioactive material, charging fees that range from $50 to $400 per day, depending on the trafficking route and the nuclear commodity. At times, ex-government workers such as trade officials, intelligence agents, and diplomats augment nuclear trading channels. In a bizarre 1994 case in the lakeside city of Como, an Italian deputy prosecutor was arrested and convicted on illegal nuclear trade charges, despite his record of devoting years to investigating cases of nuclear smuggling between Switzerland and Italy (as discussed in chapter 5).

Some networks develop outward from specific enterprises, as thieves and their associates seek buyers for stolen nuclear merchandise. For example, in a not-untypical Russian case in March-April 1994, a welder named M. Rogov persuaded his first cousin, V. V. Luagachev, who worked at Elektrostal', to pirate 1.76 kilograms of uranium from shop 46 at the plant. Once the theft was executed, Rogov asked his friend Yu. V. Taimakhin to serve as the middleman for the sale. Taimakhin in turn contacted a friend named Fahid, and together they located a buyer, Kharif. Unfortunately for the perpetrators, Kharif worked for the Russian Federal Security Service, and the entire group was summarily arrested.[12]

Alternatively, networks can be driven by available customers, but such contacts frequently are initiated by undercover police or security agents. For instance, the trafficking chain that transported 303 grams of plutonium-239 from Moscow to Munich in August 1994 included three former employees of the Obninsk Institute of Physics and Power Engineering (IPPE), a Moscow scientist, a Colombian medical doctor with a talent for fencing military goods, and two Spanish entrepreneurs in the construction business. This chain, however, evolved in response to an elaborate sting by the German Federal Intelligence Service and the Bavarian Land (State) Criminal Police, who offered the smugglers a $276-million bank draft to procure 4 kilograms of Russian plutonium and convey it to Munich. Other important seizures of nuclear materials in Europe in 1994 also resulted from arranged purchases by undercover police—notably the seizures in Landshut and Prague. (Both shipments originated from the same consignment of near–weapons grade uranium.)

EAST TO WEST AND MISDIRECTION

Illegal nuclear commerce is also characterized by its directionality. The principal smuggling pathways for stolen nuclear substances (at least those visible to Western police agencies) move from the East to the West, mirroring the haphazard and disorganized nature of the traffic and its economic dynamic of sellers in search of buyers.

At least 20 European countries, from Scandinavia, to Russia, to Turkey, have recorded nuclear smuggling incidents in the 1990s. However, Interpol and IAEA data suggest that the main traffic flows from Russia through Belarus or the Baltic states, to Poland, and from there to Central Europe. According to Interpol, by 1995 Polish nationals constituted the largest single subcontingent of 88 identified nuclear offenders in Europe (18 Poles, or approximately

20 percent), underscoring Poland's central role in the nuclear transit traffic between the NIS and the West.[13] The principal European destinations—that is, the countries where smugglers hope to sell the material—appear to be Germany and (secondarily) Switzerland, Austria, and the Czech Republic. According to IAEA and Interpol data, Germany alone accounted for slightly more than half of non-NIS European seizures of nuclear material between 1993 and 1996 and for almost 60 percent of such episodes between 1992 and 1995.[14] "Its geographical position makes Germany a center. Besides that, we also have solid financial structures; money is readily available here," explained a German intelligence official in response to a reporter's question about the large quantity of nuclear material cropping up in the country.[15] However, nuclear traffic is extremely widespread; at least 15 countries have documented such smuggling in the 1990s.

A well-oiled and professionally managed smuggling system would transport nuclear materials or components southward or eastward across Russia's southern tier in the direction of aspiring nuclear states such as Iran, Iraq, and Pakistan or to Middle Eastern terrorist organizations. For example, Transcaucasia and Central Asia—traditional smuggling routes for illegal narcotics and weapons—are more economically desperate than Russia and ideally could function as a wide-open transit zone for would-be proliferators. As one observer argues, "Known drugs and weapons smuggling routes from Afghanistan through Tadjikistan, Uzbekistan, Kyrgyzstan, and Kazakhstan could be reversed for smuggling of nuclear materials to countries or regions south of the former Soviet Union."[16] The Russian frontiers with Azerbaidjan and Georgia remain porous at best, and no special customs equipment for detecting nuclear contraband exists. Moreover, a Russia-Kazakhstan customs union (also including Kyrgyzstan and Belarus) has eliminated border controls between the two countries, although by now Kazakhstan may have deployed radiation monitoring equipment along its borders with non-NIS states.

A few reports suggest that a southern smuggling route does exist. For instance, an official of the Russian Interior Ministry,

General Vyacheslav Ogorodnikov, observed in October 1994 that unspecified radioactive materials were seized while en route to Central Asia from Kalmykia in southern Russia.[17] Federal Security Service sources disclosed in March 1996 that Uzbek and Kazakh metal traders had attempted to purchase HEU, plutonium, and californium while visiting unspecified nuclear facilities in Central Russia.[18] In 1996 and 1997, at least four thefts of low-enriched uranium and one beryllium theft originated at the Ulba Metallurgical Plant in Ust-Kamenogorsk; most of this material apparently was destined for China or Pakistan. According to a British journalist, quantities of uranium and "other bomb-making material" smuggled from Central Asia and Afghanistan are materializing in the city of Peshawar, in Pakistan's Northwest Frontier Province.[19] Nonetheless, judging from the published reports, nuclear smuggling along the Russian southern tier still qualifies as a trickle, although the potential for a significant flood cannot be overlooked.

Meanwhile, in the West, nuclear smuggling is on the decline, as the data in tables 1.1 and 1.2 clearly attest. In Germany, trafficking incidents decreased more than 50 percent between 1994 and 1995. The IAEA's database of monthly European smuggling cases verifies a 62 percent decline between 1994 and 1996; moreover, activity dwindled to near zero in 1997. In addition, no significant seizures of weapons-usable materials have been seized in Western Europe since mid-1995, as the discussion in chapter 5 indicates. Observers such as Peter Kroemer of the BKA speculate that the downturn is fundamentally attributable to two core factors: smugglers have grown leery after their poor record in marketing radioactive wares, and NIS authorities have improved their skills in preventing thefts and apprehending nuclear criminals.[20]

In sum, the visible manifest market for nuclear materials appears disorganized, chaotic, dominated by bumbling amateurs, and artificial in important respects; genuine buyers with real money seldom make an appearance, even in the few cases where weapons-usable materials are offered for sale. (The absence of legal buyers in the market—especially representatives of aspiring or de facto nuclear states such as Iran, Iraq, or Pakistan—is especially noteworthy.) Moreover, as evidenced by the Munich case, the nuclear materials flowing through international smuggling channels frequently are nothing more than artifacts of undercover operations. Viewed in these terms, the nuclear smuggling businesses represent a small proliferation danger—if, indeed, any danger—to the West. Furthermore, the observed dynamics of nuclear trafficking and the often amateurish behavior of the participants themselves raise serious problems of interpretation. As two U.S. proliferation experts, Barry Kellman and David Gualtieri, noted in a 1996 *University of Illinois Law Review* article, "The crucial truth about nuclear smuggling is that most of what is happening is covert, and inferring the magnitude of the flow or the intentions of the actors from a small share of the known picture very likely is misleading."[21] Furthermore, successful black-market transactions probably go unnoticed.[22] Significant smuggling chains quite possibly transfer nuclear materials that have not been recorded in open source data and in reports by Western law enforcement officials.

For instance, states with nuclear ambitions in the Middle East and South Asia have aggressively purchased dual-use materials such as beryllium and zirconium and components of both peaceful and military nuclear programs, such as ring magnets and vacuum pumps used in gas centrifuges. Iran attempted to procure a centrifuge facility for uranium enrichment from Russia in 1995. Certainly such states also would seek to acquire fissile materials, which are the sine qua non of nuclear weapons manufacturing.[23] What pathways might serve as routes for procuring such materials? David Kay of Science Applications International Corporation proffers a suggestive hypothesis. In an exchange with the author at a conference on global organized crime in Washington in September 1994, Kay noted:

> Let me look at the issue of buyers and who is interested. It is perfectly true, as Dr. Lee said, we cannot find in Western Europe many cases of North Korea, Iran, Iraq, or others buying. Quite frankly, I would be surprised if we did. You know, we have good

German policemen on the German border with Poland. We do not have very many good German policemen on the southern routes of the former Soviet Union. There are well-developed smuggling routes. There are bastions of criminality in the south, which happens to be closer to Iran and closer to North Korea. There are other ways to get material out rather than coming through Germany. In fact, you would have to be rather stupid, quite frankly, as a smuggler to go through Germany.[24]

These observations are points well taken. Certainly a distinction between dim-witted and smart smugglers seems appropriate. Professional smuggling chains undoubtedly would choose direct routes southward and eastward to states in the Middle East and South Asia rather than shipping nuclear wares through Europe. Furthermore, smart smugglers might well have cultivated ties with responsible figures, such as senior managers and engineers inside sensitive NIS nuclear facilities. If so, the composition of the traffic would vary. Unlike the largely inconsequential radioactive substances that typically are marketed, materials supplied to prospective end users probably would comprise quantities of uranium or plutonium that could be employed in weapons without substantial further enrichment or chemical separation. Nuclear contraband would follow direct routes to southern Asia, exiting the NIS via Black Sea and Caspian ports and moving overland across Central Asia. U.S. counterproliferation programs and Western security policy in general obviously must assess several crucial questions—notably whether such a crafty customer-oriented network already operates in the NIS and whether that network could deliver militarily significant quantities of bomb-building materials to end-user states.

CHAPTER 3

CAUSES OF
NUCLEAR THEFT

INTRODUCTION

MODERN-DAY NUCLEAR CRIMINALITY could not thrive in the framework of the Soviet totalitarian state. As a recent study by a group of Harvard researchers declared, "One of the few benign results of that system was the unquestioned control of weapons-usable nuclear materials and nuclear weapons." The disintegration of the Soviet order and the collapse of communism, however, gutted this apparatus of repression, exposing glaring weaknesses in NIS systems of nuclear security. Consequently, "a vast potential supermarket" of nuclear wares is increasingly accessible to would-be thieves and criminal proliferators.[1]

In the Soviet era, nuclear-materials security focused on preventing outsiders from penetrating or spying on the nuclear complex, not on deterring knowledgeable insiders from hijacking radioactive and fissile materials from the enterprises and institutes. The essential features of Soviet nuclear security emphasized multiple and overlapping internal controls (including tightly guarded frontiers and physically remote nuclear weapons complexes, far from major population centers). The noteworthy facilities for weapons design and production, the so-called secret cities, were strictly off limits to foreigners and anyone not cleared for access.

The palpable and ubiquitous influence of the State Security Committee (KGB) permeated even the civilian nuclear operations. For instance, the Kurchatov Institute in Moscow—a nuclear research reactor site housing at least 50 kilograms of 96 percent HEU and a larger quantity of less-enriched uranium—was protected as a "special military object," and KGB guards were stationed on the perimeter and in the institute's internal buildings.[2]

The physical signs of protection—fences, gates, locks, monitoring systems, and the like—ranked as modest if not primitive by Western standards and were deteriorating by the late Soviet era. Many enterprises could not acquire the specialized equipment necessary to prevent employees from simply walking off the site with nuclear materials. Nonetheless, in the authoritarian matrix of the Soviet Union, the nuclear complexes were functionally secure against break-ins. Moreover, the combination of their isolation from the outside world and the paucity of buyers and brokers for nuclear materials virtually eradicated incentives for insider thefts at such centers, at least until the declining days of the Soviet reign.

After August 1991 the crumbling of the Soviet Union coincided with the decimation of Communist control structures, the opening of formerly impenetrable borders, and significant political and economic turmoil in the NIS. These changes had catastrophic effects on civilian and military nuclear enterprises in Russia and other NIS states, leaving them vulnerable. The system of physical protection that depended on pervasive direct control by the central government began to unravel. The KGB was replaced by polyglot guard contingents of uncertain reliability, operating under a welter of auspices: MINATOM, MINATOM-affiliated companies, the MVD, the KGB's successor agencies (the Federal Counterintelligence Service and the Federal Security Service), and the individual enterprises themselves. The closed cities, which claimed no real raison d'être other than the manufacture of nuclear weapons, became virtual economic "basket cases" (in the words of one U.S. defense conversion expert).[3] At the same time, the overall security environment in the cities began to degenerate. As the city manager of one weapons development complex, Penza-19 (renamed Zarechnyy), proclaimed, "The previous system was based on regulations and ordinances which either no longer are in place or [are] not effective and/or military discipline and a sense of responsibility which no longer exist."[4] Some cities experienced an influx of thieves, profiteers, and criminals, who catalyzed the growth of nuclear-related crime. During 1992 and 1994, thefts of nuclear and radioactive materials (albeit not strategically significant) were recorded by at least four sites—Arzamas-16 (Sarov), Chelyabinsk-70 (Snezhinsk), Chelyabinsk-65 (Ozersk), and Sverdlovsk-45 (Lesnoi). The potential for more serious episodes looms ominously. By 1996 Arzamas-16, virtually untouched by crime in the Soviet period, reputedly housed 3,500 ex-convicts. "Crime is worsening" at Arzamas, reads one assessment. "How can we talk about physical protection at a nuclear facility," one resident there protested, "if criminals carrying firearms and terrorizing inhabitants with car bombings are freely walking the streets of the closed city?"[5]

Although prospects for thefts and illegal diversions of weapons-usable materials in the secret cities remain high, the bulk of such incidents were reported in civilian research institutes, fuel-cycle enterprises, and the Russian Northern Fleet storage depots for submarine fuel. Overall custody of nuclear materials at such sites tended to be less stringent than in weapons complexes. Facilities such as the Chepetsk Mechanical Plant in Udmurtia, the Elektrostal' Nuclear Building Plant, and the Obninsk IPPE experienced multiple leakages after the Soviet Union dissolved. In 1993 alone, according to the Russian MVD, employees of Russian nuclear facilities made 700 attempts to "take out strictly protected materials and important technological documents." In the same year, the MVD recorded 900 bids to gain unauthorized access to institutes and nuclear enterprises.[6] Internal controls and physical safeguards in the nuclear sector clearly were dangerously eroded.

MPC&A

Without the repressive Soviet controls, the NIS nuclear sectors are newly and painfully vulnerable to penetration and theft by outsiders. "At the overwhelming majority of facilities, physical protection of weapons-grade materials remains in a lamentable state," noted Vladimir Orlov, a Moscow-based expert on nuclear proliferation problems, in a 1997 article. Physical safeguards such as radioactive monitoring devices and metal detectors are antiquated or defective if not completely absent. Perimeter walls and fences frequently are in disrepair. For example, according to Orlov, 27 of 37 kilometers of the guarded territory of the Elektrokhimpribor nuclear weapons plant (at Sverdlovsk-45) are described as "out of order," guaranteeing "practically free access" to the facility. In addition, trucks that transport nuclear warheads from the plant can "drive in without admittance documents."[7] In another case cited by a correspondent for *Obshchaya Gazeta,* a group of ecologists in the city of Perm (near the Urals) conducted an exercise to infiltrate a nuclear weapons depot in a forest outside the city. The reputed depot proved to be ordinary aircraft hangars crammed with warheads. The mock terrorists encountered "no special difficulty" (according to the paper's account) in crossing all of the security barriers and reached the hangars within minutes.[8] At the Sevmorput submarine base in Murmansk, where 4.5 kilograms of HEU nuclear fuel were diverted in 1993, holes were evident in fences and only rusted-out alarms connected the guard post to the uranium storage building.[9] Gaining access to the fuel storehouse was child's play, according to case investigator Mikhail Kulik of the Northern Fleet's Military Procuracy, who portrayed the status of the theft site: "On the side facing the Kola gulf there was no barrier at all. You could take a small boat and sail right in, especially at night, and do whatever you wanted. On the side facing the Murmansk industrial zone there were shipbuilding plants, wood-working facilities, that is to say, an unprotected industrial zone. Here then were holes in the fence everywhere. And even if there were not any child could loosen the half-rotten boards and walk in."[10]

At certain research facilities, extremely insecure storage systems were in place before MPC&A improvements. For instance, at Building-116 of the Kurchatov Institute, no metal detectors were installed to deter theft until 1994. Employees were not searched when they entered and departed the premises. Moreover, the fence surrounding the building apparently "had holes in it that the staff often used as a shortcut to the cafeteria."[11] Similar security shortcomings infected other NIS settings. For example, at the Almaty branch of the National Nuclear Research Center in Kazakhstan, which stores HEU fuel (36 percent and 90 percent U-235), current physical protection is "at a zero level," commented an American researcher after a May 1996 visit. Buildings were crumbling; the grounds were overgrown with weeds, tall grass, and trees; and electricity was disconnected in parts of the compound to save money. "Perfunctory barbed wire had been placed around the top of the wall," noted the visitor, "but long branches of large leafy trees stretched easily over the wall and into the compound."[12]

Conditions in the larger society highlight the threat posed by lax security safeguards at nuclear enterprises. In the post-Soviet (and post-KGB) era, individual security guards are susceptible to bribes to permit nuclear materials to pass through checkpoints. "Guards will turn off any alarm system for a few moments for 1,000 rubles," proclaimed an unnamed nuclear dealer who described Elektrostal' security in mid-1993. "But if you have to bring out a kilo it will be much more expensive—and not in rubles."[13] Furthermore, in the prevailing climate of crime and corruption, police officers, security operatives, and other government officials might be tempted to accept payoffs or even to dabble in trading radioactive materials.

An additional proliferation danger arises from deficient accounting and control of nuclear materials in the NIS. Weapons-usable uranium and plutonium are stored at widely scattered sites. Principal locations include 80 to 100 facilities encompassing several institutes, fuel-cycle enterprises, weapons assembly plants, and naval fuel storehouses. (See table 3.1.) Each facility, however, may be comprised of several storage areas; hence, the Russian State Atomic Inspection Agency Gosatomnadzor (GAN) estimates that close to 1,000 individual locations may house uranium and plutonium.[14] Because GAN currently enjoys little or no access to the defense nuclear sector (weapons assembly plants, facilities produc-

TABLE 3.1

Principal Types of Nuclear Facilities
Housing Weapons-Usable Uranium or Plutonium, Russia

Type	Example
WEAPONS MATERIAL PRODUCTION	TOMSK-7 (SEVERSK)
WEAPONS RESEARCH AND DESIGN	ARZAMAS-16 (SAROV)
WEAPONS ASSEMBLY	SVERDLOVSK-45 (LESNOI)
RESEARCH INSTITUTES	OBNINSK INSTITUTE OF PHYSICS AND POWER ENGINEERING
FUEL PRODUCTION AND FABRICATION	ELEKTROSTAL'
NAVAL FUEL STORAGE	SEVEROMORSK, MURMANSK

ing nuclear explosives, naval fuel storehouses, and the like), the actual number probably ranges even higher. Thus DOE faces a daunting challenge in introducing comprehensive and up-to-date control systems at such dispersed and diverse locations. For example, at the Kurchatov Institute—an early beneficiary of the laboratory-to-laboratory MPC&A program—only 2 of 28 storage areas for bomb-grade materials were covered by the program in late 1996. Similarly, at the Obninsk IPPE, 10 experimental reactors operating with HEU (including weapons-grade HEU) still were not enrolled in that institute's cooperative project by the end of 1996.[15]

Simply tallying the material stored at different sites represents another daunting challenge. The prevailing inventory control practices in Soviet times emphasized checking documents and containers rather than actual stocks—the rigid Soviet system did not require more elaborate procedures. Today Russia still has not implemented a state system for materials accounting. Managers of laboratories and other facilities that safeguard large quantities of weapons-usable uranium or plutonium often cannot quantify the nuclear material in their facilities, so they cannot conclusively determine whether any material is missing. According to an American intelligence source, some Russian research laboratories "haven't opened up containers for decades to see if the nuclear material inside matches what was listed on their inventories."[16] Furthermore, a recent National Research Council report indicates that some Russian enterprises maintained stocks of material "off the books," suggesting that inventory records, if they exist, may be unreliable.[17] Currently many NIS enterprises are beginning the laborious process of cross-checking physical inventories at specific locations against the documented lists of nuclear materials delivered for storage. For example, the Experimental Physical Division at the Obninsk IPPE is verifying the weight and isotopic content of fissile materials and other elements in the roughly 70,000 to 80,000 fuel disks used in various combinations in the institute's experimental reactors. By December 1996 nearly 33,000 disks had been examined and marked with bar codes, using special U.S.-designed measuring equipment. IPPE managers stress that a thief could easily pocket one or several uninventoried disks and replace them with substitutes containing lead, sodium, or some other nonradioactive metal.[18]

A related problem stems from the Soviet practice of using standard projections of rates of loss during fissile materials production rather than measuring actual losses. For instance, at the Elektrostal' Machine Building Plant, "estimated disappearance of uranium in one production line reached 100 kilograms per year; such a wide error margin allowed prospective thieves to remove large amounts of material from production with a fairly small risk of detection."[19] At the Luch' Scientific-Production Association in Podolsk, an engineer removed 1.5 kilograms of weapons-grade uranium from the plant in an astonishing 20 to 25 separate diversions between May and September 1995. Laboratory procedures at Luch' authorized a certain percentage of "irretrievable loss" of nuclear material in technical operations; moreover, no radiation monitors guarded the doors of the plant. The thefts thus went undetected (although the perpetrator was later arrested at the Podolsk railway station, carrying the uranium to Moscow in search of a buyer).[20]

During the Soviet era, material control systems were not used to establish custody over and monitor nuclear material. According to U.S. nuclear experts, four main elements make up such systems: (1) equipping containers and vaults with seals that indicate possible tampering, (2) using badges and personnel identification equipment to control access to nuclear material areas, (3) installing television cameras to maintain surveillance over nuclear inventories, and (4) requiring two or more authorized people to observe the removal of materials from storage.[21] Only recently have NIS nuclear facilities begun to introduce such procedures.

As mentioned in chapter 1, the United States is funding a significant initiative to improve MPC&A at approximately 80 to 100 NIS facilities that house direct-use nuclear material. Approximately $570 million was allocated for this program through January 1999. The new systems incorporate an array of technical and administrative features designed to prevent nuclear thefts—portal monitors, coded locks, bar codes and seals, video surveillance cameras, computerized accounting, and "integrated planning, implementation, and effectiveness evaluations."[22] The importance of MPC&A in deterring leakages of nuclear materials is widely acknowledged; nevertheless, the program represents an imperfect technical response to a multidimensional threat. Several program limitations must be addressed. First, the program was implemented slowly. Overall U.S. expenditures—including Department of Defense and Department of Energy funding—on MPC&A in Russia was a minuscule $3.8 million in 1994, supporting mainly three pilot projects at Arzamas-16, the Kurchatov Institute, and IPPE.[23] The program accelerated in later years; however, MPC&A upgrades were in place at only 17 NIS facilities by the end of 1997 and are scheduled for installation at 10 additional sites during 1998. A huge window of opportunity clearly beckoned would-be nuclear thieves in the immediate post-Soviet years, and that window is closing only gradually, as documented in figure 3.1. Second, as Dr. Thomas Cochran of the National Resource Defense Council notes, the new equipment and technical procedures primarily offered protection against "the single outsider acting on his own to divert material: a lower level employee."[24] Technical fixes are less effective against collusive arrangements among senior managers, guards, and criminals or corrupt officials outside the plant. Managers at Obninsk, Kurchatov, and other Russian nuclear enterprises readily admit that well-placed insiders can act in concert to circumvent the safeguards. In the last analysis, an effective custodial system depends on coherent institutions and a stable order in the society at large, preconditions that to a large extent ruptured as a result of social and economic upheaval in the NIS countries. Third, as William Potter argued, Russia lacks a fully developed safeguards culture that observes technical norms and procedures, activates alarms and sensors, and maintains equipment; in the absence of such a culture, the new systems will not achieve their objectives. According to Potter, an educational curriculum is required to alter habits that compromise nuclear security, such as "undervaluation of physical protection rules and regulations" and "an avoidance of individual initiative and the neglect of employee safety." An influx of money alone will not solve the problem, he concluded.[25] The downsizing of the nuclear industry catastrophically corroded employee well-being and morale, greatly increasing the risk of nuclear theft—a reality that U.S. and Western policymakers imperfectly recognize.

THE ECONOMY OF THE NUCLEAR SECTOR

Hard times befell the individual member states of the former Soviet Union after the collapse of the Soviet order. In Russia, home to the vast majority of nuclear sites that store weapons-grade materials, real gross domestic product (GDP) plunged an average of more than 10 percent per year between 1991 and 1995 and continued the downward spiral through 1996, when GDP fell 6 percent.[26] The

FIGURE 3.1

Development of MPC&A Programs, 1994–1998

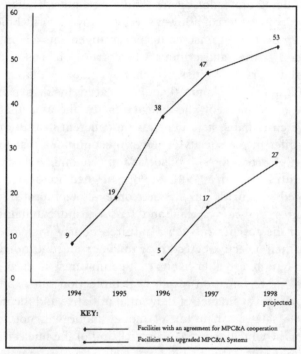

KEY:

◆———— Facilities with an agreement for MPC&A cooperation
●———— Facilities with upgraded MPC&A Systems

Source: DOE.

Russian economy recorded a small gain of 0.4 percent in 1997, but fell 4.6 percent in 1998. Much of the industrial economy of the Soviet era is virtually pulverized. Defense orders in Russia plummeted 68 percent from 1991 to 1992.[27] The machine-building industry shrank by more than 80 percent from 1992 to 1996.[28] General economic decline and the dearth of new orders for nuclear weapons compelled a major downsizing of the atomic energy industry. Consequently, the entire nuclear fuel cycle is paralyzed by insufficient funds. According to a December 1996 report in *The Moscow*

Tribune, Russia's nuclear complex (exclusive of power stations) still is owed $564 million for products already supplied to the state and for other purchases; concomitantly, unpaid wages in the industry total $100 million.[29] At the Kurchatov Institute, fully 73 percent of recent invoices were still outstanding by late October 1996, and payments on many accounts were promissory notes (*tsennye bumagy*) rather than cash.[30]

The forced downsizing of the nuclear complex and a generally poor economic outlook have devastated employee well-being and morale. Once the cream of Soviet society, scientists cleared for work in nuclear enterprises enjoyed a higher standard of living than their colleagues in nonsecret lines of work. Today the salaries of nuclear scientists rank among the worst in Russia—as low as $50 per month. According to Vladimir Orlov, for personnel working with nuclear weapons and weapons-grade materials at Arzamas-16 (Sarov), compensation exceeded the minimum subsistence level by a factor of 4.5 in 1991 but sank to an average of only one-third subsistence throughout 1996. "And this is for people with nuclear bombs in their hands," he remarked.[31] As table 3.2 documents, the 1996 salaries at some MINATOM facilities totaled only one-third to three-fifths of the national average, although employees in the Ministry of Defense direct chain of command fared somewhat better. The head of the Russian nuclear inspection agency stated in early 1994 that "highly qualified specialists who work in secret nuclear towns earn less than the cleaning women who work in the Moscow subway."[32] The payment schedule for wages tends to be irregular, but such erratic remuneration also characterizes most of the rest of the Russian military-industrial complex. These problems apparently have precipitated monthly strikes and work stoppages in several of Russia's so-called secret cities. In October 1996, nuclear industry workers drew public attention to their plight by picketing the Ministry of Finance in Moscow. In December, more than a dozen employees of the St. Petersburg nuclear power plant, which generates most of the city's electric power, commandeered the control room and threatened to close down the plant unless months of back wages were paid. The

TABLE 3.2

Average Monthly Base Salaries in Russia at Different Types of Nuclear Enterprises, 1996

Types of Enterprises	Salary
MILITARY EMPLOYEES, 12TH DEPARTMENT OF MINISTRY OF DEFENSE (FOR NUCLEAR SECURITY)	$335
CIVILIAN EMPLOYEES, 12TH DEPARTMENT OF MINISTRY OF DEFENSE (FOR NUCLEAR SECURITY)	$205
ATOMIC POWER STATIONS	$180
RUSSIAN AVERAGE	$160
ELEKTROSTAL' MACHINE BUILDING PLANT	$155
RESEARCH OR WEAPONS DESIGN FACILITIES:	
Obninsk Institute of Physics and Power Engineering (IPPE)	$90
Kurchatov Institute, Moscow	$80
Chelyabinsk-70	$50

Sources: interviews and Russian press articles

Russian government immediately flew more than 1 billion rubles in cash to the facility, staving off the crisis for the time being.[33]

Psychological impairment—a sense of loss of function and purpose among employees—also exacerbates the soaring rate of nuclear crime. The Kurchatov Institute's security director, Nikolai Bondarev, describes nuclear workers as "unneeded and unwanted, forlorn and forgotten."[34] As Yevgeniy Korolev, a former nuclear scientist who heads a trading consortium in Yekaterinburg, told this author in September 1994, "In just a few years, these people have gone from being valuable and respected members of society to being superfluous. They are stealing not just to make a living, but also because they are angry."[35]

The quality and reliability of the nuclear workforce constitute additional concerns. Nuclear enterprises are coping with a hemorrhaging of talent, especially younger professionals. For new employees, security clearances are perfunctory or are waived entirely, in contrast to the Soviet era, when prospective employees were subjected to extensive background checks by the KGB.[36] Moreover, discipline and control in the nuclear workforce have deteriorated markedly, because many employees must hold second jobs just to make ends meet. According to Kurchatov security chief Bondarev, by 1994 fully half of all the institute's employees moonlighted in various commercial operations, joint ventures, and laboratories.[37]

The general malaise afflicting NIS nuclear complexes has engendered criminality and corruption at varying levels of nuclear decision making. The rash of thefts of nuclear and radioactive materials from NIS facilities represents the most obvious manifestation. However, the lines between criminal behavior and deliberate state policy are not always so easy to draw. "The Atomic Energy Ministry and other ministries working with [it] have a broad range of international contacts. Foreign associates come in from abroad, and all sorts of tempting offers are made. The materials that the Atomic Energy Ministry controls can certainly be the goal of serious business deals, and such deals are not always legal," says Aleksandr Emelyanenkov, deputy editor of the Moscow magazine *Observer.* He and others suspect that ostensibly private companies established under the aegis of MINATOM have served as conduits for the undercover export of nuclear materials, technology, and expertise.[38] One MINATOM creation, the Chetek Company (*Chetek* is an acronym for the Russian words for man, technology, and capital), at one time proposed selling "peaceful" nuclear explosives in order to eliminate radioactive and toxic waste. The apparent objective of generating hard currency by pressing retired nuclear weapons into service ranks as an abominable creative marketing ploy by almost any standard.[39]

In the view of U.S. specialists, MINATOM's insouciance about the danger of lax nuclear security and consequent proliferation is evidenced in the ministry's nuclear cooperation agreements with Iran—a country that reputedly is actively procuring technology and components for the manufacture of atomic weapons. For instance, in a 1995 protocol with the Iranian Atomic Energy Organization, MINATOM agreed to complete a 1,000-megawatt nuclear reactor for a power plant in Bushehr, equip a uranium mine, negotiate the sale of a gas centrifuge facility for uranium enrichment, supply a light-water reactor (30 to 50 megawatts) for research purposes, supply 2,000 tons of natural uranium, and train Iranian nuclear specialists at Russian higher educational institutions. Negotiations also are under way to build a second nuclear reactor at Bushehr and to construct two 440-megawatt nuclear reactors for a power plant in northern Iran. The total estimated value of signed contracts and planned deals with Iran ranges between $3 billion and $8 billion.[40] MINATOM apparently was convinced that the hard-currency streams produced by these arrangements clearly outweighed the risks of advancing Iran's technology and skills for manufacturing nuclear weapons. Under strong diplomatic pressure from the United States, Russia later reneged on the centrifuge transaction and canceled the light-water research reactor deal. However, the Bushehr reactor and other components of the Russian-Iranian package apparently are still progressing, although MINATOM chief Victor Mikhailov reports that, as of mid-1997, construction at Bushehr was delayed by problems with "financial flows."[41]

MINATOM cash-flow concerns also prompted the planned sale of two light-water reactors to India—a de facto nuclear state that has refused to sign the nuclear nonproliferation treaty (NPT)—for an estimated $3 billion to $4 billion. As Mikhailov explained, "We must expand our exports . . . we will use the export earnings to repay our debts." Washington views the proposed sale as a violation of the 1992 suppliers' agreement that forbids exports of nuclear technology to nonnuclear weapons states that do not subscribe to the NPT and do not allow international inspections of key nuclear facilities.

However, the Russians contend that the sale will not enhance India's military potential. Indeed, since India exploded a nuclear device in 1974, conducted two more rounds of nuclear tests in May 1998, and already has stockpiled enough plutonium to make an estimated 60 to 80 atomic weapons, U.S. proliferation concerns probably are misplaced or irrelevant in this case.[42]

Nonetheless, U.S. policy legitimately advocates preventing or discouraging Iran, Iraq, and other aspiring nuclear states from acquiring the technology to produce nuclear weapons. U.S. objections to Iran's acquisition of centrifuge enrichment technology are particularly well founded—more so than its concerns about Bushehr and other power reactor projects in that country.[43] According to some researchers, existing international controls and U.S. diplomatic pressure have significantly impaired Iran's plans to develop an independent uranium enrichment capability. Cases in point include the cancellation of the Russian centrifuge deal and China's September 1997 decision not to sell Iran a uranium hexafloride plant. (Uranium hexafloride is a raw material that can be enriched in centrifuges to weapons-grade uranium.)[44] Two U.S. analysts, Andrew Koch and Jeanette Wolf, deduce that tightened export controls in supplier countries and increased international awareness of proliferation risks have "played a large role in restraining Iran's nuclear ambitions." They conclude, "Unless it secures weapons-grade fissile materials on the black market, Tehran is unlikely to have the ability to field even simple nuclear weapons for the next 10 to 15 years."[45] Of course, this caveat constitutes a huge "if." Iran's clandestine procurement of fissile material already may have accelerated that country's timetable for developing nuclear arms, as I argue later.

PROXIMATE CAUSES

The intimidating structural problems that confound Russian nuclear enterprises—weak and ineffectual physical safeguards, primitive accounting practices, and an economically desperate and increasingly undisciplined workforce—create a fertile environment for insider thefts of nuclear material. Some anecdotal evidence, however, suggests that nuclear criminality among enterprise employees and their outside associates is aggravated by media hype about the escapades of nuclear criminals and the allegedly fabulous prices secured for stolen wares and is incited to some degree by police infiltration of the market to trap unwary thieves and smugglers. For instance, Yuriy Smirnov, the engineer who absconded with 1.5 kilograms of weapons-grade uranium from the Luch' Scientific Production Association, recounts that "as luck would have it, I came across an article in *Komsomolskaya Pravda*" (a Moscow newspaper) about "several people who stole uranium" weighing 1,200 grams. Like many Russian nuclear material thieves, Smirnov had no preexisting relationship with a broker or buyer. "I didn't think of how I would sell it," the engineer confessed. "I thought I would just wander around Moscow. There are all sorts of firms and offers there. I would just look at the names."[46]

The media certainly deserves a share of the blame for adventurous nuclear criminal acts, especially when it inflates the expectations of prospective nuclear criminals. Published reports typically do not cite actual black-market prices for nuclear contraband because money rarely changes hands. (In Germany, for instance, the BKA cannot confirm a single such sale in the 1990s.) The media therefore list figures sought by sellers or offered by undercover police buyers. Table 3.3, compiled from data published in *Komsomolskaya Pravda,* lists the sums supposedly fetched by different nuclear commodities in Germany in early 1994. Most of these prices can be considered nominal or fictitious rather than genuine proceeds.

Purchases arranged by law enforcement officers are another proximate cause of nuclear theft and smuggling. A classic Western sting operation culminated in the previously mentioned seizure of plutonium in Munich in August 1996. BND and Bavarian state police operatives offered the suppliers a bank credit of $276 million to bring 4 kilograms of plutonium from Moscow to Munich; the confiscated 363 grams were the first installment. A MINATOM

TABLE 3.3

Nominal Black-Market Prices of Nuclear and Radioactive Commodities in Germany, Early 1994

Commodity	Price (per kilogram)
URANIUM: Enriched Highly Enriched	$100,000 TO $1 MILLION $1 MILLION TO $60 MILLION
PLUTONIUM	$700,000 TO $1 MILLION
CESIUM-137	$100,000 TO $1 MILLION
CESIUM-133	$30,000 TO $50,000
OSMIUM-187	$70 MILLION
RED MERCURY	AROUND $300,000
RADIUM-226	$100,00 TO $1 MILLION
LITHIUM-6	$10 MILLION
SCANDIUM	$50,000
YTTERBIUM-168	$50 TO $100 MILLION
EUROPIUM-151	$50 TO $100 MILLION
ZINC-68	$50 TO $100 MILLION

Source: Sergei Pluzhnikov, et al., "Redkii Metall Doletit do Serediny Ozera Bodenzee," *Komsomolskaya Pravda,* May 6, 1994, p. 5.

official initially described this affair as a provocation designed to discredit Russian nuclear safeguards and to force Russia to accept Western specialists and technical assistance to plug the leak. "They want our nuclear industry to be under international control," declared MINATOM public relations head Georgiy Kaurov.[47] Indeed, only one of the four primary Western smuggling cases in 1994—the discovery of more than 6 grams of nearly pure plutonium-239 in a businessman's garage in Tengen-Wiechs, Germany—could *not* be attributed to a sting operation. In that case, police were investigating the businessman, Adolf Jaekle, for a totally unrelated crime.

The overarching issue here is that police and security services largely create the black market that they are charged with suppressing. Mark Hibbs, the Bonn correspondent for *Nucleonics Week*, recounts a 1996 case in Germany where a local criminal secured "a handful of natural uranium, absolutely useless for any nuclear weapons purpose." The criminal diligently searched for a client willing to make a million-dollar purchase. However, as Hibbs explained, "the only people he found who were willing to pay 1 million dollars for useless nuclear material were the German police," who immediately arrested him.[48]

The paucity of buyers for black-market nuclear goods has provoked numerous contentions that police operations are generating an artificial demand for radioactive materials and that the operations are driven by bureaucratic or political motives. As Josef Jaffe, a knowledgeable German observer, puts it, the nuclear market largely includes "gamblers, amateurs, and decoys installed by the state, who pretend that there is a market in order to shine with rapid investigative successes or to suggest an atmosphere of danger, which is very well suited to increasing state powers."[49] In Germany, the Munich plutonium seizure precipitated a full-blown investigation by the Parliamentary Control Commission of the Bundestag (parliament) into the legality of offering money to smugglers to buy foreign plutonium. Relatively light sentences were meted out to the three smugglers in the Munich case—three years; three years, nine months; and four years, ten months—compared to the ten-year maximum prescribed under German law. The men "were provoked to commit the crime," the presiding judge pronounced at the trial.[50]

In Russia, bureaucratic warfare has erupted between MINATOM and law enforcement agencies over appropriate methods for controlling nuclear leaks. MINATOM chief Viktor Mikhailov bitterly denounced MVD "provocateurs" who prey on the economic vulnerabilities of nuclear workers. In a February 1995 interview, Mikhailov cited his impressions of a recent visit to the Chepetsk Machine Building Plant in Glazov, Udmurtia. Chepetsk manufactures nuclear fuel and, after extracting part of the uranium-235, stores "hundreds of tons" of depleted uranium in waste dumps. The local police exploited this setting to their advantage, according to Mikhailov:

> The price of these wastes is a few dollars per kilogram on the world market. Then suddenly mysterious people arrive and offer the workers 10, maybe 100 dollars a kilogram, instead of 1 to 5. This can be tempting, naturally. I asked the MVD minister of Udmurtia, "Why are you doing this?" He answered, "We need to identify possible channels." At this I answered him, "You understand, this is real provocation." They have a few people under investigation now, and they will be brought to trial. These are laborers, mechanics, installation workers. They delivered sample batches and received their dollars, but they did not even make it home to share their joy before their hands were bound, the dollars confiscated, and they were put in jail. And the MVD people change clothes and receive promotions in rank. This is very troubling.[51]

Nuclear brokers and middlemen also have been the unwitting targets of sting activities in Russia. By mid-1995 the Federal Counterintelligence Service (now the Federal Security Service) was operating ten small trading fronts in Moscow to detect smuggling channels for radioactive materials and specialty metals used in bombs. Similar shell companies were established in Yekaterinburg and in various nuclear defense centers in Russia, despite the questionable utility of such networks. A Federal Security Service spokesman claimed that they failed to prove their worth, not surprisingly trapping only petty criminals handling nuclear radioactive junk. By the end of 1995, the system of front companies had been largely dismantled.[52]

CHAPTER 4

THE ORGANIZED CRIME CONNECTION

INTRODUCTION

THE ILLEGAL NUCLEAR TRADE tends to be supply-driven, the product of desperate economic forces in NIS nuclear complexes. Nuclear-material thieves usually are identified as enterprise employees, their friends and relatives, and local opportunists who reside near vulnerable facilities. Networks of small traders, often specialty metals brokers, take delivery of the merchandise (many times on terms highly unfavorable to the seller) and arrange to smuggle the goods out of Russia. Trafficking networks develop outward from the enterprise in the search for a broker or a buyer—that is, spontaneously rather than according to a preconceived plan.

Yet such haphazard nuclear crime transpires in a wider criminal context. Indeed, President Boris Yeltsin is quoted as saying in 1994 that Russia is "the biggest mafia state in the world" and "the superpower of crime," and in 1997 Moscow mayor Yuriy Luzhkov (a possible successor to Yeltsin) remarked that Russia faces "unlimited criminalization of the economy . . . and of the government itself."[1] Such statements constitute obvious hyperbole, but they nonetheless highlight a disappearing distinction in Russian society between the criminal and the lawful. Russia is gripped by a widespread privatization mentality and by a general deterioration of moral standards, both of which are associated with the increasing ascendancy of Russian organized crime. An amorphous phenomenon, organized crime is subject to multiple definitions, but the Russian variant typically includes important criminal actors such as mafia-type syndicates that approximate traditional Western stereotypes of organized crime as well as configurations of bureaucratic profiteers who employ state resources and connections to criminal advantage. The influence of such actors eventually could transform the dynamics of nuclear smuggling. As the criminalization of Russian society progresses, the currently relatively disorganized business could evolve into a sophisticated and lethal supply chain for nuclear wares.

Organized crime in its various guises already dominates parts of the Russian economy, including enterprises in the former Soviet defense complex. The wealthier and better-organized syndicates probably possess the capability to "buy off a military commander, a nuclear scientist, or someone else with access to weapons-grade material and to nuclear weapons," Senator Sam Nunn remarked in a 1994 hearing.[2] To be sure, capabilities are not necessarily congruent with incentives. Nuclear trafficking poses substantial risks for the criminals involved, and the rewards are neither as immediate nor as certain as those of other illegal operations. Such limitations, however, are subject to change: For example, an improved infrastructure of cross-border smuggling, increased availability of weapons-grade fissile materials, and the appearance of genuine end users in the nuclear marketplace could considerably modify the economics of the underground nuclear trade, attracting a more significant and lethal class of players.[3]

According to a September 1997 *Nezavisimaya Gazeta* article, the MVD's new action program for 1998 to 2000 cites a depressing forecast: criminals might exert control over "entire branches" of the national economy, including the financial sphere and extending to small, medium, and large business enterprises. Furthermore, according to the *Gazeta* account, the MVD expects that criminal groups will "lobby their interests by bribing people in power and by moving their own members into leading positions in government." The effect on Russia will be profound, entailing "mass dissatisfaction with the struggle against organized crime, withdrawal of foreign investors, and a slowdown in the transition toward market relations."[4]

Moreover, Russian criminal networks and ventures have metastasized well beyond the confines of Russia, spawning an array of new threats and challenges for Western nations. The MVD's International Crime Department reported in 1997 that more than 100 Russian criminal groups conduct illegal activities in the territories of foreign states. "These groups are the most secret. They have huge financial resources and are well-equipped technically."[5] Citing closed testimony before the U.S. Congress in 1997, a Russian source asserts that 40 percent of the $110 million distributed to Russia by international organizations and foreign banks in that year now resides in foreign bank accounts and is controlled by Russian criminal structures.[6] New patterns of collaboration have developed between Russian syndicates and transnational crime groups such as the Colombian cartels and the Sicilian Cosa Nostra. As will be discussed, such partnerships currently are trading narcotics and sophisticated military hardware, but they could be reconfigured to traffic in nuclear materials if a promising business opportunity arises. Some sources document symbiotic ties between Russian mafia groups abroad and active and former members of the Russian Foreign Intelligence Service—a nexus that also exacerbates the risk of nuclear proliferation from Russia.

TRENDS IN ORGANIZED CRIME

The prominence of organized crime scarcely represents a new development in Russia and other former Communist states. Organized crime took root in the fertile irrationalities of a planned economy and prospered in the vast black and gray markets that emerged in the last two decades of Communist rule. However, the precipitous demise of the Soviet empire, the ongoing transition to a market economy, and the sudden opening of borders to the West gave organized crime in the East an unforeseen opportunity to gain increasing prominence and influence. Moreover, this newly invigorated criminal enterprise is showing an increasingly malevolent face. Organized crime's more nefarious business lines—such as extortion rackets, contract murders, trafficking in weapons and narcotics, and, in selected cases, smuggling of nuclear materials and components—threaten the public safety and well-being of populations. In addition, the violence, corruption, and predatory behavior associated with emergent mafia formations jeopardize the progress of Russian reform and undermine the authority and legitimacy of the state.

The following specific vital statistics currently characterize these criminal organizations. According to the MVD, Russia's criminal community in 1997 comprised 9,000 gangs with 100,000 or 150,000 members (different ministry spokesmen give different numbers), an average of 11 or 17 members per gang, respectively.[7] The largest Moscow and St. Petersburg crime groups lay claim to hundreds or even thousands of members, although actual numbers obviously are difficult to determine.[8] Following the lead of world-class criminal organizations everywhere, Russian syndicates are amassing considerable muscle and clearly are well equipped with sophisticated weapons and advanced communications and surveillance equipment. (For example, the Moscow Soltsevskaya gang, Russia's largest, reportedly maintains an arsenal of 500 Kalashnikov rifles, 1,000 automatic pistols, and a number of antitank weapons.)[9] Furthermore, the criminal underworld is exploiting the implosion of Russia's military-industrial complex to gain access to an unusual array of talent, including former KGB and public officials, military specialists, and university-trained chemists, managers, and economists. New criminal entrepreneurs clearly have emerged from the ranks of government—for instance, former KGB officers manage narcotics and nuclear smuggling ventures, and parts of the Russian military engage in arms and drug trafficking and in "illegal diversions of huge financial and material resources."[10]

The widening influence of organized crime and its increasing symbiosis with government pose a significant challenge to the former Soviet republics, currently staggering under the multiple burdens of creating a functional private economy, nurturing a struggling young democracy, and crafting a new political system. Unfortunately, the mafia views privatization as a boon. The criminal syndicates are successfully wielding their vast economic resources and superior power, often squeezing out legitimate entrepreneurs, who find it difficult to muster the needed start-up capital and all too frequently must borrow funds from mobsters at extortionate rates of interest. Senior officials in the Russian MVD estimate that organized criminals own or control some 40,000 businesses in economic spheres ranging from retail trade to heavy manufacturing, including 500 to 600 of the roughly 3,000 banks in Russia. Loosely defined, the shadow or informal economy apparently accounts for some 20 to 40 percent of the Russian GDP, although this figure largely reflects unregistered activities of legal businesses (which strive to avoid confiscatory taxes in Russia) rather than clearly illegal machinations of organized crime groups.[11] One meticulous 1997 study of the shadow economy projects that it constitutes 23 percent of Russia's total GDP (legal plus nonlegal and illegal activities); however, that share varies widely by economic sector, ranging from 9 percent and 11 percent in transport and communications, respectively, to 63 percent in trade. Moreover, according to this study, the informal economy is dynamic, more than doubling in size between 1994 and 1996, while the formal GDP dwindled by 10 percent during the same period.[12]

Russian organized crime apparently casts a wide economic shadow that encompasses even heavy industrial sectors such as mining, metallurgy, and machine building. For example, Minister of Internal Affairs Anatoliy Kulikov contends that leaders of crime groups control almost all business deals at large aluminum plants in Bratsk and Krasnoyarsk and that key nickel manufacturing plants at Norilsk and Murmansk are heavily infiltrated by crime factions.[13] According to a Yekaterinburg business leader interviewed by the author, in Sverdlovsk oblast (province), an important organized crime bastion in the Urals, three mafia clans collaborated to acquire a significant or controlling interest in 22 local industrial enterprises, including an armaments factory and a company that manufactures equipment for nuclear plants.[14] Such extraordinary developments underscore the close links between organized crime and the state in Russia. (In other countries, criminals usually avoid investing in heavy industry, preferring more short-term, speculative, and liquid investments.) In addition, the mafia's extensive economic and financial influence sets a disturbing precedent, laying the groundwork for possible penetration of the troubled Russian nuclear sector.

By some calculations, the criminal sector is thriving at the expense of legal economic activity. More than 70 percent of businesses report spending approximately 10 to 20 percent of gross revenues in organized crime extortion payoffs. According to the Russian Chamber of Commerce, this figure substantially outstrips the percentage of businesses that pay taxes in Russia. A U.S. Treasury Department official estimates that bribes and protection money equal 15 percent of total wages in Russia.[15] Obviously the protection "tax" dampens consumption and harms normal economic activity. A recently published Russian study of organized crime calculates that losses to the Russian economy from financial fraud schemes totaled $5 billion in 1994; moreover, some 90 percent of the swindlers avoided prosecution because of loopholes in existing criminal laws.[16] Networks of criminals, corrupt officials, and military officers are heavily involved in smuggling ventures for materials (such as petroleum, non-ferrous metals, precious gems, and various biological substances) that are in high demand on international markets. Many Russian resource export businesses are wholly owned subsidiaries of mafia gangs. In 1995 alone, Russian authorities successfully prevented the illegal export of 71,000 tons of oil products, 33,000 tons of metal, and 18,000 cubic meters of timber, together worth more than $500 million; much larger quantities of these commodities undoubtedly crossed Russian frontiers undetected. Economic losses from export businesses derive from uncollected taxes or tariffs and—because criminals tend to bank illicit trading proceeds in the West—from capital flight, which tallies $12 to $15 billion per year, according to a 1997 estimate by the Russian Central Bank.[17]

Many observers have commented that Russia's large organized crime sector creates an uncertain environment for investment, scaring away foreign business and, in effect, jeopardizing Russia's economic future. Foreign investment in Russia, excluding portfolio investment, from 1991-1996 was twenty-two times less than investment in China ($7 billion compared to $150 billion) despite Russia's relatively larger size and resource base.[18]

Organized crime reputedly is exerting increasing influence in the state structures of Russia and other post-Soviet states. MVD figures suggest that more than 7,100 criminal proceedings were initiated against officials of the Russian government during 1995 and 1996. Approximately 70 percent of these cases focused on government officials, 20 percent on law enforcement officers, and 3 percent on elected representatives. (The balance might represent military officers, but this conclusion is uncertain.) This number doubtless understates the extent of the criminal-political nexus in Russia. For example, Federal Security Service data apparently demonstrate that almost 80 percent of Russian organized criminal groups cultivate ties with the bureaucracy. Russian MVD Minister Kulikov estimates that criminal gangs expend 30 to 50 percent of their profits on bribing state officials, an uncommonly high percentage. (In contrast, in Colombia, projected outlays for bribes and enforcement costs probably do not exceed 10 percent of narcotics profits, according to a 1994 U.S. government study.)[19] Criminal interests also undermine the legislative process in Russia and other NIS countries. The Russian parliament (or Duma) reputedly is riddled with de facto representatives of criminal syndicates who diligently work to block or water down any significant anticrime legislation. Russian MVD chief Anatoliy Kulikov confirms that some 85 suspected criminals ran for election to the Duma in 1995.[20] If all of these candidates had won seats, the criminal bloc would have amounted to more than one-third of the parliament. According to American University researcher Louise Shelley, a member of the Duma's powerful Committee on State Security has been imprisoned twice for serious offenses, "neither of them linked to the shadow economy, but instead to the crimes characteristic of members of the criminal world." Moreover, as Shelley observes, in both Russia and the Ukraine, so-called politicians often seek election to the parliament because of the immunity from prosecution conferred by a parliamentary career.[21]

Furthermore, Russian mafia organizations increasingly assert their power through intimidation and murder. Approximately 80 Russian bankers were assassinated between mid-1993 and mid-1997, many by organized crime figures seeking to penetrate and manipulate the Russian financial system. The MVD records almost 1,100 contract killings in Russia in 1995 and 1996; most of these murders have not been solved. In 1995 alone, victims included 4 Duma deputies and 46 businessmen, according to the government.[22] In 1997, a reformist party deputy governor of St. Petersburg, Mikhail Manevich, was gunned down in his car, and, in typical mob fashion, an AKM assault rifle was abandoned at the scene of the crime. Three highly publicized slayings in 1995 and 1996 may have been related to mob takeover attempts—that of Valentin Smirnov, who headed a missile design bureau in the Kalinin missile assembly plant in Yekaterinburg; Anatoliy Ivanov, deputy director of the Baranov engine plant in Omsk, which makes engines for MiG-29 fighter planes; and Paul Tatum, the American part owner of the Radisson Slavyanskaya Hotel in Moscow. Contract murders may simply reflect sheer criminal vindictiveness. For example, in April 1994 parliamentary deputy Andrei Azderis was shot to death in an apparent contract hit near his home in the Khimki section of Moscow. The deceased deputy was the editor of a Moscow newspaper, Who's Who, that had published the names of 266 Russian mafia dons the previous month—a move that evidently did not resonate well in some criminal quarters.[23]

Following the Colombian pattern of the late 1980s and early 1990s, Russia is experiencing an upsurge of random violence attributable to organized crime. In 1996, there were 886 criminally inspired bombings, compared to 46 in 1995 and 18 in 1994. The

1996 explosions, many in Moscow, killed 141 people and wounded 553.[24] A particularly vicious bombing attack massacred 14 people at Moscow's Kotlyakovskoye cemetery in November 1996. Referring to that incident, Russia's First Deputy Interior Minister commented, "To attain their goals organized crime resorts to terror."[25] The political or financial motives that breed such violence, however, remain obscure.

Russia seemingly is incapable of countering this insidious rise in criminal activity. To date, government responses are characterized more by rhetoric than substance. In a February 1993 speech, President Yeltsin decried organized crime as "a direct threat to Russia's strategic interests and national security" and protested that "corruption in the organs of power and administration is literally eating away the body of the Russian state from top to bottom."[26] Yet by 1998 the government still had not taken sufficient action to police or contain the organized crime sector and to punish the perpetrators of major crimes, such as contract murders. Laws on the books punish official corruption and organized crime activity, and various anticrime edicts are aimed at strengthening the Russian government's power to enforce the laws and prosecute criminals. Few resources are available to implement such measures, however, and the Russian leadership's commitment to them is somewhat suspect. "Today's government lacks the will to fight organized crime," succinctly noted Aleksandr Moldovets, the deputy chief of the MVD Economic Crimes Division.[27] In general, Russian institutional weaknesses and the precarious state of the Russian economy argue poorly for a successful crackdown on the country's organized crime sector—at least in the near term.

The criminal world's usurpation of functions traditionally associated with the state and the law further complicate law enforcement. In Russia today, organized crime is substituting for ineffective commercial codes and courts by arbitrating property disputes, helping businesses to collect debts, and performing other services vital to the functioning of a market economy. Like Latin American drug lords, Russian criminals also buy social recognition and political support by contributing to various charitable causes. In his book *Comrade Criminal*, Stephen Handelman observes that the Uralmash gang in Yekaterinburg organized fashion shows to raise money for children and sponsored a girls' soccer team in the city. He also recounts the case of a schoolteacher-turned-mobster named Anatoliy Vladimirov, who donated money and equipment to the poverty-stricken Institute of Theoretical Astronomy in St. Petersburg. Scientists at the institute thereupon named an obscure star discovered 20 years earlier Anvlad, immortalizing their criminal benefactor.[28]

Progressive criminalization of the economy and of state functions has exacted a psychological toll on Russians. Not surprisingly, a sense of defeatism and hopelessness pervades the Russian government's crime-fighting units. Many Russians believe that criminals are gaining or have secured the upper hand. In a 1993 poll that asked residents of the Urals city of Yekaterinburg to specify "who holds power" there, 4 percent of respondents named the local soviet of people's deputies, 14 percent the city administration, and 74 percent "the mafia which has bought public officials."[29] In 1995 Andrei Nechayev, cochairman of the Russian Business Roundtable and president of the Russian Finance Corporation, informed the newspaper *Literaturnaya Gazeta*, "The State has effectively given up its main functions in the protection of property and the property owners. To whom? To criminal gangs. They are already performing the functions of the arbitrators, marshals of the court, tax collectors, body guards. . . ."[30] In a 1996 interview one of the most respected Russian authorities on organized crime, Dr. Aleksandr Gurov, a retired major general in the MVD, vouchsafed that the Russian government should negotiate "some sort of treaty" with the mafia and "think through how to improve order in the state with the help of the same mafia."[31] Gurov's mind-set underlines the underworld's increasing capability to shape social and political dynamics in Russia. Apparently, a process of "Colombianization" is taking hold. In Colombia, government dialogues with the organized crime sector—the powerful Medellin and Cali cartels—have been part of the political landscape for years. Such talks conferred de facto legitimacy on the criminal elites and undermined the rule of law—hardly a viable formula for stable government in Colombia, Russia, or anywhere else.

GLOBALIZATION

In a disheartening development, Russian organized crime is expanding westward by exporting capital, establishing outposts in Western countries, and collaborating in new ways with foreign criminal syndicates. Russian criminal organizations currently conduct business independently or through local partners in at least 45 countries outside the former Soviet Union. According to a 1997 study by the Center for Strategic and International Studies (CSIS) in Washington, the 26 "principal" Russian crime gangs have secured a foothold in the United States, where they "negotiated division of labor arrangements with American, Sicilian, and Colombian crime syndicates."[32]

Growing evidence documents strategic alliances between Russian syndicates and counterpart criminal groups in the West; two high-profile international transactions are cases in point. In a February 1993 case, Russian police and customs officials intercepted almost 1.1 tons of Cali cartel cocaine in Vyborg, just across the border from Finland. Most of the cocaine apparently was destined for the Netherlands. (Modern-day traffickers commonly use Russia and Eastern Europe as a back door for smuggling South American drugs into Western Europe.) The consignment was transported to Sweden and Finland in two different commercial vessels and then moved by truck to the Russian frontier. As subsequent investigations revealed, this complex deal required wide international collaboration—the principal actors included Cali traffickers, an Israeli national residing in Bogotá, Russian mafia figures, expatriate Russians in Belgium and the Netherlands, and an Israeli trafficking group.[33] An even more astounding demonstration of Russian-Colombian criminal collaboration was detailed in a recent *Washington Post* investigative report on international transfers of advanced weaponry. According to a 1997 U.S. federal indictment, a Russian émigré group based in Miami arranged the sale of at least two Soviet-made helicopters to representatives of the Cali cartel. The purchase was negotiated at Porky's, a Miami nightclub owned by one of the criminals. Furthermore, U.S. officials interviewed by the *Post* asserted that in the discussions, the Russians proposed to provide the cartel with a diesel-powered submarine from the Russian naval base at Kronstadt (in the Gulf of Finland)—including the services of a crew of 20 for a year—for a mere $5 million. The submarine would have been an important adjunct to the cartel's smuggling operation; however, the Cali representatives backed out of the deal, "apparently feeling such an enterprise was too ambitious."[34]

Of course, these incidents testify to the widening global reach and capabilities of the Russian mafia. These unprecedented criminal partnerships could dramatically accelerate international trafficking in weapons, narcotics, and other dangerous substances, conceivably including nuclear materials. Such a scenario assumes paramount importance from the perspective of U.S. national security. However, the insidious extension of Russian crime manifests other malevolent dimensions, including transplanted Russian crime groups that possess significant wealth and international contacts and thus can undermine not only the administration of justice but also the previously sacrosanct political institutions of some host countries. Excerpts from a 1995 Israeli police report cited in *Moskovskiye Novosti* underscore this alarming trend:

> Russian criminal elements have acquired in the past few years companies in Israel and do business in the spheres of finance and real estate. They try to buy the Russian language mass media and establish contacts with the political structures. Russian criminal structures tied to the Russian mafia intend to put up their own candidates in elections to the Knesset (parliament), finance political parties that will participate in the elections, and in so doing establish control over them.[35]

In other words, Russian organized crime is replicating abroad the patterns of systemic corruption already firmly rooted in Russia.

In Israel, the large (more than 700,000) community of recent émigrés from the USSR and its successor-states represents an obvious target for Russian crime syndicates, which seem well positioned to exploit the economic and political vulnerabilities of many other countries around the globe.

VARIANTS OF ORGANIZED CRIME

Introduction

The criminal community in Russia and elsewhere constitutes a confused patchwork of associations that supply illicit goods and services, engage in predatory crimes (such as armed robbery or extortion rackets), and otherwise seek illegal gains. Traditional Western models of organized crime emphasize characteristics such as hierarchy, continuity of operations, strict division of labor, internal decision rules and codes of conduct, and corrupt ties to the authorities. The larger criminal groups in Russia probably approximate this model, but most qualify as minor gangs or ad hoc associations with no permanent structures or linkages to power. Most nuclear smuggling operations in Russia fit the minor gang stereotype. Moreover, criminal entrepreneurship in Russia does not adhere to clearly defined patterns. Traditional underworld bosses, the *vory v zakonye,* typically earned their credentials by serving prison terms, but modern-day criminal authorities are just as likely to be apparently respectable bankers, teachers, factory directors, generals, or ministry officials. An MVD official in the Organized Crime Administration told a French researcher in March 1996 that 80 percent of the Russian mafia godfathers are former high officials or factory heads. Most of these high-ranking culprits undoubtedly engage in economic crimes, such as privatization scams or customs fraud, rather than perpetrating classic felonies, such as arms trafficking, drugs, extortion, or prostitution; however, some organized criminals may be committing both types of offenses.[36]

Two broad categories of criminal groups assume particular significance for this book. First, some powerful and broadly based underworld organizations operate a range of legal and illegal businesses. Such gangs have distinct identities—Ostankino, Izmailovo, Solntsevo, Tambov, Uralmash, 21st Century Association, and the like—and maintain enduring structures, substantial enforcement capabilities, and well-defined spheres of criminal activity. Members frequently (although not exclusively) rank as career criminals with prior records as racketeers, smugglers, swindlers, or murderers. The second criminal class is comprised of active or retired state employees (such as officials, managers, military officers, and KGB operatives) who leverage privileged access and contacts to enable various criminal endeavors. In contrast to high-profile underworld gangs, the upperworld bureaucratic criminals typically can be categorized as relatively clean lawbreakers with no record of crimes or convictions. Underworld and upperworld criminals frequently interact and even collaborate as needed (for instance, in smuggling ventures, extortion plots, or financial frauds). Former CIA director R. James Woolsey admitted in December 1996 that active and former members of the Russian Foreign Intelligence Service, the Sluzhba Vneshnei Razvedki (SVR); the MVD; and the Defense Ministry "are very much in bed with Russian organized crime groups."[37] This assertion was substantiated to some extent by a German BND report published by *Der Spiegel* in October 1997, just before Russian SVR chief Vyacheslav Trubnikov made a visit to Bonn. According to the magazine, "The influence of organized crime over individual people and groups in the [Russian] intelligence service have become so intensive that one must speak of partial permeation . . . a symbiotic relationship for mutual advantage." The SVR under Trubnikov allegedly is dispatching pro forma discharged SVR agents to work in Russian mafia–owned firms abroad. From these foreign vantage points, the agents continue to supply intelligence to their former colleagues in Moscow, presumably while earning attractive incomes as mafia businessmen.[38] (*Der Spiegel* included a disclaimer that "certain proof" of a functioning connection between the mafia and special services was still lacking.) Such machinations epitomize the complexity of the criminal-official relationship in Russia. Despite such allegations of symbiosis, the underworld and upperworld are socially and analytically distinct expressions of the Russian criminal milieu, even though their criminal enterprises and activities sometimes overlap.

The Underworld

The professional criminal underworld in Russia is diversified, comprising ethnic and territorially based groups that evince a range of resources, capabilities, and business profiles. British researcher Guy Dunn identified approximately 40 prominent criminal groups based in four major Russian cities: Moscow, St. Petersburg, Yekaterinburg, and Vladivistok.[39] A multitude of smaller gangs also operate in these and many other Russian cities. According to Dunn, the largest organizations, such as the Moscow-based Solntsevo group and the Tambov and Malishev gangs in St. Petersburg, claim more than 1,000 members. The three Moscow Chechen gangs boast a combined membership of 1,500 to 3,000 members, but they are so definitively linked that they essentially function as a single entity—sharing a common fund used for bribes and for legal defense of gang members, a joint security and intelligence apparatus, and (more tenuously) a common decision-making structure. Figure 4.1 details the structure and activities of the Chechen criminal enterprises in Moscow. Large Russian gangs not only engage in traditional criminal pursuits such as drug running, arms trafficking, and extortion rackets but also manage significant legal assets and businesses. For example, the Solntsevo group reputedly exercises partial or full control over 4 hotels, 3 casinos, and 300 commercial firms and banks in the city of Moscow.[40]

The Chechen mafia, the Solntsevo gang, and other extended Russian aggregates rely on wide networks of contacts and affiliates in the NIS and various Western countries. According to the research of Dunn and others, the Chechens conduct business in various European countries and in Turkey, Jordan, Argentina,

FIGURE 4.1

Structure of Chechen Mafia in Moscow

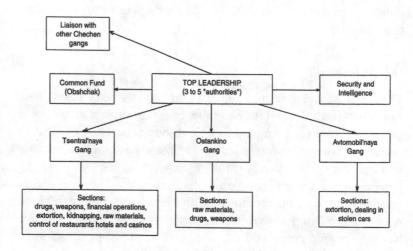

Sources: Inspired by Guy Dunn. "Major Mafia Gangs in Russia" in Phil Williams, ed. *Russian Organized Crime: The New Threat.* (London: Frank Cass, 1997) pp. 65-68.

Costa Rica, and Venezuela. An unpublished U.S. government report estimated that, by 1993, some 5,000 ethnic Chechens were managing criminal activities in Britain, Germany, Hungary, Poland, and the United States. The Solntsevo gang not only operates independently in countries outside the NIS but also seemingly cooperates with the Colombian Cali cartel to arrange the transit of South American cocaine through Russia and then into Europe and the United States. The Solntsevo group might have been the shadowy major Russian player in the previously cited Vyborg deal, although this role has not been confirmed publicly.

The larger Russian organizations maintain significant smuggling capabilities, including transit routes, corrupt or malleable officials, transport and storage facilities, customer contacts, and access to bank credits. In addition, these groups have pipelines into the Russian military establishment, as the previously proffered submarine deal attests. Black-market transactions involving sophisticated conventional weaponry and even nuclear materials and components probably fall well within the commercial scope of these organizations. If Russian criminals are positioned to sell a submarine from Kronstadt, they also might be able to supply weapons-grade uranium or plutonium from Obninsk or Chelyabinsk to foreign buyers.

The extent of Russian mafia participation in nuclear materials smuggling is difficult to gauge. Most observers see a limited organized crime presence in the market. In 1994 CIA director Woolsey informed a meeting of Washington's CSIS that "trading in nuclear weapons and materials is not the primary or secondary source of business today" for professional underworld groups.[41] Most substances offered on the black market are not weapons-quality, a fact that apparently indicates a lack of criminal professionalism. "The people seem to be naive amateurs," declared a spokesman for the Federal Counterintelligence Service who was interviewed by *Der Spiegel*. "If the mafia were involved it would dig out precisely what is needed for a nuclear bomb."[42] Furthermore, nuclear smuggling likely entails significant opportunity costs, at least at the low-value end of the business. "Why drag across multiple frontiers kilograms of uranium that require years of reworking and enrichment and then spend months looking for a potential buyer?" queries Kirill Belyaninov, a longtime observer of the Russian criminal trends. "Why not just ship non-ferrous metals out of the country or make millions from banking manipulations and ruble-dollar exchange transactions?"[43]

Such arguments are inherently persuasive and doubtless give some comfort to proliferation analysts. Nonetheless, more threatening scenarios must be assessed. Serious clients probably are calculating the value of contraband nuclear and radioactive material—for example, international metals traders,[44] nations conducting covert nuclear programs, industrial and medical organizations, and possibly the larger and more ambitious terrorist groups. The seller's credibility represents a primary high-ranking concern. As a French nuclear analyst recently explained, clients are unlikely to commit themselves to "radioactive bargains with third-level dubious smugglers."[45] As my research verified, the nuclear marketplace is heavily populated with disorganized peddlers, scam artists, and naive opportunists. Nevertheless, the attention of prospective buyers might be captured by a criminal organization that is well connected to the nuclear establishment (perhaps listing nuclear scientists on its payroll), operates through appropriate and reliable front companies, and thus can guarantee the quality of proffered nuclear merchandise.

Assuming that such a black market actually can be cultivated, the central question then becomes identifying the entry strategies that the criminal syndicates are most likely to employ. One such strategy might focus on exporting dual-use materials—that is, nonradioactive substances such as beryllium or zirconium that are used in nuclear programs but also can be adapted for civilian nonnuclear applications. For example, zirconium is incorporated not only in nuclear reactor rods, but also in linings of furnaces and ceramic products. International markets for dual-use materials are broader and better established than those for radioactive nuclear materials, and buyers are easier to contact.[46] A more daring strategy might be entering the high-value end of the nuclear materials business by procuring or exporting such wares as weapons-grade uranium or plutonium, specialty reactor fuels, and radioactive isotopes that are valuable for medicine and research. Access to such exotic substances theoretically poses a challenge, and markets for such materials are narrow and rarefied. However, high per-unit prices—a pound of plutonium reputedly can fetch $275,000 to $550,000 on the black market—can justify the necessary investments in developing requisite supply chains, refining smuggling capacity, and establishing links to end users.[47]

In sum, the nuclear smuggling game is made up of major unknowns. The motives of actors, incentive structures, and modes of operation are ill-defined and variable. Many criminals will write off this business as complex, high risk, and low profit—but a few adventurous entrepreneurs may perceive a challenging commercial frontier, concomitantly lucrative potential returns (given the right buyer and smuggling connections), and even prospects for a modicum of power. Chechen groups might harbor ideological and economic motives for risking the nuclear trade, particularly in light of their state's historical antipathy to Moscow. Indeed, my research tentatively supports the notion that Chechen and other organized crime gangs already have made forays into the nuclear black market. For proliferation analysts, this dismaying conclusion (documented and analyzed in chapter 1) is perhaps not surprising considering the covert and occasionally bizarre dynamics of the nuclear smuggling business.

Bureaucratic Criminals

Russian organized crime groups also rely on corrupt networks of active or former members of the state bureaucracy, state-controlled enterprises, and the military and security apparatus. Such networks often are characterized by a very small number of people acting in concert and thus rank as relatively unobtrusive compared to most underworld gangs. For example, unscrupulous military personnel seemingly conspire to sell stocks of weapons and equipment, contraband raw materials, and even illegal commodities such as drugs. According to U.S. military analyst Graham Turbiville, the Russian mafia-in-uniform has included general officers, aircraft pilots and crews, members of combined arms units and commands, organized military traders, and individual soldiers on combat assignments.[48] The arms-trafficking chain also subsumes civilian weapons traders (many linked to underworld groups), corrupt government officials, and combatants in regional conflicts—for instance, in Chechnya, Tadjikistan, and Nakhichevan.

The banks stand at the end of the military smuggling chain. In 1995, according to a *Novaya Gazeta* account, military intelligence (GRU) officials, top managers of the state arms trading company Razvooruzheniye, and heads of a Moscow commercial bank collaborated in a scheme to launder $400 million earned from illegal black-market sales of Russian armaments and military equipment. The plan was to transfer funds from Lebanese banks to the Moscow bank, convert the dollars to rubles, float the money in Russian interbank loan markets, convert the funds back to foreign exchange, and then transfer the formerly dirty money to foreign bank accounts "via Baltic banks or under the pretext of pseudo-import contracts," the newspaper reported.[49]

Several recent examples of military criminality in the 1990s can be documented. From the late 1980s to the mid-1990s, the Western Group of Forces in Germany and other force units in Eastern Europe and the Baltics orchestrated an underground trade that featured tons of ammunition and heavy equipment ranging from armed vehicles to MiG aircraft. In October 1995 the Federal Security Service charged Anatoliy Kuntsevich, a former general of the Chemical Troops and presidential advisor on chemical disarmament, with delivering approximately 800 kilograms of FX nerve gas precursors pilfered from military facilities to Syria in November 1993 and with attempting to deliver another 5.5 tons of chemical agents to an unidentified Middle Eastern country the following year. The charges against Kuntsevich subsequently were dropped, however.[50] According to Turbiville, the commander of a long-range aviation division (one of the Russian nuclear strike forces) in the Russian Far East, Major General Vladimir Rodionov, and his deputy converted the division operating base "into a transshipment point for moving commercial goods and businessmen" between cities of the former Soviet Union and China. Bomber pilots and crews in the division shared the profits generated by the illegal enterprise.[51] Criminality in the armed forces even extends to supplying weapons to opposing combat forces. The Russian newspaper *Argumenty i Fakty* announced in April 1996 that members of the 166th Russian infantry in Chechnya sold a tank and an armored personnel carrier to Chechen fighters for $6,000. Turbiville states that paratroopers from the 104th Guards Airborne Division were arrested in May 1995 for attempting to sell plastic explosives, grenade launchers, and ammunition to Chechens.[52]

Top echelons of the Russian government may have participated in the weapons proliferation game—and therein lies a gruesome tale. In April 1997 the so-called intelligence chief of the Japanese

Aum Shinrikyo terrorist cult testified at his trial in Tokyo that, in the fall of 1993, the Secretary of the Russian Security Council at that time, Oleg Lobov, delivered to the cult blueprints and technical documents for the production of the nerve gas sarin. The cult allegedly paid Lobov, who held his post from September 1993 to June 1996, 10 million yen (about $80,000) for the technology. These allegations have not been proven. (One FSB spokesperson termed the charge "total nonsense.")[53] Nevertheless, Lobov allegedly maintained a relationship with Aum leaders that lasted from the end of 1991 through 1995; during this period Aum was cultivating connections with Russian military, scientific, and political figures and was seeking data for its various weapons programs. According to one recent study, Lobov pocketed anywhere from $500,000 to $1,000,000 from Aum, possibly to support the group's military procurement aspirations.[54] Aum also successfully acquired a Soviet-made M1-17 military helicopter from Russia, possibly with the intention of disseminating chemical or biological agents over Japanese cities. According to a Japanese Diet (parliament) member, Aum bribed a former Russian parliamentarian from the Caucasus to arrange the transfer of the helicopter via an air carrier based in Azerbaidjan.[55]

In addition, military crime embraces an array of opportunistic illegal ventures based on nonmilitary commodities. For example, commercial export firms employ military planes and pilots to fly loads of contraband metal to the Baltic countries. "We cannot penetrate the Army," complained a senior Russian customs official. "The generals give the command for the planes to go and come back." Drug smuggling apparently constitutes another favorite military pastime. Moscow's *Obshchaya Gazeta* reported in late 1996 that Major General Yuriy Vyunov, Chief of Staff of the Russian Peacekeeping Forces in Tadjikistan, had been indicted by the Russian Main Military Procuracy for smuggling 109 kilograms of opium in a military helicopter.[56]

Not surprisingly, military criminality in Russia has spread to nuclear materials, although with modest strategic implications to date. Naval fuel storehouses serving the Russian submarine fleet represented the high-priority targets of opportunity. At least six attempted diversions of weapons-usable HEU were substantiated in the Murmansk-Arkhangelsk region between mid-1993 and early 1996. The two best-documented thefts, at Sevmorput and Andreeva Guba (both near Murmansk), could not be classified as major conspiratorial acts; the perpetrators were, respectively, three naval officers and a pair of radiation safety workers. Nevertheless, these incidents highlight serious security problems in the Russian naval forces. The Sevmorput scheme was instigated by a captain, a lieutenant, and a retired officer. The smuggling disease apparently has metastasized to the Pacific Fleet, where roughly 7 kilograms of HEU reportedly were stolen from a base at Sovietskaya Gavan' in January 1996; 2.5 kilograms of this material later materialized on the premises of a metals trading firm in the Baltic city of Kaliningrad, some 5,000 miles distant.[57] Links between such thefts certainly fall within the realm of possibility, at least insofar as the Northern Fleet is concerned. A military prosecutor attached to the fleet declared in a 1995 *Yaderny Kontrol'* article that a Murmansk–St. Petersburg criminal ring that smuggles nuclear contraband through the Baltic states had approached Russian naval officers, offering $400,000 to $1,000,000 for each kilogram of HEU that they obtained.[58] The Russian General Procurator's office has not confirmed the operation of that criminal organization, but its existence cannot be discounted out of hand. The decaying military infrastructure in the region, staggering inventories of radioactive waste, sloppy fuel storage practices, and widespread local trafficking in nonnuclear military gear and ammunition have nurtured a suitable environment and associated incentives for criminal nuclear proliferation on a major scale. Members of the current military criminal chain have honed unusual skills, assembled an array of international contacts, and are well positioned to locate prospective buyers for illegal commodities.

Active and former members of the KGB and its successor agencies have been credibly connected to an impressive catalog of criminal pursuits: heroin trafficking, drug-money laundering, currency speculation, clandestine weapons sales, computer smuggling, and even nuclear trafficking. For example, in 1995 the Moscow-based Feliks research firm chronicled a particularly well-documented case of criminal behavior by former intelligence operatives. According to Feliks, in the fall of 1991 several former KGB officers established a so-called Moscow narcotics group, centered in Moscow but composed of agents in Afghanistan, Laos, London, and the Cayman Islands. (Interestingly, Feliks itself is composed of KGB veterans.) The Afghan and Laos affiliates were responsible for procuring drugs, principally opium and morphine. The London and Caribbean branches performed two functions: arranging the delivery of narcotics to foreign criminal organizations (in Colombia, Italy, Mexico, and others countries) and investing the proceeds of narcotics sales in legal businesses. In other words, the Moscow narcotics group created the rudimentary components of an international trafficking and money-laundering structure. The group worked closely with Chechen criminal gangs in Moscow and Chechnya. Indeed, Chechnya apparently was a linchpin in the group's operations. According to Feliks, a modern chemical-pharmaceutical enterprise in the republic's Shalinsky region converted opium and morphine into high-quality heroin and packaged the drug for export. (Feliks claims that the complex was destroyed in January 1995 following the Russian invasion of Chechnya; yet the researchers maintain that the Moscow narcotics group and the Chechen mafia plan to establish a new refining base, possibly in the Uzbekistan oblast of Samarkand.) Disturbing elements of the Feliks report, particularly the Moscow narcotics group's global connections, seem exaggerated. Nonetheless, certain propositions seem generally plausible—for example, that former KGB officers are exploiting their international contacts to peddle narcotics and that the Chechnya government capitalized on the drug trade and other criminal activities to support its pretensions to independence.[59]

The evidence supporting an intelligence connection to nuclear smuggling is sparse but nonetheless disturbingly suggestive, as illustrated by three specific cases in point. First, a Europe-wide consortium, Kuzin Group International, operated on the continent in the early 1990s. Founded by Aleksandr Kuzin, reputedly a former KGB colonel, the Vienna-based group legally traded goods such as petrochemicals, fertilizers, and diagnostic medical equipment. However, some companies associated with Kuzin also maintained illegal sideline businesses that reputedly included hawking uranium, plutonium (in microgram quantities), so-called red mercury, heavy weapons, explosives, and other strategic commodities with origins in former Soviet bloc countries. (Kuzin left Vienna in 1993 after the Austrian police issued a warrant for his arrest; he was finally apprehended in Switzerland and charged with document fraud in January 1995.) Second, a mysterious trafficking episode was detailed in mid-1994 by the Moscow newspaper *Moskovskiy Komsomolets.* The Russian Federal Counterintelligence Service (FSK) reportedly arrested one of its own captains and a former FSK warrant officer for possession of about 2 kilograms of "highly radioactive" uranium.[60] The FSK denied the incident and demanded a retraction, but the newspaper's editors stood by the story.

The German magazine *Focus* published a more startling and bizarre tale in February 1997, a follow-up to the previously cited criminal case involving the smuggling of 363 grams of 87 percent plutonium-239 and 201 grams of lithium-6 aboard a Lufthansa flight from Moscow to Munich in August 1994. According to *Focus,* the German state intelligence coordinator, Bernd Schmidbauer, asserted that the Colombian smuggler who carried the dangerous materials had been an agent of the Illegals Directorate (the S directorate) of the Russian SVR. Moreover, the procurement and planned sale of the material "were no state action but rather a private deal by high-ranking officers of the S directorate." Several S directorate officers were fired after the bungled plutonium deal— which was, in fact, an elaborate sting operation perpetrated by the German authorities; among them was the department head, Yuriy Shuravlev.[61] Not surprisingly, the SVR labeled the report a U.S.-German provocation, but one high Russian official—MINATOM chief Viktor Mikhailov—confirmed in a recent interview that both "the sellers and the buyers [of the Munich plutonium] were members of special services [the term Russians used to describe intelligence agencies]."[62] The Munich smuggling affair thus is disturbing in the extreme, as it intimates possibly endemic corruption in parts of the Russian intelligence establishment and exacerbates the risk of criminal nuclear proliferation from Russia.

Finally, Western intelligence agencies have attempted to link a Vienna-based commodities firm, Nordex, both to money-laundering by Soviet or Russian intelligence and to traffic in nuclear materials. A January 1995 BND report (cited in the Western media in different versions) allegedly claims that the company was set up with the "aim of bringing the foreign currency accumulated by the KGB and top communist party officials into the West." *Time* magazine quotes the report as saying that "evidence suggests [Nordex] involvement in the international arms trade as well as the smuggling of narcotics and nuclear material across the Baltic." Nordex's participation in nuclear and drug smuggling remains unproven, however, although many Western authorities believe that the company maintains extensive criminal connections in Russia, Ukraine, and Europe.[63]

CONCLUDING OBSERVATIONS

Russia and other NIS nations are confronting a criminal proliferation threat of enormous proportions. This threat is largely the by-product of the deteriorating economic environment in NIS nuclear complexes. As U.S. Senator Sam Nunn remarked in the previously cited May 1994 hearings:

> Today in the former Soviet Union we have a situation where literally thousands of nuclear scientists do not know where their next paycheck is coming from or how their families will be fed. Today in the former Soviet Union we have a situation where thousands of military personnel who have access to highly sophisticated conventional weapons, and even nuclear warheads, are faced with drastic reductions in their standard of living. Under these conditions it is no longer too fantastic an idea to imagine a scenario in which chemical

or biological weapons, missile technology, nuclear materials or know-how, or even nuclear weapons themselves could fall into the hands of criminal elements.[64]

As already noted, such criminal operations typically rely on some combination of underworld mafia-type organizations and upperworld groups with connections to the bureaucracy or the military. Corruption at the highest levels of government also may contribute to serious proliferation episodes, as the Aum Shinrikyo's Russian connections attest. To be sure, disincentives abound in the nuclear field; for example, principal organized crime business lines are highly profitable and far less risky than nuclear smuggling, and they present fewer technical problems. Nevertheless, the major challenges of the nuclear smuggling business—obtaining weapons-usable material in quantity and developing contacts with potential buyers—probably are manageable preconditions for today's increasingly sophisticated Russian criminals. In any case, the risk of serious nuclear diversion has reached an uncomfortably high level and could well continue to escalate as the decade nears an end and Russia's expanding criminal business sector seeks new profit centers.

CHAPTER 5

THE VIEW FROM THE WEST

THE EUROPEAN SETTING

EUROPE, INCLUDING RUSSIA AND THE WESTERN NIS STATES, constitutes the principal venue for the illicit trade in nuclear materials. IAEA and Interpol data for the 1990s record only a handful of confirmed radioactive smuggling cases outside of Europe—in Kazakhstan, Ecuador, Brazil, India, and Canada. Flow patterns for the materials demarcate the distinct logistical and geographical preferences of aspiring nuclear traders: For 1993 to 1996, of 104 non-NIS nuclear smuggling incidents identified in the IAEA database, 85 (or 82 percent) occurred in six countries—Poland, the Czech Republic, Slovakia, Germany, Austria, and Switzerland.

On its face, the general pattern of nuclear smuggling in the West poses a very modest proliferation threat. European press sources and law enforcement officials report 15 separate seizures of plutonium between 1991 and 1995, as listed in table 5.1. The aggregate weight of the seized plutonium did not exceed 375 grams. Moreover, a single smuggling event—the previously mentioned Munich case in August 1994—accounted for more than 363 of the 375 grams. Six of the cases involved quantities of plutonium-coated capsules (or buttons) and screws used in Russian gas analyzers or smoke detection systems; the combined plutonium content in these cases totaled slightly more than 1 gram. In at least

4 of the 15 seizures, the plutonium originated in a Moscow industrial concern, Izotop, which also exports fuel for nuclear reactors. These materials were legally shipped to Bulgarian companies in Vienna and Sofia and subsequently were diverted or stolen.[1]

Uranium smuggling was more prevalent than plutonium diversions but unremarkable in strategic terms. According to Interpol and IAEA data, seizures of illegal uranium shipments in the West totaled approximately 200 tons in 60 separate cases between 1991 and 1996, but nearly all of that material was classified as natural, depleted, or slighted enriched uranium (no more than 5 percent U-235). In 1994 to 1995 in Central Europe, four smuggling cases were documented that entailed uranium enriched to 87.7 percent U-235, but the materials were technically not weapons-grade and weighed less than 3 kilograms total. Furthermore, the seizure of 2.73 kilograms of HEU in Prague in December 1994 accounted for the bulk of the 3 kilograms. All four of the Central European uranium smuggling cases and the Munich plutonium smuggling episode were traced to a single supplier in Russia, an engineer who formerly worked in the Obninsk IPPE near Moscow.

Table 5.1 summarizes all nuclear smuggling incidents of more than passing interest in Europe. When measuring the significance of such traffic, the quantity of fissile material required to build a nuclear weapon assumes critical importance—but the range of uncertainty is great. According to the IAEA, manufacturing a 20-kiloton device (roughly equal in size to the bomb dropped on Nagasaki) requires a minimum of 25 kilograms of weapons-grade uranium or 8 kilograms of plutonium. However, according to a recent estimate, a similar bomb could be developed by using only 6 kilograms of weapons-grade plutonium or 16 kilograms of uranium. Dr. Thomas Cochran of the Natural Resources Defense Council contends that a small fission weapon with a 1-kiloton yield could be manufactured using as little as 1 to 3 kilograms of plutonium or 3 to 8 kilograms of HEU. Viewed in those terms, the plutonium smuggled to Munich fell well below the threshold required to make a nuclear bomb, although the HEU confiscated in Prague approached the minimum requirement for manufacturing a weapon.[2]

TABLE 5.1

Plutonium Seizures in Western Europe, 1990s

Date	Location	Quantity	Form
UNKNOWN	DENMARK	2.83 GRAMS	UNKNOWN
OCTOBER 16, 1991	COMO, ITALY	200 MILLIGRAMS	PLUTONIUM TABLET
NOVEMBER 27, 1991	AUSTRIA	300 MILLIGRAMS	PLUTONIUM SCREWS
MARCH 23, 1992	SWITZERLAND	1.5 MILLIGRAMS	50 PLUTONIUM SCREWS
JULY 8, 1992	BERLIN, GERMANY	500 MILLIGRAMS (5.1 GRAMS)	300 PLUTONIUM CAPSULES
OCTOBER 29, 1992	BULGARIA	200 MILLIGRAMS	140 PLUTONIUM CAPSULES
1993	SWITZERLAND	UNKNOWN	PLUTONIUM SCREWS
MARCH 10, 1994	TENGEN-WIECHS, GERMANY	5.8 GRAMS, 99.75 PERCENT PU-239	IN CONTAINER WITH 56.3 GRAMS OF NONHOMOGENEOUS POWDER
JULY 24, 1994	MUNICH, GERMANY	240 MILLIGRAMS, 87.7 PERCENT U-239	466 MILLIGRAMS PLUTONIUM-URANIUM MIXTURE
1994	MUNICH, GERMANY	SEVERAL HUNDRED MILLIGRAMS	384 METAL PIECES
AUGUST 10, 1994	MUNICH, GERMANY	363.4 GRAMS, 87.7 PERCENT PU-239	CONTAINER OF 560 GRAMS OF MIXED-OXIDE FUEL
AUGUST 12, 1994	BREMEN, GERMANY	50 MILLIGRAMS	MIXTURE OF PLUTONIUM AND AMERICIUM
AUGUST 30, 1994	BULGARIA	UNKNOWN	CONTAINER WITH BERYLLIUM AND PLUTONIUM
SEPTEMBER 1994	VERONA, ITALY	1 GRAM	UNKNOWN
MAY 1995	WEIMAR, GERMANY	UNKNOWN	SMOKE ALARMS CONTAINING PLUTONIUM

Sources: Interpol; European press articles; Monterey Institute of International Studies, nonproliferation databases.

Outflows of radioactive material from the NIS represent a proliferation threat of sorts, but the magnitude of this risk must be viewed in perspective. The military value of most stolen radioactive goods is rated as low; the nuclear black market is characterized by many sellers and few legitimate buyers; and the organized crime connection to the market, at least in Europe, is weakly developed. In addition, the nuclear smuggling pattern for reported cases in Europe seemingly is less directly relevant to weapons production than other proliferation milestones. For example, U.S. and Western European firms contributed significantly to the Iraqi uranium enrichment program before the 1991 Persian Gulf War. Figure 5.1, compiled by the Monterey Institute of International Studies, recounts the chilling supply chain for specific components of gas centrifuges. Western firms also supplied specialty equipment and materials for the Iranian nuclear program. State-sponsored commercial transactions by nuclear powers also probably pose a greater proliferation hazard than nuclear materials smuggling. Take, for example, the above-mentioned Russian proposal in 1995 to sell a gas centrifuge facility to Iran, or, more alarmingly, Chinese transfers of ring magnets, missile components, a "special industrial furnace" (probably used to mold uranium into a bomb core), and possibly blueprints for an atomic bomb to support Pakistan's military buildup. (Note: Pakistan conducted its own series of nuclear tests, answering India's, in May 1998). Nevertheless, the conspicuous appearance of contraband uranium, plutonium, and other radioactive substances in the West is alarming, to say the least, and admittedly jeopardizes affected countries and populations. As an Interpol report declares, "Trafficking in radioactive substances represents a real danger for people and their environment and a potential threat in terms of terrorism."[3] Moreover, for many Western experts, such nuclear smuggling raises the specter of "loose nukes" spirited away from insecure nuclear complexes in the NIS. Consequently, the current low-risk smuggling flow could loom as a harbinger of more serious proliferation risks.

FIGURE 5.1

Companies Reported to Sell Iraqi Gas Centrifuge Components

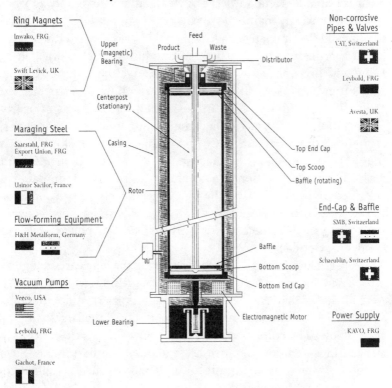

Source: William C. Potter, Center for Nonproliferation Studies, February 1991. Based on technical drawing from William Domke, Lawrence Livermore National Laboratory and data from databases of Center for Nonproliferation Studies, Monterey Institute of International Studies.

THE ACTORS

Trading networks comprising opportunistic businessmen and smugglers are well established in Western countries. According to one Italian news account, European law enforcement officials have identified approximately 600 criminal entrepreneurs who operate behind the shield of 200 front companies and serve as middlemen for nuclear smuggling ventures. As University of Pittsburgh researchers Phil Williams and Paul Woessner conclude, many nuclear traffickers tend to "treat nuclear material as simply another commodity worth trading"—that is, they supply legal and illegal products indiscriminately.[4] Williams and Woessner cite the example of Emrullah Gungor, a Turkish uranium trafficker arrested in 1994, who previously was convicted of smuggling historic artifacts and antiquities. German businessman Adolf Jaekle, arrested in Tengen-Wiechs in May 1994 in possession of 5.6 grams of nearly pure plutonium, formerly had imported and exported shoes, cigarettes, counterfeit currency, and equipment for making french fries. Aleksandr Vanous, an accused Czech heroin smuggler and dealer in counterfeit money, also illustrates this common pattern. Detained by Czech authorities in December 1994, Vanous is suspected of being the middleman in an earlier misguided scheme to deliver a single sample of 87.7 percent U-235 to police buyers in Landshut, Germany.

In Germany, the apparent epicenter of the nuclear smuggling business in Europe, at least 60 percent of trafficking suspects in 1995 were identified as foreigners, mainly from Russia, Poland, Lithuania, and the Ukraine. Russians reportedly represented the largest contingent, followed by Poles. Some traffickers have formed close working relationships—"group commercial structures," to borrow BKA terminology. Moreover, a significant number of nuclear traffickers qualify as repeat offenders. The BKA explains that the German criminal justice system treats suspected nuclear criminals lightly, imposing negligible sentences of a year or less or simply releasing them for lack of evidence. Widespread police activities in the black market might conceivably create judicial sympathy for nuclear offenders, although the relative novelty of nuclear smuggling and the usually trivial composition of the smuggled materials may be prominent factors in the lenient sentences.[5]

Apparently no specialized criminal organization or nuclear mafia operates in Central Europe. Nuclear traffickers generally vend nuclear wares as a sideline business. Indeed, such participation in nuclear commerce may be almost inadvertent. For instance, Gustav Illich, implicated in two nuclear smuggling ventures in Germany in 1994, usually dealt in advanced-design MiG aircraft, automatic pistols, and nonferrous and rare-earth metals. Illich boasted of "good friends in the government and in the military" in Russia and also claimed "a lot of friends in atomic research." As he informed a PBS interviewer in November 1996: "One director of a company producing uranium and plutonium asked me whether I could help [his company] sell their things . . . the state didn't give them anything and the state asked them to get actively involved in selling things that could be sold. Simply they were told to sell uranium and plutonium to official Western buyers."[6]

Walter Boeden, an undercover agent of the Bavarian Land (State) Criminal Police (LKA), contacted Illich and offered to pay as much as $1 million per kilogram for HEU containing more than 90 percent U-235. At Boeden's urging, Illich procured a sample of HEU extracted from a larger uranium shipment that was smuggled from Moscow to Prague in late May or early June 1994. Illich, Alexander Vanous, and an unidentified colleague delivered the sample (which later analysis confirmed was 87.7 percent U-235) to Boeden in Landshut in June. Illich was arrested in July in Fierhofen, Germany, in connection with another undercover purchase of uranium—this time reactor fuel pellets enriched to 4 to 6 percent HEU—organized by the same LKA operative. The LKA had hoped to seize a larger quantity of the same material delivered at Landshut but were disappointed.[7]

The European nuclear materials traffic is managed primarily by various small metals and arms dealers, opportunistic businessmen, and petty smugglers who barely rate a mention in the annals of international crime. However, a few high-profile operators do augment the ranks of typical nuclear smugglers, including active or former government officials and other so-called responsible actors. A few such cases depict the high end of the European nuclear smuggling business.

In October 1991 an official identified as the Honduras honorary consul in Zurich, Frederic Renfer, was detained in that city with seven other suspects in a nuclear sting operation organized by Swiss police. A police search detected 29.5 kilograms of mostly depleted uranium hidden in the diplomat's car. The suspects were soon released, apparently because Switzerland at that time had no laws proscribing traffic in nuclear materials.[8] In a 1992-1993 case in Poland, a former deputy minister of culture and a former security services official were arrested after offering 30 kilograms of weapons-grade uranium and 6 kilograms of plutonium to German television journalists "posing as agents of a country under an international arms embargo." No nuclear materials were actually seized in this case, although the arrests produced a treasure trove of diaries and notebooks replete with the names of NIS traders in rare metals and radioactive materials, according to Polish news reports.[9]

Aleksander Viktorovich Kuzin—a notorious, although perhaps overrated, nuclear criminal and a reputed former KGB colonel—was associated with a network of ostensibly legal trading companies in Europe and the Middle East, as noted in table 5.2. According to uncorroborated testimony by a former associate, Kuzin and several KGB officers masterminded a continentwide system for trading Soviet-made armaments, strategies, and radioactive materials and nuclear technology.[10] However, European police investigators can definitively tie Kuzin to only two illegal nuclear transactions, a plutonium screw case in Austria in November 1991 and an unspecified deal for a sample of red mercury. U.S. intelligence services contend that Kuzin was essentially a scam artist who, like other nuclear traffickers of the period, marketed nuclear wares of little or no strategic or commercial value.[11]

One important case that signals possible high-level involvement in the nuclear traffic features Romano Dolce, an Italian deputy prosecutor in the city of Como. Dolce was arrested in May 1994 on a charge of "criminal conspiracy for the purpose of introducing nuclear material into Italy."[12] Ironically, Dolce had spearheaded several investigations into trafficking in uranium, plutonium, and red mercury in the early 1990s. Moreover, he was one of the first European officials to sound the alarm about the

TABLE 5.2

The Kuzin Network

Firm	Location
BIOKOR INTERNATIONAL SA	SOFIA, BULGARIA
BIOKOR	QATAR
BIOKOR INTERNATIONAL	LIECHTENSTEIN
GFK BIOKOR	MOSCOW, RUSSIA
IMPEX	VIENNA, AUSTRIA COMÓ, ITALY
KUZIN INTERNATIONAL GROUP	VIENNA, AUSTRIA
KUZIN ITALIA	UDINE, ITALY
KUZIN SYSTEMS	COLOGNE, GERMANY
KUZIN UNITRADE	UDINE, ITALY MUNICH, GERMANY COLOGNE, GERMANY
SOVITRADE	TRIESTE, ITALY
TAHER KUZIN INTERNATIONAL, LTD.	DUBLIN, IRELAND

Sources: Claire Sterling, *Thieves' World* (New York: Simon and Schuster, 1994) pp. 219-220; Interpol interviews.

inflow of radioactive materials from the East. "With the disintegration of the Soviet Union you can be sure that the illegal trade will increase massively," he proclaimed in a January 1992 interview. Dolce's investigations gave rise to much hot air but no radioactive seizures of any consequence. His accusers emphasized this point, unkindly suggesting that his maneuvers were, in fact, an elaborate deception designed to divert authorities' attention from more important nuclear deals that Dolce himself helped to orchestrate.

Dolce told a different tale to PBS *Front Line* correspondent Eric Nadler, namely that he was framed to cover up a nuclear trafficking conspiracy in the Italian intelligence services. He claimed to be on the verge of proving such a plot when he was arrested. Dolce currently is at liberty pending the outcome of his trial, which could take years in Italy.[13]

The relationship between nuclear smuggling and transnational organized crime—a subject of considerable speculation—also requires some elaboration. For example, rumors abound that Russian and Italian crime syndicates are cooperating in nuclear smuggling ventures. Reports surfaced in 1993 of a crime summit in Prague in late 1992, where Italian and Russian representatives discussed various prospective drug operations, money-laundering schemes, and possible exchanges of weapons and nuclear merchandise for Western narcotics, especially cocaine. In a 1994 Washington speech, CIA director James Woolsey confirmed that such a meeting occurred but mentioned only the drugs topic. "The Italians agreed to provide know-how for the acquisition and distribution of illegal drugs, while the Russian groups pledged to provide security along with transit and distribution routes," he said.[14]

The House Republican Research Committee posits an even more imaginative account, claiming that Italian and Russian crime syndicates are collaborating to acquire radioactive materials that originated in the NIS and then transship them through Europe to radical Islamic states in the Middle East. "Uranium smuggling into Western Europe now comes atop 'the traffic in suitcases full of rubles and gold from Russia,'" observes the committee document. The Italian mafia then ships the nuclear goods through the former Yugoslavia (the document refers to "radioactive storage facilities in Croatia"), receiving in exchange drugs and Iranian-produced counterfeit dollars.[15]

Despite these accounts, the connection between organized crime and the visible black market in nuclear materials seems insubstantial. The poor quality of most diverted nuclear substances correlates with a disorganized market rather than one manipulated by professionals. Firm conclusions on this point are difficult to draw, however. A recent case in Italy documents a possible connection of the Sicilian mafia or its affiliates to nuclear materials smuggling. In March 1998, a police sting operation in Rome netted a fuel element or rod containing 200 grams of reactor-grade uranium of relatively high enrichment (19 percent U-235). Rather oddly, the uranium did not originate in the former Soviet Union, but was part of a batch of 9 rods manufactured by a San Diego–based U.S. company, "General Atomics," and sent to Zaire for use in the company's TRIGA Mark II reactor there. According to Italian press reports the reactor never actually was built and the rods "ended up" in Italy in the hands of the Cosa Nostra, which intended to sell the entire consignment for 200 billion lire ($112 million). In negotiation with the criminals police offered to buy one of the rods for 23 billion lire ($13 million); the whereabouts of the rest of the material still is not known. Reportedly 15 people were arrested in the case, several of whom had connections to the Catania (Sicily) Santapaola family and the Roman Magliana gang, considered to be an arm of the Cosa Nostra.[16]

The Rome case, though, stands apart from the general European smuggling pattern. An alternative hypothesis is that Italian organized crime groups function more as service agents in the black-market nuclear trade (collecting fees, say, for cross-border smuggling or for ditching radioactive waste) than as brokers of nuclear goods. In May 1997, I interviewed an Italian official, Major Francesco Bruzzese, who heads the Nucleo Operativo Ecologico, a joint unit of the Ministry of Defense and the Ministry of the Environment that is responsible for investigating environmental crimes in Italy. Bruzzese contends that the Neopolitan Camorra (one of Italy's four mafia crime groups) operates an illegal transnational scheme to dispose of toxic radioactive waste that originated in Central Europe (primarily Germany). Bruzzese postulates that the Camorra transports the waste to southern Italy, floats it into the Mediterranean, and deep-sixes it in the Gulf of Naples or off the western coast of Sicily. Of course, in these instances the Camorra claims no commercial interest in the nuclear materials per se; however, the major's account suggests that the group possesses more than a passing familiarity with the nuclear business, including the capability to containerize dangerous radioactive cargoes and manage their transport through covert channels. Other organized crime groups may participate in this dangerous traffic. An account in the London *Observer* cites a prosecutorial investigation in Reggio Calabria linking the Calabria-based 'Ndrangheta gang to radioactive dumping off the "toe" of Italy. The gang reportedly took the waste out to sea in tramp steamers; then "the crews would be ferried to safety and the steamers scuttled." (According to a Naples-based environmentalist group, at least 5 billion curies of radioactive waste from European power plants have been ditched illegally in the Mediterranean in the past 20 years. Italian organized crime may well have a sizeable share of this business.)[17]

Clearly international mafias cultivate the capability to smuggle virtually any type of material. In addition, transnational collaboration among crime groups to distribute narcotics, money, and other commodities is on the rise, a fact that undoubtedly will lead to expanding opportunities and channels for moving radioactive substances. At this time, evidence is difficult to amass and still murky on whether organized crime has developed a compelling commercial interest in trading radioactive materials.

THE EARLY 1990S

Although generating some understandable hype, early nuclear smuggling in Europe largely conveyed unmarketable materials that were practically devoid of strategic significance. One of the first European judicial investigations into the illicit nuclear trade began in the northern Italian city of Como in October 1991. At that time, Deputy Prosecutor Romano Dolce reportedly acquired information about a "large international clandestine traffic" in nuclear goods from two informants—Danish businessman Jorgen Nielsen and Yugoslav Dmitrije Nikolic—who themselves served as middlemen for nuclear traders. Nielsen and Nikolic financed another trafficker, Swiss businessman Karl Friedrich Federer, who subsequently was arrested in Como on October 16 while carrying a small cylinder (a so-called tablet) that held 200 micrograms of plutonium. (According to a Moscow newspaper, the tablet was used to set gauges for working with fissionable materials and originally was exported by Techsnabexport, the official Russian trading agent for nuclear materials.) Federer was hauled before Dolce and, during interrogation, detailed the specifics of a forthcoming nuclear deal in Switzerland that would transfer 30 kilograms of uranium and 10 kilograms of plutonium. Dolce alerted the Swiss police, who crafted a sting operation to flush out the traffickers. As noted previously, the operation netted eight suspects, including the honorary consul of Honduras, and 19.5 kilograms of severely depleted uranium—in fact, the black-market uranium contained less of the U-235 isotope than natural uranium (0.4 percent U-235 compared to 0.7 percent) and commanded a market value of only $31 to $33 per kilogram. If any plutonium actually was included in that shipment, it disappeared without a trace.[18]

The following January in Milan, Dolce oversaw another over-blown investigation developed on the basis of testimony from the same Danish informant (Jorgen Nielsen) who had led authorities to Karl Federer in Como. The upshot of the case was the arrest of three Hungarians and a naturalized Austrian at the Milan Hotel Capitol after they arrived "in their Mercedes from Budapest" with two glass jars marked with Cyrillic script that harbored roughly 2 to 5 kilograms of red mercury. Dolce's raid also netted 600 million lire in "checks payable to the bearer" and a quantity of scandium, a rare earth metal. The authorities had hoped to seize 5 kilograms of plutonium in the bust; however, as the story goes, the traffickers had just consigned the plutonium to a Libyan agent, who made good his escape. Two Italian nuclear energy laboratories subsequently analyzed the enigmatic red mercury (or whatever it really was), but the results were never made public. In any event, the suspects were quickly released, apparently because they had committed no crime.[19]

One of the men arrested in the Milan caper, naturalized Austrian citizen and electrical engineer Dezider Ostrogonac, testified before Dolce. Ostrogonac reputedly related a fabulous narrative, describing a multifaceted underground trade in Soviet weaponry that was permeating Europe and dealt in "machine guns, fighter aircraft, tanks, red mercury, scandium, and radioactive and strategic materials, as well as nuclear warheads and nuclear technology." Ostrogonac claimed that this traffic was the brainchild of "agents of the KGB, officers of the Red Army and high officials of the Russian government." He identified international trader Aleksandr Kuzin as the central player in this network. (Ostrogonac reportedly had administered several of Kuzin's front companies.) Ostrogonac also named as accomplices nine other purported KGB agents (whose status as active members of successor Russian intelligence agencies is unknown) and five Russian military officers.[20]

Ostrogonac's account conformed closely—suspiciously so—to Magistrate Dolce's own conspiratorial views. However, the concept of a KGB-led conspiracy seems farfetched given the disorganized, chaotic pattern of nuclear smuggling in the early 1990s. Of course, Kuzin's trading conglomerate existed, at least on paper, but its activities were less than meets the eye. Law enforcement thought of Kuzin as a preeminent international fraud, but with few proven ties to the nuclear smuggling business.

In late 1992 one of the most ludicrous incidents in the annals of nuclear smuggling transpired in Sofia, Bulgaria. In early November the Bulgarian Interior Ministry issued a report that a traveling bag containing a box of 140 plutonium capsules was abandoned in the cloakroom of the Sofia Sheraton Hotel. However, Bulgarian officials ultimately identified the perpetrator as Barrie Penrose, a British journalist with the London *Sunday Express*. Penrose protested that he was researching the activities of a gang of armed merchants ("a British arms dealer, a Swedish businessman, and two Polish entrepreneurs") who offered to deliver 80 kilograms of plutonium, priced at $1 million per kilogram, to the Iraqi embassy in Sofia. Penrose and several colleagues had managed to insinuate themselves as intermediaries in the transaction, which, in the journalist's words, "went dramatically wrong for the gang because we passed the first box of plutonium, worth $378,000 (240,000 pounds sterling) to the Bulgarian authorities." At this point, extrapolating the arithmetic is an intriguing exercise, because the 140 screws weighed one-third of a kilogram, but the combined plutonium content totaled only 200 milligrams. Evidently the sellers intended to charge their purported Iraqi clients an actual price of $1.89 billion per kilogram ($1,890 per milligram) for the plutonium. Compounding the confusion, the capsules—fuel gas analyzers produced by Moscow's Izotop—had been exported legally to a Bulgarian company and subsequently were stolen from one of its warehouses. The entire affair reads like a gigantic journalistic hoax designed to exploit stereotypical public fears of loose nukes, doomsday arms merchants, and evil Islamic bomb builders.[21] Of course, it could be totally factual, an amazing chapter in the fantastic saga of nuclear smuggling.

NONSTRATEGIC CONCERNS

On the whole, nuclear smugglers in Europe in the early 1990s were a ludicrously inept crew who, as might be expected, could not contact serious customers for the plutonium screws, depleted uranium, and other radioactive junk that they hawked. Nevertheless, some hazardous radioactive isotopes were vagabonding across the continent, creating a potentially serious threat to public health. In a high-profile case in October 1992, German police discovered 20 grams of a mix of cesium-137 and strontium-90 in a metal cylinder stashed in a locker in the main Frankfurt railway station. A subsequent investigation detected an identical container concealed in the trunk of a car with Polish license plates that was parked in front of Frankfurt's Mondial Hotel.[22] In a conclusion fraught with irony, European police view the *absence* of a market for radioactive materials as an important force behind the environmental threat. The presumption is that frustrated nuclear vendors who misjudge the market for their wares may simply abandon them in public places (as the Frankfurt cases may suggest) or ostensibly employ them as leverage in extortion schemes against the government.

Indeed, threats to deploy radioactive materials for political or financial gain were fairly common in the 1990s. The BKA recorded at least 16 such episodes in Germany between 1993 and 1995, including the following five rather bizarre cases. First, an extortionist promised to destroy four German cities by exploding "thermonuclear warheads" unless he received 100 million Deutschmarks (DM) from the State Lottery Administration. Second, unknown offenders demanded 250,000 DM from a German casino, threatening to detonate a nuclear device near it if the money was not forthcoming. (The extortion letter was signed by "the Russian mafia," but more likely it was composed by a gambler who was seriously down on his luck.) Third, an anonymous caller informed police of a nefarious Serbian plan to fire a grenade filled with radioactive waste in Munich if German troops were deployed in Bosnia. Fourth, a group calling itself the "German People's Liberation Army" insisted on the evacuation of German territories held by Poland since 1918. Otherwise, the group warned, the Polish parliament and the president of Poland would be exposed to radiation from a kilogram of plutonium already concealed somewhere in Warsaw. And fifth, an anonymous caller cautioned a German government department that six nuclear warheads were buried on former East German territory and offered to disclose the location of the weapons for 1 million DM. In a follow-up call, he threatened to detonate one device by satellite. In this case, the offender was actually traced and later arrested in Italy. According to the BKA account, "He hanged himself while being held in detention prior to his trial." Although such extortion strategies carry little credibility—and seem contrived if not infantile—in the European environment, they contributed to the general paranoia and nervousness about nuclear smuggling.[23]

In general, Europeans assess nuclear smuggling as an environmental crisis aggravated by malevolent human actors (typically would-be extortionists or political nut cases).[24] In contrast, U.S. policymakers are more concerned about the strategic dimensions of the threat—the possibility, even if remote, that rogue states or terrorist groups might just procure the means to manufacture finished nuclear weapons. Moreover, several consequential smuggling cases in Europe in 1994 provided some substance for these concerns. The nuclear material in question apparently was not liberated from Russian atomic bomb stockpiles; nonetheless, it clearly was suitable for weapons. The following sections analyze these smuggling operations and their implications for nuclear proliferation.

SIGNIFICANT EPISODES

Introduction

Central European authorities conducted four important seizures of weapons-usable materials in 1994, three of which were definitively linked to undercover sting operations. Two seizures of HEU in 1995 apparently were offshoots of the Landshut and Prague HEU cases in 1994, but no other reliable details are available. Five of the six cases are traceable to a supplier or suppliers in Obninsk, Russia, who formerly worked for the Obninsk IPPE. Table 5.3 summarizes basic information about the cases—specifically, location and date of seizures, characteristics of the materials, and probable Russian origins.

Tengen-Wiechs

On May 10, 1994, in the small town of Tengen-Wiechs (near Stuttgart), police searching the home of Adolf Jaekle, a businessman under investigation for counterfeiting, unexpectedly discovered in the garage a cylinder containing 56.3 grams of nonhomogeneous powder. On analysis, the powder proved to be mostly high-grade mercury, antimony, and iodine, but 10.28 percent, or approximately 5.8 grams, tested as plutonium-239.[25] Moreover, the material was extraordinarily pure; in fact, the percentage of plutonium exceeded that of any known bomb ingredients.

TABLE 5.3

Important Seizures of Weapons-Usable Materials in Central Europe, 1994[*]

Date	Location	Material Seized	Most Likely Source
MAY 1994	TENGEN-WIECHS, BADEN-WUERTTEMBURG, GERMANY	5.6 GRAMS, 99.75 PERCENT PLUTONIUM	A RUSSIAN WEAPONS LABORATORY (POSSIBLY ARZAMAS-16)
JUNE 1994	LANDSHUT, BAVARIA, GERMANY	0.8 GRAMS, 87.7 PERCENT U-235	TRACED TO A FORMER EMPLOYEE OF THE OBNINSK INSTITUTE OF PHYSICS AND POWER ENGINEERING
AUGUST 1994	MUNICH, BAVARIA, GERMANY	560 GRAMS OF MIXED OXIDE FUEL WITH 363 GRAMS OF PLUTONIUM AND 210 GRAMS OF LITHIUM-6	THEFT TRACED TO THREE FORMER INSTITUTE OF PHYSICS AND POWER ENGINEERING EMPLOYEES
DECEMBER 1994	PRAGUE, CZECH REPUBLIC	2.73 KILOGRAMS, 87.7 PERCENT U-235; SAME ISOTOPIC COMPOSITION AS LANDSHUT	SAME AS LANDSHUT
JUNE 1995	PRAGUE, CZECH REPUBLIC	0.415 GRAMS, 88.7 PERCENT U-235; SAME ISOTOPIC COMPOSITION AS LANDSHUT AND PRAGUE	SAME AS LANDSHUT AND PRAGUE
JUNE 1995	CESKE BUDEJOVICE, CZECH REPUBLIC	16.96 GRAMS, 87.7 PERCENT U-235; SAME ISOTOPIC COMPOSITION AS LANDSHUT AND PRAGUE	SAME AS LANDSHUT AND PRAGUE

Sources: Institute of Physics and Power Engineering, Obninsk; IAEA; William Potter, "Nuclear Smuggling from the Former Soviet Union," Testimony prepared for the U.S. Senate Committee on Government Affairs, Permanent Subcommittee on Investigation, March 13, 1996, p. 5; IAEA databases.

[*] One Western intelligence source that I interviewed mentioned a seizure of nuclear submarine fuel in non-NIS Europe in 1995. No information about that seizure was ever published and further details are not available.

Some analysts contend that the plutonium had been produced for research rather than weapons, possibly by a Russian research laboratory, such as Arzamas-16 or Chelyabinsk-70. However, scientists at the Institute of Trans-Uranic Elements in Karlsruhe, Germany, asserted that a small amount of gallium in the sample indicated a nuclear weapons source. (In atomic bombs, gallium is alloyed with plutonium to stabilize the warhead under different temperatures and pressures.)[26] The origin of this powerhouse plutonium has never been satisfactorily confirmed, at least publicly. Regardless of its genesis, the Tengen-Wiechs seizure marked the first verified instance of bomb-quality material making its way into European smuggling channels and thus assumed some strategic significance.[27]

Jaekle was arrested and jailed, charged with both atomic smuggling and counterfeiting. (Ironically, the latter offense actually ranked as the more serious crime.) In November 1994 he was sentenced to three years and four months for counterfeiting and two and a half years on the nuclear charges. Interrogated about his contacts, Jaekle claimed that he received the container from a Swiss businessman in Basel, Willy Jetzler—but, in a subsequent deposition, Jetzler denied the transaction, stating that he had not seen Jaekle in years. Then, in an evident plea-bargain maneuver, Jaekle intimated that the Tengen-Wiechs material was part of a huge consignment of as much as 150 kilograms of plutonium that previously had been transported to Switzerland from Russia. He also mentioned stashes of HEU in Switzerland and Austria and even detailed specific smuggling storage sites in Switzerland. However, the leads proved fruitless; Swiss police searched business establishments and warehouses belonging to Jaekle's contacts but apparently returned empty-handed.[28]

Jaekle probably fabricated the tale of the enormous plutonium shipment as an alarmist ruse and a bargaining tool. As William Potter of the Monterey Institute of International Studies observed in his March 1996 Senate testimony, "Extraordinary costs associated with the production of such pure plutonium make it unlikely that more than a few kilograms of the material was ever produced, much less stolen and exported."[29]

In fact, Jaekle's business connections constituted a tangled web. Some 3,500 names and addresses in his notebooks and card files implied that his multifarious trading activities spanned Germany, Switzerland, the Balkans, Russia, the Arab world, and the Far East. Different theories were posited about his buyer and supplier contacts: Perhaps he purchased the plutonium with bank credits supplied by a bank in Vienna, Austria, owned by North Korea; possibly Jaekle was a link in a nuclear supply chain connecting Russian military and intelligence officers, Balkan weapons traders, and Iraqi buyers. In the latter hypothesis, Iraqis reputedly used a numbered account in the Banco Exterior in Zurich to pay for shipping the plutonium from the Bulgarian port of Varna to Athens and thence to Switzerland and Germany. Neither interpretation seems especially persuasive. Iraqi or North Korean buyers would be unlikely to pursue the high-risk and geographically irrational option of procuring plutonium via a supply network that wound through Central and Western Europe.[30]

Nevertheless, Jaekle undoubtedly participated in some very unsavory business dealings. According to the newspaper *Welt am Sonntag,* his contacts included one Bulgarian businessman (Mitko M.) who represented an unnamed German industrial company in Sofia and another Bulgarian (Dina N.) who operated a Moscow company called Otozhenka Ltd. A Russian newspaper, *Argumenty i Fakty,* later identified the Bulgarians' last names as Mitkov and Nakova and reported that Mitkov and Nakova were acquainted. In conversations with *Welt's* investigators, both traders proclaimed that they could supply plutonium. "I can deliver plutonium to you. That is no problem," said Mitkov. Nakova, who boasted high-level KGB and military contacts, asserted that she could deliver plutonium in two to four weeks but demanded payment in U.S. dollars. Mitkov reputedly maintained "friendly relations" with the director of Kintex, a Bulgarian trading company with a history of smuggling weaponry and other strategic goods to Iran and Iraq. According to *Argumenty i Fakty,* Jaekle confessed from prison that Mitkov had promised to sell him an unlimited quantity of radioactive materials through Kintex. However, the notion of an established Kintex-Iraqi nuclear smuggling chain stretching through Switzerland and Germany seems far-fetched, as already explained.

A more likely scenario includes a prearranged plan; perhaps Jaekle brought the plutonium to Germany with the intention of later marketing it (or a larger consignment of the material) to Iraqis or other interested buyers. Indeed, documents in Jaekle's house verified that he had been trying to contact Iraqi agents. Alternatively, the sample might have been smuggled to Europe for testing and certification, while the main shipment was destined for a more direct delivery route to the end users. However, the scheduled sequence of actual and unrealized events in this complex case probably will never be substantiated.[31] In another interesting twist, the business card of a member of Moscow's Kurchatov Institute was discovered among Jaekle's effects, leading to speculation that the sample had been stolen from the institute. Kurchatov spokesmen, of course, denied the allegations.

Operation Hades

The second significant case of plutonium smuggling in the West was detected in Munich exactly three months after the Tengen-Wiechs seizure. On August 10 Bavarian LKA officers at Munich's Franz Josef Straus Airport confiscated a black suitcase being unloaded from Lufthansa flight 3369, arriving from Moscow. Inside the suitcase, the LKA unit found a cylinder containing 560 grams of mixed-oxide fuel that included 363.4 grams of plutonium-239, 87.6 percent pure. The case also held a plastic bag with 201 grams of nonradioactive lithium-6, a metallic element used in making tritium, a component of thermonuclear weapons. Bavarian authorities arrested both the apparent owner of the valise, a Colombian national named Justiniano Torres Benitez, and a Spaniard, Julio Oroz Eguia, who met Torres at the airport. Another Spanish suspect in the case, Javier Bengoechea Arratibel, was arrested later at a nearby hotel.[32]

The smugglers displayed all the characteristics of quintessential amateurs. As Phil Williams and Paul Woessner observed,

"None of the three seems to have had a background that would have led to the creation of a highly sophisticated smuggling operation."[33] Torres had received a Russian medical degree at the University of Kuban in the mid-1980s. He practiced medicine in Colombia for a time but seemingly tired of the profession. In 1990 Torres returned to Russia hoping to become a successful entrepreneur in a nation undergoing accelerated change. Together with a Russian partner, an Aeroflot executive based in Bogota, he opened a company (EMIS-21) in 1991 to export helicopters and other military equipment mainly to the Colombian military; however, when that business soured, Torres then turned to trading anything that he could sell—caviar, cement, fertilizer, animal hides, and ultimately plutonium. Torres's accomplices, Oroz and Bengoechea, are described as unsuccessful entrepreneurs in the construction business. Oroz had operated an import-export business between Russia and Spain, and Bengoechea occasionally handled deals for Russian helicopters. Both men had accumulated large debts; indeed, all three Munich conspirators apparently viewed plutonium smuggling as an opportunity to extricate themselves from serious financial difficulties—which might have been true if the buyers had been legitimate.[34]

In fact, the Munich case was the outcome of a complex international sting operation principally orchestrated by the Bavarian LKA and the German Federal Intelligence Service, the BND. A Spanish BND undercover agent, Rafael Ferrera Hernandez (Rafa) arranged a July 25 meeting in Munich for Oroz, Torres, and a "rich merchant from Munich." The purported buyer actually was LKA agent Walter Boeden. At the meeting, the traffickers delivered to Boeden a 240-milligram sample of plutonium smuggled by train from Moscow to Munich on July 9. According to an article in *Der Spiegel*, Torres requested payment for the sample so that he could compensate suppliers in an unidentified factory in Russia; however, Boeden objected, declaring "I have received so many samples and then I did not get any more. The people just disappeared with the money." Torres countered by informing Boeden "If you want, we will go to Moscow and I give it to you there. . . . Everything is ready. There are 11 kilograms there." Boeden then paid Torres 7,000 DM for the sample and for expenses but did not make the trip to Moscow.[35]

In subsequent negotiations, Boeden and the plutonium vendors reached an agreement—$265 million for 4 kilograms of plutonium and an additional $11 million for 2.5 kilograms of lithium-6.[36] The agent showed Torres and Oroz a letter of credit from the Bayerische Hypoteken und Wechsel Banke in Munich that read in part, "Dear Mr. Boeden: Taking your assets and your excellent reputation into consideration, we are ready, able and willing to guarantee payments of up to $276 million for your business transactions." (A bank spokesman later pronounced the letter a forgery.) In any event, the July discussions precipitated the next month's events in Munich. The 363.4 grams of plutonium and the 201 grams of lithium-6 apparently were the first installments of the quantities promised to Boeden by the sellers in their July deal.[37]

The BND side of the affair, known as Operation Hades, unfolded in Madrid, Moscow, and Munich over several months. In Madrid, Rafa met with a Spanish arms broker, an associate of Bengoechea named Jose Fernandez Martin, and posed as an intermediary who was fully prepared to buy plutonium suitable for nuclear weapons. (The rationale for using Spain as the initial venue for Hades is not clear; perhaps the BND hoped to uncover a link between nuclear smuggling and a Basque terrorist group, the Basque Fatherland, and Liberty, or ETA, but such a connection was never established.) In late May and early June 1994, Rafa and an undercover colleague held business discussions with Bengoechea and with unidentified Spanish businessmen, also in Madrid. These contacts set the stage for the July negotiations with Walter Boeden in Munich, which in turn culminated in the large plutonium seizure and the arrest of Torres and his companions the following month. The arguments used by the BND operatives to convince Torres and his partners that the plutonium deal had to take place in Munich remain one of the enduring mysteries of the case.[38]

The source of the plutonium also poses a challenging question. The best available evidence suggests that Torres's network of military contacts in Moscow also extended to the atomic energy industry. The Russian Federal Counterintelligence Service (FSK) proposed one version of events in an October 1995 letter to the German Ministry of Justice. According to the FSK, Torres, through a Moscow acquaintance named Gennadiy Nikiforov, managed to contact three Obninsk residents—E. V. Baranov, O. V. Astafyev, and I. I. Penkov—intending to purchase "radioactive material." In June Torres bought a 2-gram sample of material for $2,000; in August he acquired another 400 grams. (This account varies from that of Western sources, which reported that 560 grams of mixed-oxide fuel were seized in Munich.)[39] Torres reportedly told his German interrogators that the plutonium was stolen from a fissile material inventory at the Obninsk IPPE. The head of the IPPE international relations department, Gennadiy Pshakin, confirmed that Baranov, Astafyev, and Penkov were former employees of the institute. The men had left a year or more before the Munich transaction. Penkov was a nuclear scientist, Baranov a research engineer, and Astafyev an engineer in charge of a materials storage facility.[40] When and how the plutonium was hijacked from the institute and where the material was secreted before mid-1994 cannot be ascertained from the available data.

Aftermath of Munich

The Munich incident prompted both consternation and controversy in Germany. A public opinion poll in late August 1994 indicated that 71 percent of Germans ranked trafficking in nuclear materials as a direct threat to their personal safety and security. At the same time, concerns were voiced over the BND and LKA roles in stimulating demand for nuclear materials. "We have to be careful that our [intelligence] services don't create the market for plutonium they aim to combat," warned Peter Struck, a parliamentary leader of the opposition Social Democratic Party.[41] The hypothesis that the Munich deal was largely the product of a provocation by the intelligence services was borne out by testimony at the 1994-1995 trial of the three smugglers. This testimony detailed the subterfuge used to entrap the smugglers, including Boeden's $276 million fake line of credit. A senior BND official code-named Sybille confirmed under oath that the BKA and the LKA offered to pay Rafa $215,000 in cash if he succeeded in obtaining foreign plutonium from a would-be smuggler.[42]

Meanwhile, the bureaucrats were busily covering up their own exposure in the affair. The heads of the BND and the Bavarian Interior Ministry (which controls the LKA) each denied responsibility for organizing the Munich sting. A parliamentary Investigatory Commission is evaluating the legality of offers to buy foreign plutonium and assessing whether senior government officials were aware of these tactics. As of this writing, a report from the commission is still being prepared.[43]

Although Munich clearly was the result of undercover police work, the episode created widespread alarm, fueling suspicion that Russia cannot monitor and control its nuclear stockpiles. "This is a serious danger not only for us but for many," said German Chancellor Helmut Kohl in an August 1994 television interview. One week after the Munich bust, Bavarian Interior Minister Gunther Beckstein claimed that Russia's entire nuclear safeguards system "was not functioning at all." Germany's finance minister, Theo Waigel, darkly hinted that future German aid to Russia would be contingent on Russian efforts to thwart nuclear smuggling.[44]

On the other hand, official Russian reactions ranged from outright denial ("not a single gram of plutonium is missing from storage," emphasized an FSK spokesman) to accusations that the West was looking to embarrass Russia and impose its own control and inspection regime on Russian atomic enterprises.[45] A MINATOM spokesman, Georgiy Kaurov, claimed that the German Secret Services placed the plutonium on board the Lufthansa plane in Munich to discredit Russia. In a March 1995 seminar in Munich, Kaurov asserted that the material unaccounted for at the MINATOM production facilities "is not in the realm of tons or kilograms but grams. You might not agree with this, but it is a fact."[46] The head of the MINATOM Main Scientific and Technological Administration, Yevgeniy Mikerin, detected an "economic motivation" behind the Munich sting. "By convincing the whole world that the proper control is lacking in the Ministry of Atomic Energy, the West is trying to impose on us its assistance in constructing new storage facilities and imposing its own control systems. And that means multimillion-dollar orders for the suppliers' firms."[47]

Russia and Germany later tried to mend their differences: In late October, three days of talks between the German minister of state for security issues, Bernd Schmidbauer, and the FSK chief, Sergei Stepashin, produced a memorandum of understanding to cooperate against nuclear smuggling. "Both sides believe it is vitally important to halt international trafficking in nuclear and radioactive materials, irrespective of where they originate, by all possible means," stated the memorandum. The Germans and Russians agreed to exchange intelligence information on the origins, routes and methods, and potential customers for the black market in nuclear materials.[48] The combination of German and Russian cooperation and the general publicity surrounding the Munich operation may have deterred serious smugglers from peddling their goods in Germany. In any event, no important seizures of radioactive materials have been recorded there since the Munich case, implying a possible shift in the dynamics of the traffic.

Landshut, Prague, and Beyond

Despite the gap between the June and December 1994 seizures of uranium in Landshut and Prague, these events actually represent separate sections of one large case. Although conflicting versions describe events surrounding the case, several conclusions seem clear. First, the HEU seized in Prague in December was smuggled there from Russia (via Minsk and Warsaw) in late May or early June 1994. Second, the 800-milligram sample of HEU delivered to Walter Boeden in Landshut was chemically identical to the Prague consignment, doubtless because it was extracted from the same cache. Third, a link exists to the Munich plutonium episode, because the Russian supplier of the HEU was Eduard Baranov, one of the three former IPPE employees who provided the plutonium to Justiniano Torres. Fourth, Landshut and Prague both were associated with undercover operations, although the shipment of HEU to Prague may have occurred independent of police offers to purchase the material. Reports surfaced that "German middlemen" had conducted sales negotiations with North Koreans, Spaniards, and Nigerians, but such discussions, if they occurred, were unsuccessful.[49] According to a Senate staff report, "The North Koreans allegedly canceled negotiations because they obtained the material they wanted from other sources; the Spaniards were willing to pay five times the middlemen's asking price, but wanted to use counterfeit dollars; and the Nigerians allegedly did not want to pay in cash, but with drugs."[50] I doubt the authenticity of the negotiations. The so-called middlemen, no doubt German undercover police, probably wanted to impress the uranium traffickers that they were actively searching for buyers.

The identified smuggling participants in the Landshut-Prague affair constituted a loose polyglot grouping of at least 14 people of differing nationalities and professions. The principal players in the case were Jaroslav Vagner, a Czech national described as a "former nuclear institute worker who had migrated into the bakery business," Gustav Illich, a Slovak musician and part-time arms dealer, and Aleksander Scherbinin, a Russian or Tadjik national (accounts differ) who at one time resided in Obninsk. Other participants included Zdenek Cech, the head of a Prague transport company, Autotransport, and a "high-ranking" Prague policeman, Zdenek Sindlauer.[51] One person implicated in the Landshut sting, Alexander Vanous, was arrested in late 1994 for heroin trafficking. Illich and Vagner represented key figures in the events at Landshut and Prague, respectively, but seemingly maintained separate smuggling networks; yet the two men obviously were in contact. ("I talked with him several times. I did not like him at all because he drank a lot," Illich told a PBS interviewer in November 1996.) Illich apparently acquired the 800-milligram HEU sample, delivered to Boeden at Landshut, from Vagner or his associates.

Gustav Illich had held earlier negotiations with Walter Boeden before his meeting with the LKA agent on June 13. In late April

Illich offered to supply Boeden with "plutonium, highly enriched uranium, nightscopes, MiGs and 1,000 Scorpion automatic pistols." In a second meeting, Boeden informed Illich that he had "solved the plutonium matter" (possibly because preparations for the Munich sting operation were already under way) and that he wanted 90 percent HEU, for which he would pay as much as $1 million per kilogram. (Illich also was conducting discussions with a German businesswoman, Krista Klein, who apparently sought to be the intermediary in his arrangements with Boeden. Klein was later arrested but received only probation.)

In late May or early June, Illich notified Boeden about the large HEU cache in Prague. Subsequently, Illich told Boeden that several kilograms of HEU (3.3 or 6.0 kilograms, according to different police reports) were secreted somewhere in Prague. After obtaining the sample at Landshut, Illich and Boeden and Boeden's "secretary," another police operative, met at a bank in Prague. Boeden displayed a safe deposit box to Illich that held 340,000 DM. A meeting was arranged in Fierhofen in early July, where Boeden hoped to flush out the rest of the cache. As noted, the bust netted only pellets of reactor-grade uranium, but police were forced to arrest Illich and two colleagues, because they were technically guilty of transporting radioactive material.[52]

The former scientist Jaroslav Vagner, who once worked in the Czech Nuclear Research Institute at Rez, represented the first European nuclear professional implicated in atomic smuggling. The deal was really Vagner's—he negotiated the purchase of the uranium (Baranov was asking $800 per gram) and arranged its transport to Prague. Aleksander Scherbinin and Zdenek Cech acted as couriers for the uranium. Scherbinin also was linked to Obninsk and at one time was Baranov's neighbor; he apparently functioned as the intermediary in Vagner's dealings with Baranov. He is described as "suffering under mounting debts from a business deal gone bad—a typical pattern in the illegal nuclear trade."[53]

German undercover police continued to work on the case after Landshut. They managed to contact Scherbinin, dangling the prospects of a buyer (imaginary, of course) who was seeking a steady supply of 5 kilograms of HEU per month. Scherbinin conveyed this information to his Russian contacts, who claimed that they could supply much larger quantities of the material—40 kilograms in a short time and as much as a ton over a longer period. Police negotiated with the smugglers from July through November, trying, without success, to locate and capture the main uranium shipment. Apparently, an additional offer of $4.5 million was made to the dealers in December, after which they proceeded to retrieve the smuggled uranium from a bank vault. On December 14, Vagner, Scherbinin, and a Belorussian named Valera Kunickiy (the latter an employee of Autotransport) were arrested with 2.72 kilograms of uranium while sitting in a car in front of a Prague restaurant waiting for the promised buyer.[54]

Five others were arrested later, among them Sindlauer and Cech. In 1997, the Prague city court sentenced Vagner (who claimed to be only a "consultant" in the attempted deal) and Scherbinin each to eight years in prison. Cech and Sindlauer (who allegedly had stored the material in his apartment for a time) received two-and-a-half and one-and-a-half year sentences, respectively. However, both men will remain free because of time served before the trial. Four other accused conspirators in the case, including Kunicky, were acquited.[55]

Sample-size quantities of the same Prague consignment have surfaced since December 1994, suggesting that Vagner and his colleagues conducted a wide search for possible buyers. The IAEA database reports two incidents in the Czech Republic in June 1995 involving, respectively, 415 milligrams and 16.96 grams of HEU that were identical in composition to the Prague material. How and under what circumstances the police discovered the samples—and whether arrests were made in these cases—still are not public knowledge.[56]

Evaluation

The events of Tengen-Wiechs, Munich, Landshut, and Prague did not in themselves pose a grave danger to Western security. The quantities of material involved, except perhaps those in the Prague case, were too small for bomb-making purposes. The buyers and end users never materialized. In three of the cases, police obviously created a false market; in the Tengen-Wiechs episode, the smuggler probably was searching for a buyer. Almost all of the participants ranked as amateur criminals, many confronting hard times financially. Yet aspects of the cases are distinctly troubling. For example, the suggestion was advanced that weapons-usable material had escaped from Russian government control; Torres allegedly informed Boeden that 11 kilograms of plutonium were available for purchase in Moscow, and the Scherbinin Russian sources seemed ready to supply tens if not hundreds of kilograms of HEU to interested buyers. Such claims may be exaggerated but nonetheless are worrisome: Just how much uranium and plutonium currently rest in the hands of private dealers or rogue officials in Russia?[57] How much uranium has been exported successfully or still is wandering the globe in search of a buyer?

Moreover, the possibility (discussed in chapter 4) that officials of the Russian Foreign Intelligence Service connived in the Munich plutonium smuggling affair would lend a different cast to the events and the actors. Justiniano Torres and the Obninsk suppliers might knowingly have worked for Russian Intelligence (although the deal could have been managed from the Russian side to disguise the intelligence connection). In addition, Baranov's participation in both the Munich case and the Landshut-Prague cases might indicate an SVR investment in the HEU deal as well. The questions that remain unanswered about these smuggling incidents leave a great deal of room for interpretation.[58]

EPILOGUE

The specter of loose nuclear materials continues to haunt Western authorities. A June 1997 article in the German magazine *Focus*, citing a confidential BKA report, contends that plutonium dealer Justiniano Torres Benitez—who returned to Colombia after being deported from a German prison—again has offered nuclear material for sale. According to *Focus*, the BKA's Peter Kroemer traveled to Bogotá in May to meet with a Colombian informant who claimed to be Torres's intermediary. The informant stated that Torres had stashed 5,000 grams of plutonium in 5 containers and 2,300 grams of uranium (enrichment level not mentioned) in a warehouse in north Bogotá and that he intended to sell the merchandise for a total of $40 million to the Communist government in Cuba. (Why the Cubans would buy such material is not clear; perhaps they could resell it at a profit to some Middle Eastern country.) The same source reports that Torres declared he had another 9 kilograms of uranium and plutonium hidden somewhere in Germany.

Attempts by the BKA and Colombia to verify these allegations proved disappointing. Samples of radioactive material were obtained from the informant and other Torres emissaries, but analysis by a nuclear forensics expert flown in from Germany confirmed that the material was natural uranium laced with strontium-90, not plutonium or HEU. *Focus* cites evidence suggesting that Torres intermediaries maintained ties to a Colombian guerrilla group, the Ejercito de Liberación Nacional. The case is still unresolved, and the whereabouts of the plutonium smuggler and his reputed caches of fissile materials—if, indeed, the latter exist—remain a mystery.[59]

CHAPTER 6

THE VIEW FROM RUSSIA

INTRODUCTION

MOST OF THE INTERNATIONAL FLOW of nuclear contraband originates in nuclear facilities in Russia. Troubled conditions in the
atomic energy complex—including catastrophic declines in living
standards and disintegrating morale—have prompted this bizarre
criminal traffic. In addition, the nuclear trade phenomenon is
attributable to important systemic changes in the NIS, including the
collapse of the Communist control system, the social strains generated by economic restructuring, and the increasing transparency of
NIS borders. Controversy abounds in Russia about the significance
of the nuclear traffic. Officials stress that most incidents "are not
significantly harmful to society or to public health,"[1] that theft-and-
smuggling chains are characterized as spontaneous and disorganized, and that free markets do not apply to radioactive substances.
(As described previously, MINATOM argued that the propensity of
nuclear workers to steal is aggravated by police sting operations and
by media reports of apparently fabulous but actually hypothetical
prices for such goods on international black markets.) Several
features of the illegal nuclear business in Russia apparently support
this interpretation. For example, of the hundreds of radioactive
thefts recorded in Russia since the beginning of 1992, only the
handful listed in table 6.1 involved weapons-usable uranium or
plutonium. Moreover, none of these incidents culminated in a sale or

seemingly were linked to organized crime activities. Russian officials also claim that thefts from nuclear facilities have declined in recent years. This reduction in criminal diversion might be explained by the improved safeguards at many enterprises and by the mounting recognition by nuclear workers that little or no market demand can be documented for such stolen substances. The claims apparently are corroborated by the dwindling quantities of nuclear materials arriving in Europe, although nuclear traffickers may simply be shipping their wares through other trading channels.[2]

The possibility remains, however, that the visible record of black market nuclear trade obscures a more complex and dangerous reality, as the following observations confirm.

First, the magnitude of fissile material stolen from nuclear stockpiles in Russia may outstrip by a considerable margin the recorded quantities seized in Russia and in Europe. Reported statements of nuclear criminals arrested in Europe in connection with the Munich and Prague cases lend some credence to this hypothesis. If this gap is genuine, the overriding issue becomes whether such materials are stored in the vicinity of the originating enterprises, are concealed at other locations, or already have been shipped abroad through covert channels.

Second, not all important diversion cases necessarily are acknowledged by the government or publicized in the Russian media. Several submarine fuel thefts at different Russian naval bases between 1994 and 1996 fall into this category, as does the pirating of nuclear warheads from a weapons assembly plant in the Urals in 1993.

Third, diversion patterns and sequences are evolving, becoming more sophisticated. This chapter cites anecdotal evidence that nuclear technical elites—scientists, managers, and senior engineers—are playing an increasingly important role in illegal nuclear transactions. Such testimony documents not only the operations of independent elite entrepreneurs who seek to market weapons-usable materials to foreign customers but also informal alliances of nuclear managers and organized crime groups in international nuclear trading schemes.

TABLE 6.1

Reported Diversions of Weapons-Usable Materials in the NIS, 1990s

Source Facility	Date of Theft	Location and Date of Seizure	Material
UNKNOWN (PROBABLY A RUSSIAN NAVAL FUEL STORAGE FACILITY)	UNKNOWN	KIEV, MARCH 1996	6 KILOGRAMS URANIUM, PROBABLY 20 PERCENT U-235
OBNINSK INSTITUTE OF PHYSICS AND POWER ENGINEERING	EARLY 1990S	MUNICH, AUGUST 1994	363.4 GRAMS OF PLUTONIUM
POSSIBLY OBNINSK INSTITUTE OF PHYSICS AND POWER ENGINEERING*	EARLY 1990S	LANDSHUT, PRAGUE, OTHER CZECH LOCATIONS; JUNE 1994, DECEMBER 1994, JUNE 1995	2.75 KILOGRAMS HEU, 87.7 PERCENT U-235 (TOTAL OF ALL SEIZURES)
ELEKTROSTAL' MACHINE BUILDING PLANT	FEBRUARY 1994	ST. PETERSBURG, JUNE 1994	3.05 KILOGRAMS OF HEU, 50 TO 90 PERCENT U-235
MURMANSK AREA GUBA ANDREEVA FUEL STORAGE SITE	JULY 1993	MURMANSK AREA, AUGUST 1993	2 FUEL RODS, 1.8 KILOGRAMS OF HEU
MURMANSK AREA SEVMORPUT FUEL STORAGE SITE	NOVEMBER 1993	MURMANSK AREA, JUNE 1993	3 FUEL RODS, 4.34 KILOGRAMS OF HEU, APPROXIMATELY 20 PERCENT U-235
MOSCOW INSTRUMENTATION RESEARCH AND DEVELOPMENT INSTITUTE (OREL BRANCH)	UNKNOWN	OREL, APRIL 1993	75 GRAMS OF PLUTONIUM
LUCH' SCIENTIFIC PRODUCTION ASSOCIATION	MAY-SEPTEMBER 1992	PODOLSK, OCTOBER 1992	1.5 KILOGRAMS OF HEU, 90 PERCENT U-235

Sources: Russian press sources; *PBS Front Line,* "Loose Nukes," November 20, 1996; Monterey Institute of International Studies Nonproliferation Databases.

*A former Institute of Physics and Power Engineering employee, Eduard Baranov, one of the suppliers of the Munich plutonium, was also linked to the seizures of HEU in Landshut and Prague. It is not clear, however, whether the uranium was stolen from the institute or from some other facility.

Fourth, the environmental consequences of nuclear theft—although minor compared to Chernobyl-type accidents at nuclear facilities—nonetheless are troubling. At least one contract killing in Moscow was attributed to the use of radioactive material, which was planted in the desk chair of a company director who died agonizingly from radiation burns. Such material also has been associated with terrorist threats in at least three locations: a Moscow park, an atomic power station in Lithuania, and a submarine repair facility near Murmansk.

Thus, despite official denials and assurances, Russian nuclear breakout and criminal proliferation scenarios must be taken seriously. Unfortunately, Russia and the West apparently assign different priorities to halting the nuclear traffic. As noted in chapter 5, Western leaders express alarm at Russia's apparent inability to secure nuclear laboratories and production sites, while Russian officials depict such concerns as a smokescreen for Western attempts to discredit Russia in the world nuclear marketplace and to penetrate and control Russian atomic enterprises—although such rhetoric has softened somewhat in recent years. Russian organized crime experts, observing little mafia affiliation with nuclear threats, tend to discount the importance of these episodes altogether. According to one report, in 1995 the MVD and the Federal Security Service both cut the number of officials assigned to nuclear smuggling investigations, redeploying them to the higher-priority conventional organized crime cases—narcotics, contract murder, financial fraud, and the like.[3]

Nuclear thieves are widely perceived as victims of economic circumstance (or of Western police entrapment) rather than as true criminals whose acts jeopardize much wider populations. Many theft cases are quashed before they reach the courts, and even major offenders apparently go scot free. For instance, Yuriy Smirnov of Luch' fame was sentenced to only three years' probation, and Eduard Baranov, the point man in the Munich and Prague cases, seemingly was interrogated by Russian officials and then released to return home.[4] Even more disturbing, the new Russian criminal code, adopted in 1996, actually lowered penalties for nuclear trafficking (as opposed to theft) from "up to five years" to "up to two years." Such a step is almost tantamount to an invitation to nuclear trading and further underscores the government's unwillingness to categorize nuclear infractions as serious crimes.[5]

To be sure, pressure from the West and irrefutable evidence of leaks in nuclear facilities—for example, the Obninsk connection discussed in chapter 5—have compelled Moscow to accept a measure of Western help in retooling safeguards at nuclear enterprises. Cooperation in MPC&A and in various export control projects is proceeding apace and in time may iron out some of the problems. Moreover, by now many Russian policymakers must realize that their aspirations for partnership and equality with the West in no small measure depend on vigorous programs to throttle nuclear smuggling and related criminal activities and to implement specific policies and countermeasures. Nonetheless, for a variety of reasons, current proliferation risks in Russia remain unacceptably high. Indeed, U.S. and Russian ventures to date may have failed to prevent significant leakages of nuclear material, a proposition that is analyzed later in this chapter.

NUCLEAR TRAFFICKING IN RUSSIA: THE AMATEUR TRACK

Introduction

Part of the research for this book focused on the characteristics and dynamics of the nuclear black market in Russia, addressing questions such as the following:

- Who are the nuclear criminals, and how do they differ from ordinary criminals?
- What trading or marketing networks support the smuggling of nuclear materials?
- What actions have been undertaken to purchase nuclear materials or weapons in Russia?

- What is the relationship between established organized crime groups and the illegal nuclear business?

These issues are discussed in the following sections. In general, the illegal supply system for nuclear wares displays little evidence of careful organization or planning. Nuclear deals are generally ad hoc transactions, and stable groupings of perpetrators seldom can be discerned. Such a pattern may not fit the entire universe of black-market transactions in Russia; serious, professionally organized networks may coexist with the "amateur tracks" (but look and act quite different, as argued later). Nevertheless, available evidence documents a fair approximation of the reality of nuclear trafficking in Russia in the 1990s.

The Thieves

Nuclear thieves commonly fall into four categories—employees (mostly low-echelon employees) of nuclear enterprises and store-houses, relatives or friends of nuclear industry insiders, "local enthusiasts" (in one MVD official's term) who live in the vicinity of vulnerable facilities, and former employees of the nuclear industrial complex. According to the MVD, 90 percent of the perpetrators are "rank-and-file workers" whose principal motives are acquiring money or procuring consumer goods.[6] A theft can be executed by insiders acting alone or in concert with outsiders. For example, in 1992 engineer Yuriy Smirnov at the Luch' Scientific Production Association pilfered 1.5 kilograms of weapons-quality uranium over a period of several months, hiding the material in a jar he stored on the balcony of his apartment. This solo criminal was apprehended while boarding a train to Moscow, where he planned to search for a buyer. One local enthusiast (an unemployed recovering alcoholic) organized a theft of 100 kilograms of uranium from the Chepetsk Mechanical Factory (a natural uranium processing plant in Udmurtia) in 1992, teaming with a metalworker operating inside the plant and a driver who possessed "a [facility] pass for free entry and exit." Similarly, in November

1993 military officers of the Northern Fleet broke into a reactor fuel storeroom at a naval base near Murmansk and absconded with reactor fuel rods. In mid-1994 local residents of the secret city of Arzamas-16 solicited the assistance of employees at the Nuclear Center to enter the facility "through a hole in the fence" and steal 9.5 kilograms of uranium from a storage site.[7]

In general, Russian nuclear crime constitutes a neighborhood affair, inspired by people who work in, or have close connections to, the target enterprise. Variations of this pattern include the 1994 theft of Elektrostal' HEU (see table 6.1), reportedly masterminded by a former engineer (section chief) and technician at the enterprise, who had retired two to three years earlier and established a company with branches in Moscow and St. Petersburg to sell rare-earth metals. A machine repair worker in the shop that converted uranium gas to powder served as the inside man at the time of the crime. (According to media accounts, a butcher and a plumber were arrested in connection with the crime, but apparently they were mere couriers.) In another Elektrostal' case, a mysterious buyer arrived in the town, which is 40 miles from Moscow, in 1993 and discreetly advised plant employees of his intention to purchase a large quantity of low-enriched uranium. Several employees collected approximately 30 kilograms of uranium pellets, which they "stored in their basements and attics." The buyer accepted 1.5 kilograms on consignment and then simply vanished.[8]

Russian police and journalist sources emphasize that nuclear thieves are classified as relatively clean lawbreakers, because they typically have no criminal records, claim no links to organized crime, and do not operate other illegal businesses—that is, they epitomize the archetypal amateur criminal. This profile is not surprising. Nuclear crime retains a unique, elitist cachet, because the actual robberies in large measure can be committed only by workers and specialists who have passed some type of security screening to gain access to nuclear materials. As a rule, nuclear thieves commit the crime on their own authority, not in response to a specific order (*zakaz*) from an outside buyer or trader. Nuclear crimes therefore are supply-driven, a product of the desperate economic conditions that besiege nuclear enterprises and surrounding localities. Aspiring sellers almost invariably are arrested while carrying nuclear materials out of the plant, secreting materials in apartments or garages, or attempting to solicit buyers in major cities such as Moscow or St. Petersburg. As in the West, when buyers are located, more often than not they ultimately are exposed as undercover police operatives, journalists, or agents of security services.

Traders and Buyers

Although organized crime's role in the illegal nuclear trade is difficult to pinpoint, Russian investigators cite evidence that a small nuclear trading network emerged in the early and mid-1990s to market nuclear materials and other radioactive isotopes. By mid-1994 MVD sources contended that some 35 to 40 suspected dealers in nuclear substances were operating in the Moscow region. These dealers possessed export licenses, maintained Western bank accounts, and traded in illegal commodities such as oil, nonferrous materials, and rare-earth metals. Importantly, nuclear trafficking ranks as a sideline occupation for these operators, who accept nuclear merchandise strictly on consignment, paying no money to the supplier up front and retaining between 40 and 75 percent of the sale proceeds.[9] A few of these dealers have criminal records for currency speculation, illegal arms dealing, and other fraudulent activities.[10] The dealer network relies on a crew of couriers and guards who transport radioactive materials in exchange for the going rate in Russia, which ranged from $50 to $400 per day in early 1996, depending on the region, the route, and the commodity in transit.[11] Compared to nuclear thieves and their generally clean records, traders and transporters are more likely to have criminal pasts or ties to the criminal underworld, although not necessarily as members of organized crime groups.

Buyers for stolen radioactive materials apparently are few and far between. The MVD reports only eight actual purchases between 1992 and 1995. Only two of the cases can be detailed to any degree. In one 1992 episode, an Iranian businessman purchased 0.5

kilograms of uranium (degree of enrichment unknown) for between $10,000 and $15,000 from a small Russian import-export venture in Nizhny Novgorod. The customer paid 25 percent in cash up front for the merchandise and later wired the balance to the company's account in the Union Bank of Helsinki. In a 1993 case a German businessman staying at the Aerostar Hotel in Moscow procured 13 kilograms of cesium-137 from Moscow metals dealers for 4 million rubles—approximately $5,000 to $8,000 per kilogram, a fraction of the legal international price of $80,000 to $100,000 per kilogram.[12] However, the paucity of such examples and the rock-bottom price paid for the cesium again underscore the supply-driven character of the nuclear trade, clearly distinguishing it from more normal illegal businesses such as narcotics trafficking and arms smuggling.

Published reports can confirm would-be buyers for Russian nuclear goods, but such clients usually seek weapons rather than materials. For example, in 1991, according to *Literaturnaya Gazeta* journalist Kirill Belyaninov, the Federal Nuclear Center Arzamas-16 received a faxed letter in English, purportedly a conditional offer from the Islamic Jihad to buy an atomic bomb; the bid specified "parameters, the sum of the transaction, and the mode of shipment." In mid-1993 Arzamas-16 director Vladimir Belugin declared that "Saddam Hussein's people" had offered the center $2 billion for a nuclear warhead. A compelling question is whether these incidents should be cataloged as mere hoaxes or as ominous close calls.[13]

Organized Crime

In the West, significant speculation surrounds possible ties between the illegal nuclear trade and Russian and Eurasian crime organizations. Governments everywhere express a legitimate concern about the prospect of ruthless criminals precipitating a proliferation of dangerous nuclear materials and weapons of mass destruction. Of course, the visible pattern of nuclear thefts in the NIS to date—supplier-driven, locally inspired, and deficient in prearranged commercial outlets—argues against a strong connection to organized crime and its meticulous devotion to commercial details and projected profits. Furthermore, Russian police sources emphasize that nuclear thieves and traders display a "completely different profile" from that of criminals engaged in hard-core underworld operations such as racketeering, narcotics trafficking, car theft, or contract murder.[14] Of course, a complex and fluid enterprise such as organized crime does not accommodate rigid distinctions. The transaction proposed to Poodle and described in chapter 2 suggests that organized crime groups may be testing the nuclear trade waters, but remain wary and skeptical. First Deputy MVD Secretary Mikhail Yegorov noted at a Senate hearing in Washington in May 1994 that the MVD was investigating a possible organized crime link in one of nine recent cases of alleged theft of "highly enriched materials."[15] Still, no hard evidence can be cited that directly connects organized crime to nuclear theft. As some documentary evidence attests, organized crime groups are more likely to help broker smuggled nuclear materials that cross borders.

CASES

Published sources in Russia and other NIS countries furnish some information on the origin of bootlegged radioactive materials. Published reports and my own interviews with Russian government officials document that the nuclear enterprises most vulnerable to theft fall into the following three categories:

- Scientific research and weapons design institutes, such as Arzamas-16, the Obninsk Institute of Physics and Power Engineering, and the Luch' Scientific-Production Association in Podolsk near Moscow. The plutonium and possibly the HEU seized in Europe in 1994-1995 originated in Obninsk.
- Enterprises engaged in the nuclear fuel production cycle, such as the Elektrostal' Machine Building Plant in

Moscow oblast; the Chepetsk Mechanical Factory in Glazov, Udmurtia; and the Ulba Metallurgical Plant in Ust-Kamenogorsk, Kazakhstan. Chepetsk and Elektrostal' were sites, respectively, of six and three reported uranium thefts between 1992 and 1994. At least five such thefts occurred at Ulba between 1994 and early 1997.

- Industrial enterprises unrelated to the nuclear industry that are end users of gamma radiation sources such as cesium-137 and cobalt-60. (Such substances are widely used to calibrate instruments and to measure the thickness and density of industrial materials). Published reports and Interpol data suggest that cesium-137 is the most commonly stolen substance in this category. Cesium thefts have been recorded in end-user enterprises such as the Guryev oil refinery in Kazakhstan, the Fosforit chemical association in St. Petersburg, and the asphalt-cement Kaliningradavtodor complex in Kaliningrad oblast.

Exceptions to this pattern can be noted. Several thefts or attempted thefts of HEU occurred at Russian submarine bases between 1993 and 1996. Plant managers conspired to remove nonfissile radioactive isotopes from the Elektrokhimpribor weapons assembly plant in the early 1990s, a case discussed in detail later. Two atomic power plants—the Chernobyl plant in Ukraine and the Ignalina station in Lithuania—also experienced thefts of fuel rods and components in 1992 and 1993. According to one Russian report, in the Ignalina case, the thieves made off with a 7-meter assembly containing highly radioactive spent fuel.[16]

Table 6.1 (page 107) shows important cases of diversion in the NIS. The Obninsk episodes are included in the table, even though the actual seizures occurred in Central Europe. Little information can be acquired on the Orel case. According to an article in *Komsomolskaya Pravda,* the institute's employees tried to sell the plutonium for $100,000.[17] Perpetrators in the Kiev case were identified as "former servicemen in the Russian army." According to William Potter of the Monterey Institute, an analysis of the material by the Kiev Institute for Nuclear Research indicated a 20 percent enrichment level, "consistent with much naval reactor fuel."[18]

As noted previously, the Elektrostal' theft might have been instigated by former plant employees; the inside man was a worker who repaired machinery in the shop where uranium hexafloride gas (UF_6) is converted into uranium oxide powder. According to one Elektrostal' spokesman, a total of 5 kilograms of material were stolen. "He must not have taken out the material all at once, but rather in small amounts," commented the spokesman.[19]

The Luch' and Murmansk cases are quite well documented. Yuriy Smirnov's theft at Luch' has been discussed previously. According to Smirnov, economic reforms beginning in 1992 forced prices to rise much faster than salaries. "I was at a loss," he explained. "I could buy nothing—no furniture, no clothing, nothing. So I simply panicked." The engineer pilfered 1.5 kilograms of weapons-grade uranium in small 50 to 70 grams lots over four months and was arrested in October at the Podolsk Railway Station en route to Moscow.[20]

The first of the Murmansk cases occurred in July 1993 in Military Unit 90299, a secret storage facility adjoining Guba Andreeva (Gulf Andreeva) on the Kola Peninsula. The thieves broke into the storeroom and removed two fuel rods, each 2.7 meters long. Using a hacksaw on one of the rods, they extracted a core containing approximately 1.8 kilograms of HEU enriched to 36 percent HEU and then "carried their loot into the hills." A search team detected the material nine days later. Two naval servicemen, Pavel Popov and Dmitriy Antonov, were arrested. Popov apparently had a criminal record for petty theft, a rarity among nuclear thieves. In testimony before the fleet's military procuracy, he implicated two superiors, Captain of the Third Rank Oleg Bakshanskiy and a fellow officer, as organizers of the theft. (The officers promised him 10 million rubles, he reported.) An ambitious military prosecutor, Mikhail Kulik, contended that Bakshanskiy, a Seventh-Day Adventist, planned to sell the uranium through religious cohorts in Norway and Western

Europe. As noted in chapter 4, Kulik also believed that a gang of uranium buyers from Murmansk and St. Petersburg had offered to buy HEU from officers of the Northern Fleet. However, after 19 months of investigation, 11 volumes of 300 pages each, hundreds of interrogations, and dozens of examinations, the case against the officers was dismissed for lack of evidence. In November 1995 Popov and Antonov were sentenced to prison terms of five and four years, respectively. No prospective client for the uranium was ever identified, and no mafia link was ever established. Nevertheless, important details of the case still have not come to light. (I attempted to interview Kulik while he was on leave in Moscow in late 1996, but he is under direct orders from his superiors not to talk to anyone about the affair.)[21]

The second theft, in late November 1993, was accomplished at Military Unit 31396 at the Sevmorput shipyard near Murmansk city by three naval officers of the Northern Fleet: Captain Second Class Aleksei Tikhomirov; his younger brother, Senior Lieutenant Dmitriy Tikhomirov; and a retired officer, Oleg Baranov. According to various accounts of the theft, Aleksei Tikhomirov slipped through an unprotected gate into the shipyard, sawed through the emergency door in storage unit #3-30, and broke off parts of three reactor core assemblies from a 671-design Yersh nuclear submarine. The rods included almost 4.5 kilograms of HEU enriched to approximately 20 percent U-235. Dmitriy, an engineer with a knowledge of reactor fuel assemblies, furnished technical guidance for the operation. Baranov, supposedly the brains behind the scheme, stored the material in his garage and assumed responsibility for selling it. Baranov later alleged at the trial that he had been approached by "strangers" six months before the theft who were prepared to offer $50,000 per kilogram for the uranium. Apparently, however, he had not lined up any firm buyers—perhaps the group expected to market the material among the local mafia elite in Murmansk.[22] The theft was soon discovered—Tikhomirov carelessly left the door of the storage building open—but the uranium was not recovered until almost 7 months later. In late June 1994, Lieutenant Dmitriy Tikhomirov, while drinking in a local bar with a fellow officer, a Lieutenant Parolov, casually mentioned the theft and the difficulty that the group was encountering in marketing the merchandise, and then asked Parolov to help. Apparently after some soul-searching, Parolov alerted his superior officer about the request, and the latter relayed the information to the high command. The three conspirators were summarily arrested and charged with theft of radioactive materials.[23] The case went to trial in early 1995; Captain Tikhomirov and Oleg Baranov were sentenced to three and a half and three years' imprisonment, respectively, but Lieutenant Tikhomirov apparently received a suspended sentence.[24] Commenting on the case, military prosecutor Kulik noted in *Yaderny Kontrol'* in February 1995, "Criminal groups are ever more actively seeking to obtain significant amounts of material from the Northern Fleet." However, Kulik could not prove that the three culprits—who themselves had no prior criminal record—were in contact with such groups.[25]

Although organized crime involvement was not detected in the Murmansk thefts, these robberies could not be categorized as isolated cases. Rather, they manifested a pattern of poor nuclear security in the Russian submarine fleet. According to my interview sources in Moscow, at least five other actual or attempted thefts of uranium occurred at naval facilities from 1994 to 1996.[26] Table 6.2 details these incidents, which the government did not publicly acknowledge, including four in facilities in neighboring Arkhangelsk oblast and one in the Russia Far East. The infection of the Russian navy with the nuclear crime disease is disturbing but hardly surprising. Like many of their civilian counterparts, military nuclear employees largely lost their sense of purpose and function when the Soviet state collapsed and the threat of hostilities with the West receded.

Dual-Use Materials

A quasi-legal and illegal traffic is thriving for so-called dual-use materials, metals equipment and technologies that have widespread civilian applications but also are used in the production of fissile materials or finished nuclear weapons. Similar to trade in

TABLE 6.2

Submarine Fuel Thefts

Location	Date	Material Stolen	U-235 Enrichment Level	Alleged Perpetrators	Outcomes
GUBA ANDREEVA, NORTHERN FLEET FUEL STORAGE SITE	July 1993	2 fuel rods, each weighing 4.5 kg and containing 1.8 kg of HEU	36 percent	Two sailors working on radiation safety devices	Two officers also accused, but case against them dismissed for lack of evidence
SEVMORPUT, NORTHERN FLEET FUEL STORAGE SITE	November 1993	3 fuel rods, together containing 4.34 kg of HEU	Approximately 20 percent	Two captains, one lieutenant	Material recovered; alleged thieves apprehended 6 months after theft
SEVERODVINSK SEVMASH (NUCLEAR SUBMARINE CONSTRUCTION)	July 1994	3.5 kg of uranium dioxide	20 to 40 percent	Four local businessmen from Severodvinsk arrested; links to Sevmash plant workers	Trial in progress
SEVMASH	October 1994	Fuel rods	No data	No data	Alleged perpetrators arrested in Arkhangelsk, but not charged
SEVERODVINSK ZVEZDOCHKA	July 1995	Fuel rods	No data	Contract employees of Northern Fleet	Alleged culprits stopped before removing uranium from plant
ZVEZDOCHKA	January 1996	Fuel rods	No data	Contract employees of Northern Fleet	The accused carried material out of Zvevdochka, but were arrested in Severodvinsk (case under investigation)
SOVIETSKAYA GAVAN' PACIFIC FLEET FUEL STORAGE FACILITY	January 1996	Fuel rods containing at least 7 kg of HEU, 0.5 kg of zirconium, and some cesium-137	40 to 60 percent	Three workers at facility, two employees of metals trading company in Kaliningrad	4.5 kg seized in Sovietskaya Gavan'; 2.5 kg seized in Kaliningrad, part of same theft (case under investigation)

Sources: Russian press sources; interviews with Russian investigative journalists.

nuclear substances, commerce in such products is subject to export controls and guidelines in the United States, Russia, Ukraine, and other countries in the Nuclear Suppliers Group (NSG).[27] Commonly cited dual-use materials include zirconium, a cladding material for fuel in nuclear reactors, and beryllium, a tamper reflector in nuclear warheads.

Globally, governments, private companies, and organized crime groups have trafficked in different combinations of dual-use materials. In the United States, in a significant 1995 case, federal authorities arrested three employees of the New York company Interglobal Manufacturing Enterprise for attempting to sell several tons of nuclear-grade zirconium to U.S. customs agents posing as arms buyers and materials brokers from Iraq. (In this case, 5 tons of material were seized in New York, and two in Cyprus). According to William Potter, the Dneprodzhrzinsk Chemical Factory in Ukraine produced the zirconium, five tons of which were smuggled to the United States from the Ukraine by way of Germany, according to U.S. investigators.[28]

Potter also observed that the same chemical complex had been identified as the source in multiton shipments of hafnium and zirconium to Belgium and the Netherlands in 1992.[29] (At the time, however, the Ukraine was not a party to the NSG accord on dual-use exports and did not control exports of such materials.) Other less-publicized zirconium transactions also deserve mention. Russian press sources report that the breakaway government of Chechnya purchased 148 tons of zirconium tubing in late 1992 from the Chepetsk Mechanical Factory in Udmurtia (the site of numerous uranium thefts in the 1990s) and later sold the material illegally to Pakistan.[30] In an October 1996 interview, Russian customs officials cited a 1996 case where 100 tons of zirconium powder being shipped by a South African company were detained temporarily in the Russian Caspian Sea port of Astrakhan. The cargo, inexplicably contaminated by radium-226, had transited Germany, Poland, Belarus, and Russia and was en route to Iran. The cargo manifest listed the end use of the material as "ceramic plates." The zirconium eventually was released by the customs house in Astrakhan and continued on to Iran.[31] In a May 1996 case in Krasno-yarsk, the Federal Security Service arrested a former Russian scientist associated with a commercial firm in that city for illegally exporting 5 kilograms of powder riddled with hafnium and zirconium, probably to Germany. The material had been developed in a local laboratory, reputedly as a "high temperature coating in missile warheads and unmanned aircraft," and was unrelated to nuclear weapons production.[32]

Covert international trade of beryllium, a metal used as a neutron generator and tamper reflector in warheads, also warrants assessment. According to U.S. journalists Andrew and Leslie Cockburn, a U.S. inspection team visiting the Ulba Metallurgical plant in Kazakhstan in late 1994 as part of Project Sapphire (a U.S. expedition to purchase 600 kilograms of weapons-grade uranium stored in a Kazakh fuel plant under insecure conditions) found a pile of suspicious-looking containers that were addressed to Tehran, Iran, and "appeared ready for shipment." Ulba managers informed the Americans (who were prepared to purchase more than half a ton of weapons-grade HEU stored at the plant) that the containers "held only beryllium" and that they had decided not to ship the material. The U.S. discovery nonetheless suggests not only commercial links between Ulba and the Iranians but also the possibility that Iranian weapons buyers successfully procured beryllium from the plant on other occasions.[33]

The best-documented case of smuggling of dual-use materials was perpetrated between March and June of 1992 and transferred several tons of beryllium from Obninsk, Moscow, to Yekaterinburg in Russia and from Yekaterinburg to Vilnius, Lithuania. More than 4 tons of the material was seized in a bomb vault in the Vilnius Joint Stock Innovation Bank in May 1993. Parts of the consignment were slightly contaminated with HEU, apparently because the beryllium had seen service at an experimental reactor site at the Obninsk IPPE.

A pair of reporters for *U.S. News & World Report* and a news team from the CBS television program *60 Minutes* investigated the incident. According to a 1995 article in *U.S. News*, the investigation produced "irrefutable proof" that Russian organized crime masterminded the shipment. In addition, the article chose to regard the shipment as a smuggling case, but both claims require more careful examination.[34]

According to the article, the prime mover in the beryllium deal was the deputy director of the Sverdlovsk ALT Ltd. trading firm, Igor Rudenko, who coincidentally worked for a MINATOM-controlled nuclear research institute in the region. Using his MINATOM connections, Rudenko concluded that IPPE possessed a "surplus" of 4 tons of the metal, which he viewed as a business opportunity. The article claimed that no evidence implicated Rudenko in organized crime. When he needed financing, he turned to a Sverdlovsk native, Yuriy Ivanovich Alekseev, who had moved to Moscow in the early 1990s and established a number of business ventures—"sports clubs and commodity trading firms." For a time (1994-1995) Alekseyev, apparently a rising young political star in the region, also served as the deputy governor of Sverdlovsk oblast.[35]

The article calls Alekseyev a "suspected racketeer" who "operates in the group zone that exists in Russia between the underworld and the official world." Evidence for this assertion is based on allegations by unnamed police officials and seems unconvincing.[36] Alekseyev himself regards the characterization as libelous. In a December 1996 interview, Alekseyev protested, "There should be a special international tribunal tasked with judging and punishing irresponsible journalists who defame decent citizens." He also contends that he financed the transaction as a favor for a friend and that he had no idea who was purchasing the material.[37] Whether or not, like many new Russian capitalists and politicians, Alekseyev has any links to, or dealings with, organized crime—the truth may never be known—the suggestion that he was fronting for organized crime in the beryllium transaction seems farfetched. (In fact, his political enemies may have played a role in shaping the story. Charges of racketeering and links to the mafia are part of the common currency of political mudslinging in Russia.) In any case, Alekseyev, who had no prior arrest record, was interrogated in connection with the transaction but never was prosecuted.

The organized crime link is only slightly better established later in the *U.S. News & World Report* account. The actual export of the beryllium was managed by a trading firm, the Urals Association of Business Development. The association reputedly was backed by the Tsentral'naya organized crime gang in Yekaterinburg, which was associated with prostitution, drug trafficking, metals smuggling, and arms dealing. In addition, the company boasted a prior history of exporting zirconium, although the specific infraction in April 1992 probably involved the avoidance of customs duties rather than the illegal export of a restricted material.[38]

The Russian government opted not to regard the beryllium transaction as a crime. At the time of the various transfers of the material, regulations governing exports of dual-use materials apparently were not yet in place. Also, the article in the Russian criminal code (Article 78) that proscribes and punishes the export of materials that can be used in construction of atomic weapons was not adopted by the Russian parliament until 1993. Consequently, designating the beryllium deal as a smuggling venture seems inaccurate; indeed, customs documentation for the shipment was filled out, if incompletely.[39] The ultimate buyers of the beryllium remain shrouded in mystery. Intermediate purchasers identified in the article's investigation included a Lithuanian company, VEKA, and later an Austrian firm, A. Kontor. A shadowy buyer in Switzerland reputedly offered $24 million for the shipment—approximately 10 times the market value of $600 per kilogram—but evaporated after the beryllium was seized.[40]

Loose Weapons

Widespread thefts of nuclear and radioactive materials and the generally sorry state of the atomic energy industry in the NIS raise troubling questions about the security of nuclear arsenals in those states. Rumors of diversions of finished weapons abound, although most of them are not particularly credible. For example, according to different press reports, the Ukraine sold the Palestine Liberation

Organization two nuclear warheads for $10 million in 1993, and Kazakhstan brokered three tactical nuclear warheads to Iran in 1991 for between $130 million and $150 million. Western intelligence experts cannot confirm such transactions, and Kazakhstan and the Ukraine naturally deny making the transactions.[41] A March 1995 report in *Soldier of Fortune* magazine declares that the Lithuanian police busted a ring of former Soviet GRU (military intelligence) agents who were smuggling Special Atomic Demolition Munitions—i.e., backpack nukes—out of Russia.[42] The bad news, noted the magazine, was that the group already had shipped several such weapons to Iraq and possibly North Korea. This information is attributed to a former sergeant in the U.S. Special Forces who had participated in a police training mission inside Lithuania. While the story lacks corroborating detail and is difficult to take seriously, it is unsettling nonetheless.

Separating fiction from fact in such nuclear scare stories represents a difficult exercise. Yet successful diversions of nuclear weapons rank as more than a hypothetical possibility in post-Soviet states. Russian spokesmen insist that nuclear weapons have not been stolen and cannot be secured illegally in Russia. In May 1995, for example, General Yevgeniy Maslin, the head of the Defense Ministry's 12th Department responsible for nuclear security, proclaimed in an interview, "Till now not a single nuclear warhead has been lost or stolen."[43] In December Maslin described the MPC&A system for nuclear weapons and weapons-grade materials as "intact."[44] Nevertheless, in November 1993, according to Russian nuclear policy expert Vladimir Orlov, the head of a proliferation research center in Moscow, a pair of workers of the seventh section of "Factory X" removed two nuclear warheads from the plant's second industrial site. Other sources confirm the theft at the Zlatoust-36 Instrument-Building Plant facility (in the Urals, west of the city of Chelyabinsk), which assembles nuclear weapons. Fortunately, the warheads were recovered from a garage in a nearby residential site, and the thieves were apprehended. Orlov cited the incident at an April 1997 international conference in Bonn, Germany, on improving security safeguards at nuclear enterprises.

Official denials were immediately forthcoming; an enraged deputy minister of atomic energy, Nikolai Yegorov, denounced the Orlov account. "This is really idiotic. I have never heard anything more idiotic."[45] Yet according to Orlov, the Russian General Prosecutor's Office supplied the data on the Zlatoust affair, indicating a high probability that the theft actually took place as reported.[46] Few credible assurances, then, can be proffered that warhead assembly plants—which to date have not received upgraded U.S. MPC&A systems, although agreements exist for such projects—are secure against insider thefts or that other more successful diversions have not already been executed at such facilities.

Moreover, accounting and control systems for nuclear weapons apparently function imperfectly. Despite agreements to concentrate control of tactical nukes in Russia, the possibility of holdouts cannot be dismissed entirely. For example, two representatives of the 12th Department, Major General Vladimir Kosorukov and Colonel Vladimir Karimov, reportedly notified a journalist in Moscow in early 1996 that thefts or losses of strategic nuclear weapons constitute "a practical impossibility" but that "problems could arise" in inventorying tactical arsenals. A specific concern mentioned in the interview identified some 150 nuclear artillery shells that the Ukraine navy supposedly returned to Russia by 1991. The weapons were formally accounted for, but the officers suspected that the Ukraine still retained them. "Of course, this fact is impossible to confirm," the journalist commented.[47]

In June 1997 former Russian Security Council chief General Alexander Lebed told a visiting congressional delegation in Moscow that, while serving in the Kremlin, he had conducted an inventory of 100 or 132 former Soviet suitcase-size nuclear bombs (accounts differ on Lebed's actual statement) but could locate only 48. A CBS *60 Minutes* broadcast in September provided additional details about the suitcases, which weighed 60 to 100 pounds each, had a yield of approximately 1 kiloton, and could be armed in 20 to 30 minutes without secret military codes. According to General Lebed, the weapons had been developed for use by Special Forces units of the Main Intelligence Directorate of the Soviet General Staff.[48] Lebed hypothesized in that interview that the missing weapons could be stored in the Ukraine, Georgia, and the Baltics—that is, no longer under Russian military control. U.S. and Russian security officials question the veracity of Lebed's claim and express skepticism that such weapons even exist. Prime Minister Victor Chernomyrdin labeled Lebed's statement "absolute nonsense," while the official government newspaper *Rossiiskaya Gazeta* sneered, "Such superfantasies can only be the product of a diseased imagination." General Yevgeniy Maslin of the Ministry of Defense Twelfth Department issued a characteristic denial, asserting "Owing to strict supervision it is impossible for nuclear ammunition to fall into unauthorized hands." Nevertheless, Alexei Yablokov, a corresponding member of the Russian Academy of Sciences and a former Yeltsin advisor on environmental protection, wrote a letter to *Novaya Gazeta* that affirmed "a real basis" for Lebed's claim. He affirmed that a "suitcase variant" of atomic weapons had been built to order by the KGB (not for the GRU, as Lebed claimed) for "terrorist purposes" in the 1970s, that such weapons did not fall under Ministry of Defense supervision, and that they were not factored into the process of Russian arms control negotiations with the United States. However, Yablokov could not verify that any such weapons were missing.[49] Moreover, former Lebed aide Vladimir Denisov supplied partial substantiation for the story. Denisov, who had headed a working group established by the general to investigate the situation, told the Interfax news agency that no Russian military unit incorporated nuclear suitcases in its arsenal but that "there was no certainty that no low-yield nuclear ammunition had not remained on the territory of Ukraine, Belarus, or the Baltic countries, or that such weapons had not appeared in Chechnya."[50] Nevertheless, the actual military significance of the missing suitcases remains in doubt. "The suitcase theory is more or less bullshit," scoffs Valeriy N. Spektor, head of the Academy of Sciences (AOS) Working Group on Dual-Use Technology. "The weapons were indeed developed and tested for use by our special services, but they were never actually assembled and deployed.

The plutonium charges are stored separately from the suitcases and remain under tight Russian government control."[51]

Such conflicting accounts are difficult to reconcile. As Yablokov, Lebed, and others contend, the suitcase weapons quite possibly were produced in the Soviet era for sabotage purposes. (U.S. analysts point out that the United States built hundreds of portable nuclear devices in the 1960s.)[52] However, existing evidence does not explain who controlled the weapons, whether they were actually readied for field use, and whether any bombs were lost or misplaced. Conceivably, as a contender for the presidency in Russia, Lebed simply was trying to embarrass the Russian government and discredit Yeltsin's leadership. However, factors such as the overall state of nuclear security in Russia and Lebed's own past position as a Kremlin insider argue against entirely dismissing his assertion.[53] Furthermore, as previous experience confirms, Russian denials about nuclear leakages cannot always be taken at face value.

A Shadow Market

Russian and Western observers recently have questioned whether the visible market for nuclear materials represents the real market or simply the proverbial tip of the iceberg. Some observers advance the theory that nuclear smuggling is more professional, better organized, and more lethal than originally concluded. As explained by Russian customs official Nikolai Kravchenko, who heads a special customs section charged with interdicting nuclear contraband, "Looking at the specifics of nuclear and radioactive material, it is hard to believe that the contraband business is run by nonprofessionals in that sphere."[54] Kravchenko contrasts professional smugglers with courier "simpletons" who conceal small quantities of nuclear material in their luggage and confront a high risk of detection and apprehension. Similarly, University of Pittsburgh scholars Phil Williams and Paul Woessner argue, "Supply networks that are easiest to detect are also the least worrisome."[55] In their view, more sophisticated networks may already be operational and responsible for serious diversions of weapons-usable material.

A visible shadow market seemingly requires preconditions, such as the availability of supplies of weapons-grade or weapons-usable nuclear materials, corrupt or desperate managers and custodians, and financial and logistical mechanisms for delivering such materials to final customers. These preconditions are described in more detail later.

As the European sting operations in mid-1994 and late 1994 demonstrated, availability might not constitute a significant constraint. By happenstance, the Munich, Landshut, and Prague buyers admittedly were police, but they easily could have been Iranians, Iraqis, or North Koreans. As noted, Czech police investigating the smuggling to Prague of 2.7 kilograms of near–weapons grade HEU reportedly were informed that the Russian suppliers could deliver 5 kilograms of the material every month and 40 kilograms in a one-time shipment.[56] Similarly, Justiniano Torres assured the LKA operative Walter Boeden that his Russian sources could furnish 11 kilograms of plutonium, 30 times as much as the quantity actually seized in Munich.[57] Because the incentives for corruption are rife in NIS nuclear enterprises, the possibility cannot be dismissed that some employees might succeed—or already have succeeded—in pulling off a major theft.

As already noted, workers at Russian institutes and fuel cycle enterprises are nothing short of economically depressed. Salaries fall below or well below the Russian national average wage, and employees commonly are paid three to four months behind schedule. In addition, salaries for top management rarely exceed $200 to $400 per month in institute and design laboratories. These consequential economic incentives for diversion are compelling, because collusive relations among well-placed insiders usually can defeat internal enterprise safeguards against theft—even the advanced security systems introduced under the widely hailed U.S.-Russian laboratory-to-laboratory program. Requisite key players include employees who can gain access to storage facilities, disable alarm systems, and alter paperwork to cover up the crime. The director of the IPPE International Department, Gennadiy Pshakin, told me in a recent interview that a mere three to four responsible engineers and a perimeter guard would need to cooperate to successfully bootleg quantities of uranium or weapons-grade plutonium from the institute's most secure experimental reactor site (equipped with the latest safeguards) and subsequently to conceal evidence of the theft.[58] Mirroring this generally ominous state of affairs, the director of Chelyabinsk-70 killed himself in October of 1996, because he apparently saw (in the words of a MINATOM official) "no economic way out" for the enterprise, which depends heavily on the military contracts that represent 70 to 80 percent of its business.

The development of marketing channels for fissile materials constitutes perhaps the most difficult step in the diversion process, but enterprising employees have a number of options.

For example, some plant leaders in Russia have sought the assistance of Western colleagues in marketing fissile material. During a meeting at a MINATOM enterprise in Sverdlovsk oblast in mid-1993, the plant manager, senior technicians, and local economic officials asked British engineering consultant John Large to arrange for the certification of plutonium and enriched uranium samples at laboratories in the United Kingdom. In a public commentary Large noted, "I was asked if I knew any Western company who would want nuclear materials—they were senior plant people, nuclear scientists who saw this as a way of making money."[59] In another case British nuclear expert John Radgey was offered plutonium and other nuclear materials by two engineers and a manager working at an unidentified nuclear facility in Russia. According to Radgey, one of the three pulled a piece of plutonium "the size and shape of a 5-peso coin" out of a briefcase while the group was dining at a local Chinese restaurant.[60]

Private commercial ventures also can expedite the diversion of nuclear materials. For instance, during the early 1990s employees of legal companies affiliated with the Moscow Kurchatov Institute and the Elektrokhimpribor factory in Sverdlovsk oblast were involved in illegal exportation of radioactive, but fortunately not bomb-usable, substances. Another diversion scheme relies on evading export controls by smuggling HEU or plutonium in legal radioactive cargo. Russian customs officials believe that professional contrabandists would favor this method, because most internal customs posts in Russia still are not equipped to distinguish one type of metallic radioactive material from another.

Finally, enterprise managers might forge opportunistic ties with international organized crime groups to arrange the export of strategic nuclear materials. Nuclear elites and professional criminals make strange bedfellows, but in the dismal economic circumstances of today's Russia, such alliances are well within the realm of possibility.

Various episodes validate the potential significance of collusive managerial corruption in executing criminal proliferation scenarios. One widely publicized diversion of radioactive materials originated in the early 1990s in Elektrokhimpribor, a chemical production plant in the Urals that functioned as part of the Sverdlovsk-45 (Lesnoi) weapons assembly complex. Elektrokhimpribor produced nuclear charges for atomic weapons. The materials themselves—radioactive isotopes thallium-203 and zinc-68—were of relatively minor importance (used in medical radiography and scientific research) and were produced as a sideline in plant Shop 1. The case assumes significance because of the apparent penetration of one of the most important Russian defense enterprises and because of its scope, which eventually encompassed virtually every senior plant manager, including the director, two vice directors, two shop chiefs, and other key personnel. Several MINATOM officials also were implicated in the scheme. The stolen isotopes were marketed abroad via a succession of quasi-private companies, circumventing Technsnabeksport, at the same time the state trading arm for radioactive materials. (One of these quasi-private companies, Briz, was established by the head of Elektrokhimpribor's financial department; another firm, Stabis, was connected with researchers at the Kurchatov Institute in Moscow.) At one point, seeking higher profits, the Elektrokhimpribor conspirators sought the services of a local organized crime group to smuggle the isotopes out of Russia. However, the gang members threatened to reveal the entire scheme to the KGB. Inevitably, authorities learned of the leakage of isotopes; prosecutors and the KGB initiated an investigation; and Elektrokhimpribor managers were detained and brought to trial. According to an investigator in the case, "damage caused to the state" (probably the value of the stolen isotopes in international markets) amounted to $23 million, a tidy sum.[61]

Other recent cases highlight the increasing sophistication of nuclear smuggling chains. In August 1994, a radioisotope plant at the "Mayak" (Chelyabinsk-65) nuclear combine successfully exported two containers of iridium-192 to Great Britain without a license. The following year, the factory again shipped out two containers of iridium under license but understated the radioactivity level (number of curies) of the material by one-third. The intended recipient was a well-known British firm that trades internationally in radioisotopes for industrial and analytical instrumentation. The exporter's apparent purpose was to avoid paying additional taxes on the shipment. As in the Elektrokhimpribor case, the radioactive material was a strategically insignificant medical isotope, but the diversion mechanism itself entailed ominous connotations. Luckily, customs officials acting on a tip successfully seized the shipment at St. Petersburg's Pulkovo Airport. The architect of the scheme, the director of the plant (A. Kalinovskiy), received only a four-year suspended sentence from a Russian court.[62] The case exposed a gaping hole in the Russian export control system. "People who want to smuggle radioactive nuclear material can do so with little risk by simply substituting or increasing the materials recorded in the export license and the customs declaration," reported Nikolai Kravchenko. "Customs officials do not know what is really inside the containers—what is declared as cesium-137 could well be plutonium or some radioactive material."[63] Current speculations hypothesize that a Western firm with close ties to Islamic states might be a likely foreign recipient of such diverted fissile material. Unfortunately, as Kravchenko and his colleagues emphasize, Russia has little recourse against radioactive customs fraud. Sophisticated technology (such as state-of-the-art gamma spectrometers) can scan the contents of containers and detect such legal contraband, but Russians customs checkpoints currently lack the resources to purchase and deploy such equipment.

The prospect of collusion between senior managers of nuclear enterprises and organized crime groups with international connections poses a particularly grave proliferation threat. Such a dangerous alliance already could be unfolding in Russia. An important contributing factor is the decline of government orders in the atomic energy industry (and in other parts of the military-industrial complex) that, as already noted, jeopardizes the economic security of enterprises and the employment prospects of nuclear scientists and engineers. To compensate for reduced government procurement, certain nuclear enterprises are permitted to sign contractual agreements with agents such as foreign states and private commercial companies. Such arrangements provide a handy cover and a mechanism for a dangerous shadow business in nuclear materials. A highly placed Russian source in a research institute of the Russian Academy of Sciences who is familiar with nuclear security and weapons proliferation issues apprised me of a credible scheme, under way since early 1994, to import uranium concentrate, enrich it in Russian plants equipped with isotope separation machinery, and then export the product through southern Russia to various states in the Middle East. This threatening scenario views the shadow traffic in nuclear wares as more than surreptitiously removing fissile materials from enterprises and using fraudulent documents to transport contraband in legal shipments. According to the scientist, the core of the current Russian proliferation problem lies in uranium enrichment services contracted by Islamic (Chechen) criminal groups that hold previously negotiated arrangements with final buyers outside of Russia.

This novel idea apparently relies on the following chain of events. Uranium concentrate produced in Kazakhstan is shipped from the port of Aktau (Shevchenko) across the Caspian Sea to the Dagestan (Russia) capital of Machackala, where Chechen-controlled private companies assume control of the shipment. The uranium is trucked to staging areas in Chechnya, principally abandoned mines or unused military bases. From there the cargo is transported to nuclear plants in the Chelyabinsk region and in western Siberia. Processing arrangements are ostensibly innocuous—filling an order to produce radioluminescent paints, for example. However, technical specifications of such agreements are altered by unwritten understandings to obtain final products that are suitable for energy-grade or weapons-grade fissile materials. The brokering companies compensate the enterprise in cash for final products, which the scientist contends include enriched reactor-quality uranium, highly enriched weapons-quality uranium (weapons-grade HEU), and radioactive isotopes used in medicine and research. Experts from laboratories in Moscow and St. Petersburg certify the technical specifications of samples of the finished materials, which are then shipped back to Chechnya. (Exactly where these appraisals are done is not clear from the scientific account.) The materials eventually are smuggled across the Russian Azerbaidjan border for export via the Caspian Sea ports or are shipped out of Russia from the Black Sea port of Novorossiysk. The principal destination for the finished uranium is Iran, but other aspiring or de facto nuclear states (Israel, Iraq, and Pakistan) also are mentioned as possible end users.

But why such a circuitous transaction—why transport the uranium ore all the way from Kazakhstan when Russia itself is a producer? As the scientist explains, foreign uranium and associated products are largely outside the framework of state control: "Most favored treatment and lowest levels of control by the government are applied in these instances to orders based on the principle of 'foreign source raw material' (*daval' cheskoye siryo*). This means raw material extracted or produced not at Russia's government enterprises and not according to government orders, but to raw material received previously from private individuals and commercial enterprises and received or purchased from other countries."[64]

The cunning of this scheme is obvious: The uranium raw material is not Russian; no entries are made in Russian enterprise books; and procedures for checking storage containers to measure nuclear inventories against enterprise paperwork are ineffectual and virtually pointless. The scientist could not precisely quantify the uranium that is enriched and reexported by using this strategy but does project that the value of the traffic could approach \$1 billion per year. More than half of this value is attributable to various radioisotope products, and most of the balance is reactor-grade uranium, enriched to 12 to 16 percent U-235. The remainder, approximately 1 percent, comprises weapons-grade HEU. The scientist estimates that the quantity of HEU thus diverted amounts to 50 to 80 kilograms per year, which he contends is sufficient to make three to five nuclear warheads, each in the 30- to 50-kiloton range.[65] (According to IAEA figures, such quantities would permit the manufacture of two to three 20-kiloton weapons; however, the IAEA's engineering assumptions are conservative, as noted in chapter 5.) In the view of this prominent and well-informed specialist, this dangerous channel of nuclear diversion and proliferation reflects a catastrophic disintegration of morale and discipline in the nuclear complex. In an unpublished document on such covert activities, the scientist noted: "A part of the production and technological management of the plant cannot help but know the true nature of the production output. However, the pressures of social problems on the one hand, and criminal structure on the other, combined with a measure of personal opportunism, may force this segment of the administration not to see what is going on or to become a passive participant in a criminal conspiracy."[66]

These grave allegations correlate with important policy implications, but the credibility of such charges is subject to debate. In contrast to Lebed's story of the missing suitcase bombs, this case features no apparent reason for embarrassing or discrediting the Yeltsin government. (Indeed, the scientist told me on several occasions that no reasonable or efficient alternative to Yeltsin's policies can be posited in Russia today.) In addition, the source occupies an important position in the Russian AOS system, is a longtime observer of Russian nuclear defense problems, and apparently enjoys extensive contacts in the atomic energy sector and in the Russian intelligence and security communities. While the information might be an elaborate invention, this conclusion seems improbable. (Why go to the trouble of concocting such a tale?) The data more likely manifest a careful blend of fact and guesswork. Estimates of the total volume of the underground traffic ($1 billion per year) seem exaggerated if not surreal. However, the basic outline of the story could contain important elements of truth—in any event, the report is sufficiently coherent and detailed to warrant high-level attention by U.S. policymakers. At the very least, the scientist's account illustrates how little is known about the workings of illegal nuclear markets, especially such crucial aspects as the organized crime connection to the business, the criminal environment in the former secret cities, and emerging nuclear material smuggling routes across Russia's southern frontiers and through Transcaucasia and Central Asian states.

The AOS account and other evidence tend to reinforce the hypothesis that two basic smuggling pathways can be employed for transferring nuclear material: an overt, strategically innocuous channel and a covert channel that poses a significant security threat. Table 6.3 summarizes these two pathways. Unfortunately, neither the United States nor Russia seems prepared to deal with the sophisticated collusive patterns of diversion and smuggling that apparently are emerging in Russia today. Indeed, powerful pro-proliferation interests operating within the atomic energy ministry—and within the administrations of regions (oblasts) where large nuclear facilities are deployed—may provide cover or implicit support for such activities.[67]

ENVIRONMENTAL CONCERNS

Like Western Europe, Russia has been exposed to terrorist threats involving radioactive materials. The most widely publicized episode occurred in November 1995, when a Chechen military commander, Shamil Basayev, arranged the burial and the subsequent discovery (by a Russian news team) of a canister of cesium-137 in Moscow's Izmailovsky Park. At the time, the Chechen

TABLE 6.3

Nuclear Smuggling Channels

Principal Elements	Visible Channel	Covert Channel
ENTERPRISE PARTICIPANTS	Low-ranking employees, workers	Mid-level and senior managers
MATERIAL	Mostly radioactive junk of little military significance	Low-enriched and high-enriched (including weapons-grade) uranium; valuable radioisotopes
BROKERING MECHANISMS	Spontaneous, transaction-dependent, unstable networks	Criminal organizations; government officials, intelligence operatives, visiting foreign scientists
EXPORT ROUTES	Baltics, Belarus, Eastern Europe, Central Europe (especially Germany)	Europe, Southern Russia (Chechnya, Dagestan, Azerbaidjan) Central Asia
CUSTOMERS	Few bona fide customers	Nuclear threshold states, undeclared nuclear states
STRATEGIC SIGNIFICANCE	Low	Moderate to high

leader threatened to use the radioactive waste to turn Moscow into an "eternal desert." Basaev also asserted that he had smuggled in four such containers, two attached to explosives that could be detonated at any time. (Fortunately, the threat was not carried out.)[68] Economic desperation also can precipitate terrorist-type episodes. Captain Mikhail Kulik, an investigator for the Northern Fleet prosecutor's office, recounts such a case involving a worker at a repair facility for nuclear submarines. After not being paid for a few months, the worker decided to post a notice on the plant's bulletin board threatening to blow up a workshop containing two reactors. Although he was apprehended, the incident underscores the threat to nuclear facilities from resentful or mentally unstable insiders. Moreover, in 1994 two bomb threats were made against the Ignalina atomic power station in Lithuania. One threat was communicated by a local organized crime boss after a court had sentenced his son to death. The plant was shut down and searched, but no explosive device was detected. In another case, a Lithuanian national in Sweden claiming to represent a secret organization (NC-41W) submitted a written demand to the Swedish prime minister's office for $8 million; the letter declared that the secret organization had infiltrated the Ignalina facility and was prepared to destroy the plant.[69] Fortunately, the extortionist was arrested, tried, and convicted.[70] Such threats nonetheless have a powerful psychological impact on nearby populations, although the actual effects of detonating radiological weapons (such as Basaev's canisters) may be less damaging than commonly supposed.[71]

A bizarre event in the illegal nuclear trade transpired in the Ukraine and Sweden in the spring of 1994. A 32-year-old Swedish businessman, Erik Estenson, contacted the Ukrainian Ministry of Defense and asked to purchase four warheads of disassembled nuclear missiles for $2 billion. Estenson's stated aim was to introduce the weapons into Stockholm and then blackmail the Swedish government into supporting the Ukraine with additional technical and economic assistance. The Ukrainian authorities, concluding that they had a crackpot on their hands, arrested the man and returned him to Sweden, where he was convicted and jailed for 15 years on terrorism charges.[72]

Fears of nuclear terrorism in Russia were exacerbated by the 1993 murder of Vladimir Kaplun, director of the Russian packing company Karton Tara. Kaplun died from radiation sickness over a period of several weeks after someone inserted a radioactive substance in the desk chair of his Moscow office. "A huge ulcer on his back wasn't healing and he began to bleed internally," noted one account of this tragic episode. Radiation murder seemingly constitutes an inefficient technique for disposing of enemies, however, and thus radioactive substances are unlikely to become common weapons of choice for homicide.[73]

CHAPTER 7

CONCLUSION

NUCLEAR BLACK MARKETS
AND THE CHIMERA OF NONPROLIFERATION

AS THE PRECEDING CHAPTERS SUGGEST, the nuclear materials traffic is fraught with ambiguity. In its visible statistical and qualitative manifestations, the business embodies a relatively low and possibly diminishing proliferation risk. The observed traffic, however, may imperfectly reflect the total reality of such smuggling. Some anecdotal evidence points to the existence of a shadow market that is more professionally organized and operated than the visible market and that poses dangerous implications for international security and stability.

Of course, the public record of the traffic tells a compelling story. According to different European databases, the overall outflow of nuclear substances from NIS factories is diminishing quantitatively in response to poor market demand for NIS nuclear wares and to progressive improvements in security at NIS nuclear installations. Globally, the number of recorded incidents involving weapons-usable material is relatively small (approximately 12 by my reckoning), and several of these smuggling episodes apparently are linked to a single facility, the Obninsk IPPE. Moreover, no such cases have been documented in Europe or Russia since mid-1995.

The fraud quotient is high in the nuclear smuggling business. Sellers frequently misrepresent their wares—for example, representing reactor fuel pellets, radioisotopic sources (such as cesium-137), or plutonium-coated screws for sale as weapons-quality HEU or plutonium. The German government reported that fraudulent offers accounted for some 35 to 40 percent of trafficking episodes in Germany between 1992 and 1995. A persistent and popular nuclear scam focused on the esoteric substance known as red mercury. The U.S. DOE documents 50 such scams from 1979 to 1996. Analysis of samples of red mercury acquired by European governments have identified common compounds such as mercuric oxide or mercuric iodide (in some cases, irradiated in a reactor) or ordinary mercury mixed with red dye or fingernail polish.

Moreover, the nuclear trade does not bear much resemblance to other illegal businesses. Such trade is driven principally by the suppliers, disgruntled and economically desperate employees (or former employees) of nuclear enterprises, and local enthusiasts who reside in the vicinity of such enterprises. As noted in chapters 5 and 6, trading and marketing opportunities are fairly narrow—very few people and companies deal in these substances, and those that do treat nuclear materials as a sideline, principally engaging in the export of nonferrous metals and other raw materials. In Russia dealers usually accept nuclear merchandise on consignment only and collect enormous commissions if an actual sale is completed. Furthermore, legitimate buyers are few and far between. In Europe the principal customers apparently are not the obvious candidates such as North Korea, Iraq, Pakistan, Iran, or Islamic Jihad representatives—or, at least, purchases of nuclear contraband by such groups have yet to be conclusively demonstrated. Rather, the market as such comprises an assortment of police, undercover agents, intelligence operatives, and journalists. Indeed, European police and Russian authorities can confirm only a few actual cases of money changing hands for nuclear goods.

In addition, most nuclear smuggling networks seemingly lack the principal attributes of organized crime—a continuing criminal conspiracy, a firm organizational structure, and corrupt ties to the authorities. Relationships among sellers, brokers, and middlemen are ad hoc, deal-specific, and impermanent. Large Russian or

Western mafia syndicates evince little apparent interest in procuring, transporting, or selling nuclear and radioactive assets. Western officials and academic observers maintain that organized crime operates extremely profitable crime businesses and that a high-profile, risky, and uncertain business holds little allure for most professional criminals.

A defining characteristic of the visible market is the predominant East-West flow of nuclear contraband—mainly from Russia through Belarus, the Baltics, and Poland to Germany and other Central European states. To date, Germany represents the principal entrepôt and trading center for illegal nuclear commerce in the 1990s, accounting for half of the radioactive seizures between January 1993 and May 1997, according to IAEA data. The apparent geographical irrationality of this pattern (except, perhaps, for the export of samples to Europe for expert certification) was noted several times.

The more refined and professionally managed shadow market draws on a pattern of corrupt relationships at different junctures in the nuclear supply chain. At the enterprise level, thefts and diversions are the product of consensual arrangements among well-placed insiders, in some cases including senior managers, engineers, and scientists. In the Elektrokhimpribor scandal described in chapter 6, the architects of the illegal scheme to export radioisotopic materials were the top leaders of the plant. The legal contraband case at Mayak and the AOS report of Russian plant participation in uranium enrichment and reexport schemes also indicate a pattern of managerial complicity in diversions.

Corrupt nuclear managers can choose from a wide variety of smuggling options. In the conventional black market, smuggling chains comprise largely opportunistic traders, couriers, and scam artists—in general, an unmemorable collection of minor criminals. The shadow market, however, apparently features a more sophisticated array of actors and relationships. The clandestine Elektrokhimpribor marketing arrangement, for example, relied on MINATOM officials and MINATOM-linked private companies. My AOS source contends that Chechen criminal organizations brokered the previously cited uranium diversion scheme. Plant managers and local economic officials in Sverdlovsk sought the assistance of Western nuclear specialists to certify samples of HEU as plutonium, probably hoping to find foreign customers for fissile materials stockpiled at the plant. The Russian Foreign Intelligence Service reputedly had a hand in the 1994 diversion of plutonium from Obninsk to Munich, although the extent of such participation is not entirely clear. More speculatively, the shadow market implies direct and strategically consequential links among suppliers, broker-dealers, buyers, and ultimate end users of strategic nuclear materials. In the AOS account detailed in the last chapter, Chechen-organized smuggling routes for bomb-grade HEU crossed southern Russia and Azerbaidjan en route to prospective end-user states in the Middle East and South Asia. The AOS calculations imply that Iran, the principal beneficiary of this complex scheme, could have stockpiled enough HEU to make five or more high-yield nuclear warheads by the end of 1996.

Other aspects of the Russian nuclear proliferation threat also must be evaluated. As noted in previous chapters, the custodial system for nuclear materials in Russia and other post-Soviet states probably was the weakest in the early post-Soviet period. At that time, the old KGB-centered system of controls had collapsed, and severe economic strains at enterprises and institutes had further undermined safeguards, systems, and procedures.[1] U.S.-Russian cooperative programs to upgrade such facilities did not produce tangible results until 1995-1996, and then only at a handful of Russian enterprises. (As of early 1998, the MPC&A programs still protected only a fraction of factories and sites housing fissile nuclear materials.) Therein lies the crux of the nuclear leakage problem. Recent investigative reports on the Munich and Prague smuggling cases, including testimony imputed to traffickers, suggest that the available supplies of black-market nuclear materials potentially were much greater than the quantities actually seized. An intriguing possibility posits that Russian nuclear employees, exploiting the lax state of controls in the early 1990s, liberally helped themselves to HEU and plutonium from fissile stockpiles with the hope that customers subsequently could be identified and contacted. If this strategy was applied, in all likelihood, the stolen nuclear materials still are held privately in Russia or already have been exported successfully.

Of course, such findings and hypotheses must be thoroughly tested. Shadow trafficking networks that deal in weapons-usable uranium and plutonium cannot be authenticated by direct proof. Nevertheless, indirect evidence seems sufficiently compelling to warrant a reassessment of U.S. counterproliferation programs. The alleged disappearance of a number of suitcase-size nuclear weapons further underscores the porosity and vulnerability of Russian nuclear complexes. Official U.S. policy, of course, advocates preventing the transfer of nuclear materials (and finished weapons) to states and groups with interests inimical to those of the United States. As Thomas MacNamara, a U.S. assistant secretary of state for political-military affairs, explained in a March 1996 Senate hearing, "Nuclear smuggling is not like other kinds of illegal trafficking. We cannot afford to have even a single case of successful smuggling of enough nuclear material for a weapon."[2] Unofficially, U.S. policymakers should acknowledge that zero proliferation may have misfired as a policy and should design ongoing strategies accordingly.

A wide consensus has evolved among nuclear policy experts that acquiring a supply of adequately pure weapons-grade nuclear material constitutes a technical shortcut and a cheap route to manufacturing an atomic bomb. "Limits on access to fissile materials are the primary technical barriers to acquisition of nuclear weapons capability in the world today," argued a U.S. military analyst.[3] Yet engineering expertise also is required at other stages— for instance, in fabricating and testing the device, developing delivery vehicles, and actually deploying the weapon. More important, states that possess the requisite fissile materials may opt, for domestic or international political reasons, to reject the development and deployment of a nuclear force and even the production of a bomb. The demarcation lines between acquiring fissile materials, building a prototype weapon, and creating a full-fledged nuclear capability also create windows of opportunity for U.S. policy.[4] Strategies that isolate nuclear threshold states, particularly Iran, as rogue regimes and supporters of international terrorism will not prove viable in the long run and probably should be abandoned. (Moreover, the recent election of a relatively moderate political figure, Mohammad Khatami, as president of Iran probably enhances the prospects for an accommodation with that country.) Dialogues with these aspiring nuclear powers should be expanded whenever possible on issues such as arms control, trade, and nuclear security. For example, easing economic sanctions against Iran and broadening direct diplomatic contacts, possibly high-level contacts, with that country could serve as positive steps toward improving the likelihood of arms control and security in the Middle East.[5] Of course, Iran and other states should be encouraged to place clandestine stockpiles of HEU and plutonium under IAEA safeguards. In sum, the emerging new configuration of nuclear powers in the post–Cold War environment requires a more enlightened approach to nuclear proliferation—one that recognizes the wider availability of the knowledge and ingredients necessary for weapons production. Legalizing proliferation, however, would rank as a serious if not fatal error.[6] The international community still must discourage threshold states from joining the nuclear club or acquiring other weapons of mass destruction. Furthermore, international control regimes must be maintained and indeed strengthened to prevent nuclear materials from falling into the hands of wholly irresponsible actors such as criminal extortionists and terrorist groups.

WHAT CAN BE DONE?

Overall U.S. strategy emphasizes the containment of thefts at nuclear enterprises, but other promising lines of defense consequently may be shortchanged. For example, the more sophisticated collusive diversion scenarios outlined previously suggest that even well-guarded and upgraded facilities may not prevent the eventual (and possibly even current) diversion of sensitive nuclear materials into international trafficking and marketing channels. Nonetheless, U.S. cooperation with, and support for, Russian law enforcement is languishing, beset by both insufficient funding and legal and bureaucratic wrangling. U.S. law enforcement and intelligence officers and their counterparts in the NIS have played little role in bilateral dialogues on counterproliferation, accentuating one-sided U.S. policy. In addition, U.S. programs in the NIS suffer from insufficient focus on the core motivations that drive the supply-side diversion of nuclear materials. Better and more comprehensive economic programs must be developed to guarantee a decent livelihood for nuclear workers in post-Soviet states.

For example, prevention of thefts—the rationale for MPC&A programs—undoubtedly must be counted as a laudable and worthy objective, and substantial apparent progress was achieved on this front between 1995 and 1997. As noted, by the end of 1997, agreements for MPC&A cooperation had been signed with 53 facilities in the NIS, and a total of 17 NIS facilities had new MPC&A systems in place—an impressive success considering the legacy of hostilities from the Cold War and legendary Russian sensitivities about nuclear security and sovereignty.

Whether strengthened MPC&A systems have reduced or will significantly diminish the risk of nuclear proliferation from the NIS is less clear. In this respect, the shot glass can be viewed as half empty or half full. Justifications for skepticism certainly abound. U.S.-Russian cooperation on MPC&A programs produced few tangible achievements before 1995, and policymakers can only guess the extent of thievery and black marketeering of nuclear materials that characterized the chaotic years immediately following the breakup of the Soviet Union. MPC&A programs thus struggle to escape the uncomfortable connotation of padlocking the proverbial barn after the horse has escaped. Furthermore, the task is obviously far from complete. According to the 1996 testimony of a General Accounting Office official, the number of NIS facilities (excluding weapons storehouses) that require MPC&A upgrades could run as high as 135.[7] Many of these facilities comprise multiple individual storage sites for nuclear materials, and additional sites continue to surface as the MPC&A program progresses; the accomplishment of MPC&A hence can be described as partial at best, even at enterprises covered under the program. The National Research Council published a sobering assessment in 1997: ". . . while significant improvements have been made at selected facilities the task has not been completed at any facility and has only begun at many. The DOE estimates that *tons* of direct-use materials are contained in internationally acceptable MPC&A systems and that *tens of tons* are in partially acceptable systems; but adequate MPC&A systems for hundreds of tons must still be installed."[8]

Furthermore, the new MPC&A technologies represent an imperfect defense against the diversion-by-consensus scenarios cited earlier. Well-placed insiders working in concert can defeat such systems, or so Russian nuclear managers contend. (The improved safeguards admittedly would make it more difficult for solo thieves such as Luch's Yuriy Smirnov to remove nuclear materials from an enterprise.) The absence of technical discipline and the presence of irresponsible work habits also conspire to undermine nuclear security at enterprises. If corrupt managers can disable sensor systems, incompetent ones may simply neglect to turn them on or may fail to notice whether they are working properly. Unfortunately, as one astute observer notes, "An MPC&A system is only as good as the scientists, technicians, and guards in charge of running it. It will take years before we can accurately assess the extent to which Russia is able fully to integrate an MPC&A system jointly designed with U.S. engineers and scientists."[9]

A final point: Effective implementation of the new MPC&A safeguards will require monitoring and oversight from a reliable observer outside the MINATOM nuclear complex. U.S. and other Western nuclear specialists and advisors are not in a position to assume this responsibility. The extant Russian oversight agency, the State Nuclear Regulatory Committee (Gosatomnadzor, or GAN), lacks the statutory authority to regulate much of the complex;

specifically, the GAN mandate does not extend to facilities or parts thereof that manufacture nuclear weapons or explosive charges for such weapons, to weapons storage sites, or to naval bases storing submarine fuel. Furthermore, as the report by the National Research Council confirms, GAN "suffers from a shortage of well-trained inspectors, qualified staff, and necessary analytical and related equipment."[10] In addition, GAN is a puny instrument compared to its principal object of control, MINATOM (the hyperbolic fly and elephant). To quantify, GAN employs approximately 2,000 people, MINATOM approximately 700,000 (as of the mid-1990s). The annual GAN budget does not exceed $4 million, while MINATOM oversees billions. MINATOM exports ($2 billion in 1996) account for approximately 3 percent of Russian exports; as a domestic regulatory organ, GAN exports virtually nothing. In any power contest with MINATOM over improving regulatory controls in the Russian nuclear complex, GAN is likely to emerge as the battered loser. Moreover, although GAN does conduct inspections at civilian enterprises and institutes—29,000 violations of rules and norms were detected in 1995—the agency typically imposes only symbolic punishments (a $1 or $2 fine). GAN does possess the theoretical authority to decertify enterprises that violate safety regulations, but, not surprisingly, this power has never been exercised. In my opinion, senior GAN officials are a dedicated and competent crew, but this generally weak institution is unlikely, at least in the near term, to play a significant role in countering the proliferation forces at work in Russia.[11]

Such uncertainties and concerns about MPC&A programs argue for some shifts in the emphasis of U.S. counterproliferation policy in the NIS. One obvious recommendation is to devote greater attention and resources to strengthening the NIS antitrafficking infrastructure (that is, police, security, and customs agencies), an important second line of defense against the proliferation of nuclear materials. U.S. funding for such activities, approximately $10 million in fiscal year 1998, is a pittance—only 7 percent of the $137 million allocated to MPC&A in this year. (According to DOE projections, total expenditures for MPC&A projects will reach $800 million by the year 2002.) The world confronts a substantial risk that fissile materials will continue to escape from Russian enterprises for years to come, so law enforcement must assume a larger share of the counterproliferation burden. As the military prosecutor of the Northern Fleet, Mikhail Kulik, explained to *Yaderny Kontrol'*: "For the time being we do not count on the improvement of the system for physical protection, control, and accounting—it seems that it could take many years to implement state programs. We rely on law enforcement bodies, primarily local ones . . . we find criminals and receive stolen materials."[12]

A significantly larger share of overall U.S. counterproliferation funding in the NIS probably should be devoted to second-line activities such as training and equipping NIS law enforcement and security officials to interdict stolen nuclear materials and nuclear contraband. Police, prosecutors, security officials, and customs officers operating in the neighborhood of large nuclear complexes or secret cities—Obninsk, Mayak, Arzamas-16, Tomsk-7, and the like—probably require special assistance and support. For example, officials of the Russian State Customs Committee want to deploy 30 to 40 gamma spectrometers (which can check the contents of radioactive cargoes) at internal customs posts that adjoin large nuclear enterprises. As argued previously, such equipment might help close so-called legal contraband channels for diverting dangerous nuclear materials. To date, however, insufficient funds have been allocated for this purpose by U.S. Customs, DOE, and other agencies.[13]

Improving the capability of border agents and guards to intercept contraband nuclear material at Russian frontiers also should receive a higher priority. Such border operations represent especially important tools for states along Russia's southern periphery. Unfortunately, by late 1996 Russia had deployed no radiation monitoring equipment along its borders with Transcaucasia or the Central Asian states, and these countries (with the possible exception of Kazakhstan) have not mustered the resources to procure such equipment on their own. Russian police and customs officials have no conception of the quantity of nuclear material that might be illegally transiting the country's southern borders—the region effectively functions as a free zone for the smuggling of virtually any kind of contraband. Regrettably, U.S.-Russian customs cooperation long was in limbo because of a U.S. legislative requirement that audits and inspections of U.S.-made detection equipment be conducted by an appropriate U.S. government agency. In a typical display of sovereignty, Russian customs officials flatly refused to permit such audits. The dispute now appears to have been resolved. DOE has begun providing equipment to shore up Russian customs' second line of defense, but the delay in such assistance is certainly unfortunate.[14]

The long-standing disparity between funding for MPC&A and appropriations for countertrafficking law enforcement activities mirrors political realities in the United States. A large lobby (DOE, the National Laboratories, and many members of Congress) advocates MPC&A, but no comparable lobby has yet coalesced for law enforcement. This imbalance is reinforced and perpetuated by the common perception that NIS police and customs officials (especially the latter) are excessively prone to corruption and that managers and scientists in nuclear institutions are somehow free of the taint of criminality. This clearly ranks as a dangerous assumption, as this book documents. Both U.S. intelligence and law enforcement officials and their counterparts in Russia must be encouraged to play a larger role in bilateral dialogues on nuclear proliferation and to apply their street-smart perspectives to resolving this thorny problem. Needless to say, U.S.-Russian cooperation programs should be reconfigured to assign greater weight to such real-world evaluations.

An in-depth international response to the formidable hazards of nuclear smuggling and proliferation also requires enhanced cooperation between Western intelligence and law enforcement agencies and their NIS counterparts. As noted in chapter 1, at the 1996 Moscow summit Russia and the Group of Seven powers agreed on a collective program to combat nuclear trafficking, including pledges to exchange information on significant trafficking incidents and to cooperate in ensuring the "prompt investigation and successful prosecution" of such cases.[15] None-theless, barriers to substantive cooperation remain. Because of security and policy constraints, governments usually are reluctant to disclose intelligence data on illegal nuclear transfers and nuclear black-market transactions, so reporting on such cases still can be classified as selective and sporadic.[16] Governments' suspicions of each other's integrity and motives also dilute incentives for sharing information. From the West's perspective, the expanding influence of Russian organized crime cuts across many issues of East-West relations, including cooperation on nuclear matters. (Witness the BND's assessment that the Russian foreign intelligence service is inextricably intertwined with criminal organizations.) From Moscow's perspective, the West is simply manipulating mafia and nuclear leakage concerns to discredit Russia internationally and to weaken Russian sovereignty over nuclear weapons. Such unfavorable suspicions aside, no viable alternative can substitute for Russian-Western cooperation to control criminal nuclear proliferation. The road to such cooperation, however, undoubtedly will be littered with potholes, requiring considerable confidence building and demonstrations of good faith on both sides. Some analysts believe that an international convention or treaty against nuclear smuggling could improve East-West atmospherics, but such an instrument is likely to have little more than symbolic value at this stage.[17]

In addition, America's own intelligence capabilities to collect data on nuclear diversion episodes (and on incidents involving other weapons of mass destruction) must be significantly upgraded. According to the *Washington Post,* the CIA plans to add 100 analysts to the agency's Non-Proliferation Center to "help monitor global proliferation of ballistic missiles and chemical, nuclear, and biological arms."[18] Assigning more Washington-area analysts to these cases probably represents a necessary bureaucratic step, but what is most needed is timely information about real deals in the making. Hence, a high priority also must be placed on developing informant networks and technical collection techniques in proliferation-sensitive regions in the NIS—for example, in Russia's former secret cities and in the Caspian and Black Sea ports that figure prominently in clandestine nuclear transfers.

An additional set of issues addresses the economic underpinnings and motivations of the illegal nuclear trade. The threat of nuclear theft and diversion in Russian facilities simply will not be ameliorated by MPC&A programs that construct increasingly sturdier walls around hungry and resentful employees. In a recent book, *Avoiding Nuclear Anarchy,* Harvard scholar Graham Allison and his colleagues criticize U.S. programs for paying insufficient attention to the collapsing quality of life of nuclear workers. The authors contend that the real obstacle to removing the temptation of nuclear diversion lies in the unwillingness of the U.S. Congress to propose any support that might be construed as foreign aid or welfare spending for NIS nuclear complexes and their employees.[19]

To be sure, U.S. policy does not entirely neglect economic concerns. Some funding in the MPC&A contracts with Russian facilities is earmarked for salary supplements, although DOE does not advertise this aspect of the projects (possibly to avoid arousing the ire of Congress). For example, the salaries of some 100 employees at IPPE and 200 employees at Arzamas-16 are supplemented by U.S. funds. (At Obninsk, these subsidies amount to approximately $125 per month.) Nonetheless, as noted previously, such funds are available only to participants in the cooperative MPC&A programs, which are incompletely implemented at individual enterprises. For instance, as of year-end 1996, some 200 to 300 employees at Obninsk were not yet under the MPC&A umbrella, despite working at ten experimental reactor sites that use both reactor-grade and weapons-grade HEU. In addition, the possibility must be considered that U.S. support may be creating a class system of sorts in Russian enterprises, fueling resentments that ultimately could magnify the likelihood of nuclear theft.

Since 1994 the United States and other foreign donors have underwritten a program that provides salaries for unemployed or underemployed weapons technicians and nuclear scientists who work on nonmilitary projects. Managed by the International Science and Technology Center (ISTC) in Moscow and a parallel center in Ukraine, this program is designed more to counter the brain drain of weapons specialists and staunch outflows of sensitive nuclear technology than to reduce economic incentives to steal nuclear material. Groups of applicants submit funding proposals to ISTC, and Western supporters usually participate in the approval process. By the end of 1996, the ISTC had contributed approximately $120 million to finance nearly 320 projects employing more than 15,000 NIS scientists and engineers, "a majority of whom were previously involved in research on weapons of mass destruction."[20] However, these technical experts represent a small fraction of the hundreds of thousands of scientists and engineers associated with post-Soviet nuclear complexes (although many of the estimated 10,000 to 15,000 scientists with knowledge of strategic weapons or enrichment technologies are nurtured under the program). In addition, the ISTC grantees include chemical and biological warfare specialists and missile designers as well as nuclear scientists. More to the point, as Allison and his colleagues observed, the ISTC "does little or nothing for the guards and administrators of nuclear installations who probably pose even worse security risks than scientific personnel."[21] In addition, the ISTC clearly constitutes a temporary fix at best, not a permanent solution, and thus can alleviate only partially the suffering of nuclear elites in the NIS.[22]

In sum, more comprehensive and broadly targeted programs must be devised to improve the livelihood of nuclear workers, and benefits should be distributed more equitably within enterprises and institutions participating in MPC&A programs. The composition of the assistance—the specific mix of salary supports and other items (food and medicines, for example)—perhaps could be negotiated case by case. A more ambitious proposal, advanced by Allison, calls for the "conversion and retraining" of enterprises and individuals enduring the aftershocks of nuclear dismantlement. John Holdren, a former member of the President's Committee of Advisers on Science and Technology, advocates a large international investment in cultivating business opportunities that diversify the economic base of the former secret cities. "Major cultural changes and substantial subsidies will be required if these cities are to have any economic future independent of the production of nuclear weapons," he declared. Such ideas may be deemed impractical given U.S. budgetary constraints and congressional aversion to seeming welfare expenditures in the former Soviet Union.[23] Nevertheless, as these and other observers confirm, U.S. counterproliferation strategy is likely to be significantly more successful if accompanied by a broader program to improve the economic prospects of people handling nuclear materials and weaponry.

In general, an argument can be made for reconfiguring and broadening U.S. counterproliferation initiatives in the NIS, especially in Russia, and for more intensively addressing the root causes of nuclear leakages. Expectations for such cooperative measures, however, should be modest. In the end, Russia's Western partners can do little to control systemic proliferation risks such as corrupt enterprise management, collusive ties between nuclear managers and professional criminals, and Russian government complicity in illegal and quasi-legal nuclear transfers. The weakness of controls implemented in Russia's nuclear archipelago mirrors an array of problems in the larger society—eroding moral standards, a continuing crisis of authority, widespread economic distress, and the pervasive influence of increasingly powerful organized crime groups on the economy and the political system. How, when, and whether such problems are resolved obviously will exert a profound influence over the future success or failure of counterproliferation in Russia and other NIS states. In the meantime, concerns about loose nukes and nuclear material smuggling will continue to affect the stability of the East-West relationship, in the process damaging Russia's national self-respect and its image as a reputable nuclear power.

Furthermore, the United States and the international community must acknowledge the economic imperative driving the export behavior of MINATOM and other NIS atomic energy industries and must craft policies accordingly. As British nuclear expert John Baker observes, "This economic imperative stems from the need to compensate for the substantial loss of internal revenue sources that these industries enjoyed when they were high-priority components of the Soviet Union's military-industrial complex."[24] The United States and its allies hold a legitimate interest in containing the spread of sensitive nuclear technology and materials. Yet the West also has a vital stake in the economic health of MINATOM and the sizable community of people who depend on it. Ultimately, such economic vitality will generate the best guarantee against the nuclear theft and other diversion scenarios described in this book. Striking a balance between these concerns and prioritizing counterproliferation objectives constitute a challenging puzzle. International control regimes and associated diplomatic initiatives can focus most usefully on preventing the export of enrichment and reprocessing technologies, weapons-making expertise, and fissile materials themselves. Russia's various nuclear power projects in India, China, and especially Iran also raise legitimate concerns.[25] Nevertheless, the associated multibillion-dollar hard-currency contributions to Russia's troubled atomic energy complex eventually might translate into improved security for HEU and plutonium stocks in MINATOM custody. (This result remains to be seen.) Incidentally, a similar positive spin is advanced to justify a major 1994 U.S. agreement with Russia to buy 500 tons of blended-down Russian uranium at a cost of $12 billion over 20 years. The injection of such funds into the Russian economy reputedly will improve prospects for economic reforms, promote defense conversion, and empower MINATOM's capability "to guard the fissile material remaining in its installations."[26] Whether and to what extent MINATOM's foreign economic activities will directly benefit employees at those installations—and concomitantly minimize their incentive to steal nuclear materials—is still an open question. The only irrefutable conclusion is that the covert or criminal risk of nuclear proliferation from NIS countries cannot be treated cavalierly or overlooked, because the worst-case consequences of failure are entirely too grave and potentially widespread.

REFLECTIONS ON SUPPLY-SIDE NUCLEAR CONTROL

THE SETTING

Deteriorating economic and security conditions at post-Soviet nuclear facilities have lowered barriers to proliferation, widening the array of potential nuclear threats to global security. As Senator Richard Lugar, a key Congressional sponsor of non-proliferation efforts in the newly-independent states (NIS), formulated the issue: "Rogue states and terrorist groups no longer need their own Manhattan Project; they can now seek to buy or steal what they previously had to produce on their own."[1]

To counter this threat, the United States has invested close to $1 billion since 1994 to prevent thefts and illegal diversions of nuclear materials and weapons-building expertise originating in Russia and other new states. At the heart of U.S. containment strategy are the Department of Energy's (DOE) programs to improve "materials protection, control and accountability" (MPC&A) at sensitive nuclear facilities, and DOE- and State Department-run initiatives to help unemployed weapons scientists find productive, non-military work. Smaller programs run by other

U.S. agencies are designed to improve export controls and defenses against smuggling in the NIS. These "supply-side" efforts, however, are conceptually and technologically inadequate—and will remain so because of economic and political conditions in Russia that are largely beyond the range of U.S. influence.[2]

TOO LITTLE

Supply-side controls of illicit commodities, whether drugs or nuclear materials or weapons designs, are intrinsically difficult to implement under any circumstances. For instance, the notion that the United States might effectively protect Russian nuclear secrets against leakages is wildly optimistic. If the United States could not prevent its own closely held atomic secrets from gravitating to the Soviet Union in the 1940s, and apparently to China in the past decade, how can it possibly expect to keep Iran or Iraq from obtaining nuclear bomb-making specifications from an unemployed Russian scientist, even one receiving stopgap assistance from the United States?

Compounding the difficulty is the unrealistically high rate of interdiction that a supply-side nuclear control effort would require in order to be effective. For comparison, consider that perhaps 25 percent of the cocaine refined in Colombia is seized internationally before it reaches consumers in the United States and Europe. A 25 percent interdiction rate obviously would not be acceptable for weapons-usable uranium or plutonium; indeed, the rate would have to reach close to 100 percent for the effort to be considered successful.

Aside from patently unrealistic expectations, another general weakness of supply-side controls is that the impetus for them often comes from without rather than from within. Again, the U.S. war against drugs provides a useful analogy. In that sphere, Washington has provided both the funding and the agenda for efforts elsewhere in the world, but has had little success in countries whose own leaders lack the political will to control lucrative narcotics exports. In dealing with sovereign states, Washington is limited to the power to "decertify" them if their cooperation is found wanting. Similarly, nuclear non-proliferation programs that emanate from Washington are headed for defeat as long as the NIS leaders are principally concerned with their own countries' economic and political survival.

The DOE efforts to improve MPC&A through technological safeguards might be expected to keep nuclear materials out of reach of would-be thieves, regardless of the political will (or lack thereof) of the local authorities, but here, too, such hopes are unwarranted. First, nearly eight years after the Soviet Union's collapse, those controls have yet to be installed at most of the 400-odd Russian buildings housing nuclear materials. This is due at least in part to poor administration by the DOE, which has put at least as much of the allocated funds into U.S. weapons laboratories providing oversight as into NIS enterprises and institutes themselves. ("Welfare for the U.S. labs" is how one DOE official describes the programs.[3]) Second, the deterrent capacity of even the new systems is questionable, since they depend upon the integrity, diligence and competence of the people tending them. "I would certainly know how to remove fissile materials from here," says the director of one Russian laboratory equipped with the latest American locks and alarm systems.[4]

Moreover, material successfully removed from laboratories is not difficult to smuggle out of the country. For instance, only about one-quarter of the 300-odd customs posts along Russia's 40,000-mile border have working radiation monitors. Also, most of the equipment in the field cannot distinguish one type of radioactive metal from another, which means that smugglers could easily conceal plutonium or highly-enriched uranium in radioactive cargo that is being legally exported.[5]

The single greatest motivation for nuclear proliferation is economic gain, and even in a best-case scenario the DOE programs might have little impact in the face of widespread corruption and indifference. Just as impoverished people in the Andes flocked to the cocaine industry in search of a better future as a result of the

Latin American economic reversals of the 1980s, the current hardships in the NIS might make the lucrative black market an irresistible temptation to scientists, administrators, or security personnel with access to weapons-usable materials. Similarly, police and intelligence agents might seek a piece of the action either by demanding bribes or by participating in nuclear smuggling on their own.

Those who traffic in nuclear materials or designs can expect Russia's internal and external political situation to pose little problem, and perhaps even to enhance their chances of success. First, as stated above, when leaders are preoccupied by fundamental threats to their economic and political future, proliferation becomes a lower priority, and vigilance might relax. In addition, Russia's generally good relations with states such as Iran and Iraq make these countries important potential markets for nuclear goods—both official deals sanctioned by the government and, conceivably, black market trade without official approval. In 1995, for example, Russia signed a protocol to sell a centrifuge plant for uranium enrichment to Iran. (It backed off under U.S. pressure.) According to some accounts, plans are currently underway to transfer specialized reactors and other tools that could accelerate Iran's nuclear weapons program. Finally, increased tensions in U.S.-Russian relations arising from NATO enlargement, the bombing of Yugoslavia, and other factors may well diminish Russia's willingness to support international non-proliferation regimes for nuclear materials and other ingredients of weapons of mass destruction.

TOO LATE

Perhaps the most fundamental flaw of supply-side nuclear control is that it comes much too late. As the book describes, thefts of radioactive materials in the NIS surged in the early 1990s—well before any DOE measures had been implemented. Most of these occurrences were militarily insignificant, but a few high-profile episodes pointed to a spreading ethos of corruption within the nuclear complex. In two recorded cases, Russian managers of top-secret defense plants offered plutonium for sale to visiting foreign scientists. Elsewhere, military officers stole highly-enriched uranium fuel from a submarine base in Murmansk. In a bizarre episode suggesting a wider conspiracy, agents of Russia's Foreign Intelligence Service reportedly masterminded the delivery of almost a pound of plutonium oxide from Moscow to Munich in August 1994.

Less well documented, but nonetheless ominous are reports from Russia that large quantities of uranium and plutonium were removed from nuclear labs in the early 1990s, that scores of "suitcase"-sized nuclear weapons are missing from storage, and that certain labs are engaged in criminally-brokered schemes to enrich uranium and sell the weapons-grade product internationally. According to one calculation, Iran might have acquired enough highly-enriched uranium to make at least five high-yield nuclear warheads—as long ago as 1996. If any such reports are true, nuclear proliferation is no longer a threat, but a fact.

CONFRONTING THE DANGER

The proliferation window in the NIS is likely to remain open for some time, despite the highly-touted "lab-to-lab" programs and associated significant influence of U.S. money and security technology. Recent (February 1999) CIA testimony before the Senate Armed Services Committee referred to "reports of strikes, lax discipline, and poor morale and criminal activity at nuclear facilities" across Russia.[6] Such reports point to a crisis of authority within the nuclear custodial system, a situation that modern locks and inventory controls and workfare for scientists will do little to alleviate.

Current non-proliferation efforts can doubtless be improved at the margins, for instance, by focusing more on the immediate economic needs of nuclear workers. Nevertheless, the intrinsic limitations of supply-control regimes might justify a shift to a more demand-oriented approach to countering illegal nuclear proliferation. Such an approach has theoretical merit, but also faces problems in implementation. To intervene in the nuclear black market would require a sophisticated understanding, more than U.S. authorities now possess, of weapons development programs, of potential end users, and of users' procurement requirements and strategies. Successes in uncovering nuclear deals-in-the-making or in shutting down procurement chains are likely to be modest or ephemeral because the dynamics and modalities of nuclear smuggling systems are constantly shifting.

A demand-side strategy, though, should above all seek to modify the intentions of nuclear-prone actors and to create disincentives to weaponization. If the spread of nuclear materials and intelligence is a fact—and it is irresponsible to assume otherwise—one urgent imperative is to discourage or prevent recipient states or groups from building a nuclear arsenal. None of the economic, diplomatic or military options that might come into play will be easy to implement or free of risk, but when confronting proliferation there are no risk-free alternatives. Nor can the available options be implemented as though in a political vacuum: intractable conflicts in regions such as the Middle East, South Asia, and the Korean Peninsula continue to tear at the fabric of international nonproliferation regimes; also, NATO bombing campaigns in the Balkans and Iraq could likely heighten small states' craving for a nuclear deterrent of their own. Such realities suggest that, contrary to expectations, a more rather than a less nuclear world could be in the offing and that nuclear threats to Western security have increased even as the stockpiles of the United States and Russia are reduced.

Appendix

Protocol
of
Negotiations Between the Minister of the Russian Federation
for Atomic Energy, Professor V. N. Mikhailov,
and the Vice President of the Islamic Republic and President
of the Organization for Atomic Energy of Iran, Dr. R. Amrollahi

From January 5 to 8, 1995, the Minister of the Russian Federation for Atomic Energy, Professor V. N. Mikhaylov, visited Iran at the invitation of the Vice President of the Islamic Republic of Iran and President of the Organization for Atomic Energy of Iran, Dr. R. Amrollahi

During the visit, negotiations took place regarding cooperation in the utilization of atomic energy for peaceful purposes.

Both sides have expressed satisfaction with the results of the visit and have reached the following understandings:

1. The present protocol establishes a contract for completing the construction of Block No. 1 of the atomic electric power station "Bushehr." The protocol was signed by the All Russian production enterprise, "Zarubezhatomenergostroy," and by the Organization for Atomic Energy of Iran, dated January 8, 1995, and reaffirms that both sides will implement the contract.

2. Both sides have exchanged letters which deal with the principal issues of cooperation in completing the construction of Block No. 1 of the atomic power station "Bushehr."

3. It was agreed to use Iranian personnel at the facilities to the maximum extent possible, subject to cooperation, especially at operations dealing with the completion of the atomic power station "Bushehr."

4. Subsequent deliveries of fuel for Block No. 1 of the atomic electric power station "Bushehr" will be carried out under conditions and for purposes that are in accord with world standards.

5. The Russian side will instruct appropriate Russian organizations to submit within one month a commercial proposal for the training of Iranian personnel so that following the initial acceptance of Block No. 1 of the atomic electric power station "Bushehr," it could be operated independently by Iranian personnel.

6. Both sides will instruct their competent organizations to prepare and to sign as follows:

Within three months to sign a contract for the delivery from Russia of a light-water reactor for research purposes with an output of 30-50 MWatt

Within the first quarter of 1995 to sign a contract for the delivery from Russia of 2,000 (two thousand) tons of natural uranium

During the first quarter of 1995 to sign a contract for the training of scientific teams, ten to twenty persons per year (candidates and doctors), for the Organization for Atomic Energy of Iran at Russian institutes of learning (MIFM)

Within six months to sign a contract to equip a uranium mine in Iran and later to conduct negotiations for the signing of a contract for the construction of a centrifuge plant for uranium enrichment on conditions analogous to those concluded by Russian organizations with firms in third countries.

Both sides have agreed as follows:

To cooperate in the construction in Iran of low-power reactors for research purposes (below 1 MWatt). The Russian side will within a six-month period present the Iranian side with a technical and commercial proposal on this issue.

Both sides will examine the question of cooperation in the construction in Iran of desalination plants.

Both sides have agreed to hold at least once a year a high-level meeting between Minatom of Russia and the Organization for Atomic Energy of Iran for the purpose of organizing operational control over the progress of cooperation, especially when dealing with operations concerning the construction of Block No. 1 of the atomic power station "Bushehr."

This protocol was signed on January 8, 1995, in two copies, each in the Russian and Persian language.

Minister of the Russian FederationPresident of the Organization
for Atomic Energyfor Atomic Energy

/s/ V. N. Mikhailov/s/ R. Amrollahi

Notes

INTRODUCTION

1. U.S. Department of Energy, *MPC&A Program Strategic Plan* (Washington, D.C.: January 1998), pp. 8-9.

CHAPTER 1

1. Law Faculty, St. Petersburg State University, *Ugolovny Kodeks Rossiiskoi Federatsii* (St. Petersburg: "Severozapad" 1994), pp. 164-165. Article 223, sections 2 through 5, deals with nuclear-related offenses. Interestingly, the code fails to specify sale of nuclear materials as a crime, apparently not envisioning that possibility.
2. Personal communication from Kirill Belyaninov, March 27, 1997.
3. IAEA, "INSIDE. Technical Cooperation" (December 1996), p. 1.
4. Slawomir Sterlinski and Tadeusz Hadys, "Polish Prevention System Against Nuclear Trafficking of Radioactive Substances and Nuclear Materials" (Central Laboratory for Radiological Protection and Border Guards Headquarters, Warsaw, 1997), p. 5.
5. See discussion in Phil Williams and Paul N. Woessner, "The Real Threat of Nuclear Smuggling," *Scientific American* 274, no. 1 (January 1996), pp. 40-41.
6. James L. Ford and C. Richard Schuller, *Nuclear Smuggling Pathways: A Holistic Perspective* (Washington, D.C.: National Defense University, December 1996), p. 7.
7. Leonard S. Spector et al., *Tracking Nuclear Proliferation: A Guide in Maps and Charts,* 1995 (Washington, D.C.: Carnegie Endowment for International Peace, 1995), p. 3.
8. William Potter, "The Post-Soviet Nuclear Proliferation Challenge." Testimony prepared for the hearing on Proliferation: Russian Case Studies, U.S. Senate Governmental Affairs Subcommittee on International Security Proliferation and Federal Service, Washington, D.C., June 5, 1997, p. 4.
9. Spector et al., *Tracking Nuclear Proliferation,* p. 3.

10. William Potter, "The Post-Soviet Nuclear Proliferation Challenge." Paper prepared for the Aspen Strategy Group meeting, Aspen, CO, August 10-15, 1996, p. 10.

11. Valeriy Davydov, "Nuclear Material in the Wrong Hands Pushes Russia to Cooperate With the West," *The Christian Science Monitor,* April 26, 1996, p. 19.

12. U.S. Department of Energy, *Partnership for Nuclear Materials Security* (Washington, D.C., January 1997), p. 1.

13. Personal communication from Professor Gary Bertsch of the University of Georgia (Athens, Georgia), September 25, 1997. The U.S. Department of Commerce plays a major role in helping the new states draft export-control legislation. Personal communication from Emily Ewell of the Monterey Institute, March 5, 1998.

14. Nikolai Kravchenko, "Interviu Mesyatsa: Lish 25 Protsentov Punktov Propuska na Odorudarany Spetsialnymi Priborami dlya Presecheniya Yadernoi Kontrabandy," *Yaderny Kontrol',* nos. 20-21 (August-September 1996), p. 8.

15. The rationale for emphasizing control of fissile materials at their sources, as one writer explains, is that "once [nuclear] materials are stolen, the difficulty of finding and recovering them before they can be used in weapons rises exponentially." See John R. Holdren, "Reducing the Threat of Nuclear Theft in the Former Soviet Union," *Arms Control Today,* no. 3 (March 1996), p. 16. Telephone interview with Larry Ellis of U.S. Customs in Washington, D.C., on November 24, 1997.

16. U.S. Department of Energy, *MPC&A Program Strategic Plan* (Washington, D.C., January 1998), p. 7.

17. "Programmme for Preventing and Combating Trafficking in Nuclear Material" (Washington, D.C.: U.S. State Department briefing materials. June 17, 1996), p. 1.

18. "Statement by Boris Yeltsin" at the Moscow Nuclear Safety and Security Summit (Moscow: International Life, 1996), p. 38.

19. DOE. *MPC&A Program Strategic Plan,* p. 2. According to experts cited by DOE, the former Soviet Union produced more than 1200 tons of HEU and 150 tons of plutonium. Approximately 650 tons of this material are contained in "metals, oxides, solutions, and scrap" and 700 tons in nuclear weapons.

20. Department of Energy Nuclear Material Security Task Forces, "United States-Former Soviet Union Program of Cooperation on Nuclear Material Protection, Accounting and Control" (Washington, D.C., December 1996).

21. Tom Masland et al., "For Sale," *Newsweek,* August 29, 1994, p. 30.

CHAPTER 2

1. Some of the material in this chapter appeared in Rensselaer W. Lee, III, "Smuggling Update," *The Bulletin of the Atomic Scientists,* no. 3, May-June 1997, pp. 52-56.

2. Oral testimony of William Potter before the U.S. Senate Committee on Governmental Affairs, *Global Proliferation of Weapons of Mass Destruction: Hearings before the Permanent Subcommittee on Investigations, Part II,* 104th Cong., 2nd sess., March 13, 20, and 22, 1996, p.25.

The terms "weapons-usable" and "weapons-grade" require definition here. Weapons-grade usually connotes uranium enriched to 90 to 95 percent uranium-235 (U-235) and plutonium with 92 to 95 percent plutonium-239 (PU-239). The accepted minimum concentration of U-235 that can be used in weapons is 20 percent. For plutonium, the minimum standard is not clearly defined in the literature, but one source suggests that reactor-grade plutonium with 56 percent PU-239 could be used to make a bomb. See Richard Kokoski, *Technology and the Proliferation of Nuclear Weapons* (New York: Oxford University Press, 1996), pp. 66-69. Note that the less pure the material, the more of it is required to produce a fission chain reaction. The critical mass of uranium containing 20 percent U-235 is estimated at 250 kilograms (or 550 pounds). At 100 percent U-235, the critical mass is 15 kilograms. See Mason Willrich and Theodore B. Taylor, *Nuclear Theft: Risks and Safeguards* (Cambridge, MA: Ballinger, 1974), p. 58.

3. Interviews at Interpol General Secretariat, Lyon, October 14, 1996.

4. Personal communication from Valeriy Golodyuk of Elektrostal', December 19, 1996.

5. Personal communication from DOE Office of Non-Proliferation and National Security, June 8, 1997.

6. Interview with Peter Kroemer of the BKA in Wiesbaden, October 9, 1996.

7. Mark Hibbs, "Plutonium, Politics, and Panic." *The Bulletin of the Atomic Scientists* 50, no. 6 (November-December 1994), pp. 25-26.

8. John Deutch, "The Threat of Nuclear Diversion." Prepared statement in *Global Proliferation,* p. 310.

9. Interview with Yuriy Melnikov of Interpol, Moscow: Interpol. July 28, 1994. MVD Press-Relis, "Khishcheniye Radiaktivnykh Materialov: Realnost i Domyski," October 10, 1995, p. 1.

10. Personal communication from Kirill Belyaninov of *Ogonyek,* March 27, 1996.

11. Interview at Interpol General Secretariat, Lyon, October 14-15, 1996. "A Czech Suspected of Drug Dealing Allegedly Smuggled Uranium Too." *Rude Pravo* (Prague), February 5, 1995, p. 1. Phil Williams and Paul Woessner, *Nuclear Material Trafficking: An Interim Assessment,* Ridgway Viewpoints no. 95-3 (1995), p. 9.

12. Personal communication from Valeriy Golodyuk.

13. Interviews at Interpol General Secretariat in Lyon, October 14-15, 1996.

14. IAEA. "Second Quarter 1997—Summary Listing of Illicit Trafficking Incidents," May 12, 1997, pp. 1-6.

15. Dieter Schroeder, "To Our Knowledge a Centrally Controlled Nuclear Mafia Does Not Exist," *Suddeutsche Zeitung,* August 20-21, 1994, p. 8.

16. Emily Ewell. "Trip Report—Uzbekistan, Kazakhstan, Ukraine," Monterey Institute of International Studies, Center for Non-Proliferation Studies, (May 1996), p. 1.

17. *Nuclear Material Trafficking,* Appendix 2, p. 13.

18. Interview with Moscow investigative journalist in Moscow, March 17, 1996.

19. See, for example, Tim McGirk, "A Year of Looting Dangerously," *Sunday Independent* (London), March 24, 1996, pp. 4-8. McGirk colorfully describes nuclear materials markets in Southwest Asia. He quotes a Western diplomat familiar with smuggling in Afghanistan: "First, an Afghan offers you some beautiful old Buddha head, then a Stinger missile for $80,000 and then, if they see you're still in the game, they'll offer enriched uranium or some other nuclear goodies." McGirk reports that much of the nuclear material smuggled through Afghanistan ends up in the Pakistan frontier town of Peshawar. He interviewed an American art expert from Islamabad who went to Peshawar in search of antiquities. The American was shown inside a large house where—to his surprise—floorboards were lifted up to reveal dozens of metal containers. "They had Russian writing and looked like medicine jars. Each jar contained enriched uranium. Hidden in this house, these guys had 1,200 kilograms of enriched uranium from the former Soviet Union, which they were trying to sell," the dealer told McGirk. Evidently, the uranium originated in the Ukraine and, according to the article, "had been moved, jar by jar, along the old smuggling routes through Afghanistan and into northern Afghanistan before it crossed the Khyber Pass into Peshawar."

20. Interview with Peter Kroemer of the BKA, Wiesbaden, Germany, October 11, 1996.

21. Barry Kellman and David S. Gualtieri, "Barricading the Nuclear Window— A Legal Regime to Curtail Nuclear Smuggling," *University of Illinois Law Review,* 1996, no. 3, (1996), p. 677.

22. Graham Allison et al., *Avoiding Nuclear Anarchy* (Cambridge, MA: MIT Press, 1996), p. 10.

23. Guy B. Roberts, *Five Minutes Past Midnight: The Clear and Present Dangers of Nuclear Weapons Grade Fissile Materials,* INSS occasional paper 8 (Colorado Springs: Institute for National Security Studies, February 1996), p. 2.

24. David Kay, "Remarks." In Center for Strategic and International Studies (CSIS), *Global Organized Crime* (Washington, D.C.: CSIS, 1994), p. 89.

CHAPTER 3

1. Graham Allison et al., *Avoiding Nuclear Anarchy* (Cambridge, MA: MIT Press, 1996), p. 2.

2. N. D. Bondarev, "Analiz Kontseptsii RNTs 'Kurchatovskiy Institut.'" In *Proceedings: International Conference on Non-Proliferation and Safeguards in Russia* (Moscow: Kurchatov Institute, May 14-17, 1996), p. 146.

3. John P. Holdren, "Reducing the Threat of Nuclear Theft in the Former Soviet Union," *Arms Control Today,* no. 3 (March 1996), p. 20.

4. Mark Hibbs, "Physical Protection Reportedly Eroding at MINATOM's 10 Closed Cities in Russia," *Nuclear Fuel,* January 2, 1995, p. 13.

5. Cited in Vladimir Orlov, "Nuclear Blackmail, Threats from Enemies Within More Disturbing than Conspiracies from Without," *Nezavisimoye Voennoye Obozreniye,* no. 32, August 29, 1997, pp. 1, 7.

6. Nikolai Bondarev, "Background Report: Incidents in Russia of the Attempts for Illegal Transport of Special Nuclear Material and Their Classification for RRC KI" (Moscow: The Kurchatov Institute, November 1994), p. 8.

7. Vladimir Orlov, "Accounting, Control and Physical Protection of Fissile Materials and Nuclear Weapons in the Russian Federation: Current Situation and Main Concerns." Paper presented at the International Seminar on MPC&A in Russia and the NIS, Bonn, April 7-8, 1997, p. 9; and Orlov, "Nuclear Blackmail: Threats from Enemies Within More Disturbing than Conspiracies from Without," *Nezavisimoye Voyennoye Obozreniye,* no. 32. August 29-September 4, 1997, pp. 1, 7.

8. Alla Malakhova, "Nuclear Arsenals Kept in Ordinary Hangars," *Obshchaya Gazeta,* no. 30, July 31-August 6, 1997, p. 2.

9. Oleg Bukharin and William Potter, "Potatoes Were Guarded Better," *Bulletin of the Atomic Scientists* 51, no. 3 (May-June 1995), pp. 48-49.

10. Mikhail Kulik, "Nekotoriye Problemy Khraneniya Yadernykh Materialov na Severnom Flote," *Yaderny Kontrol',* no. 2 (February 1995), p. 12.

11. Allion et al., *Avoiding Nuclear Anarchy,* pp. 42-43; Jessica Stern; "U.S. Assistance Programs for Improving MPC&A in the Former Soviet Union," *The Non-Proliferation Review* 3, no. 1, (Winter 1996), p. 25; and interview, Nikolai Kukharin at the Kurchatov Institute in Moscow, October 25, 1996.

12. Emily Ewell, "Trip Report—Uzbekistan, Kazakhstan, Ukraine," Monterey Center for Non-Proliferation Studies (May 1996), p. 8.

13. Kirill Belyaninov, "Nuclear Nonsense, Black-Market Bombs, and Fissile Flim-Flams," *Bulletin of the Atomic Scientists* 50, no. 2 (March-April 1994), p. 48.

14. Interview with Mark Hibbs, *PBS Front Line,* "Loose Nukes," November 20, 1996.

15. Interview with Igor Matveenko at the Institute of Physics and Power Engineering in Obninsk, December 21, 1996; interview with Nikolai Kukharin at the Kurchatov Institute in Moscow, October 25, 1996; Michael Gordon, "Russia Struggles on Long Road to Prevent Atomic Theft," *New York Times,* April 20, 1996, pp. 1, 4.

16. Tom Masland et al., "For Sale," *Newsweek,* August 29, 1994, p. 32.

17. National Research Council, *Proliferation Concerns* (Washington, D.C.: National Academy Press, 1997), p. 13.
18. Interview at the Institute of Physics and Power Engineering in Obninsk, December 21, 1996. Most of the disks contain weapons-grade uranium and plutonium, MOX fuel, neptunium, and other exotic metals.
19. Interview at Elektrostal', September 5, 1994.
20. Interview with Yuriy Smirnov, *PBS Front Line,* "Loose Nukes," November 20, 1996.
21. U.S. General Accounting Office, *Nuclear Proliferation: Status of U.S. Efforts to Improve Nuclear Materials Control in Newly Independent States* (Washington, D.C., March 1996), p. 13.
22. *Proliferation Concerns,* p. 8.
23. U.S. MPC&A initiatives in the NIS for a time ran on two organizationally distinct tracks: respectively, the government-to-government programs run by the Defense Department and the laboratory-to-laboratory program sponsored by the Department of Energy. A presidential directive assigned DOE financial responsibility for all MPC&A in September 1995. See U.S. Department of Energy, *United States/Former Soviet Union, Progress of Cooperation in Nuclear Materials Protection, Control and Accounting* (Washington, D.C., December 1996), pp. 6G 1-2.
24. Interview with Dr. Thomas Cochran, *PBS Front Line,* "Loose Nukes," November 20, 1996.
25. William Potter, "Nuclear Leakage from the Post-Soviet States." Written testimony prepared for the U.S. Senate Committee on Governmental Affairs, *Global Proliferation of Weapons of Mass Destruction: Hearings before the Permanent Subcommittee on Investigations, Part II,* 104th Cong., 2nd sess., March 13, 20, and 22 (Washington, D.C.: U.S. Government Printing Office, 1996), p. 225.
26. U.S. Agency for International Development, "Monitoring Country Progress in Central and Eastern Europe and the Newly Independent States" (Washington, D.C.: September 1997), p. 30.
27. *Proliferation Concerns,* p. 34.
28. Talk by Sergei Rogov, director of USA-Canada Institute in Moscow, at the Foreign Policy Research Institute, Philadelphia, January 22, 1997.
29. Igor Zaslonov, "Nuclear Union Demands Wages," *Moscow Tribune,* December 10, 1996, p. 1.
30. Interview with Nikolai Kukharin of the Kurchatov Institute, October 25, 1996.
31. Orlov, "Nuclear Blackmail."
32. Olga Sitkova, "How About a Bomb," *Die Woche* (Hamburg), March 23, 1994, p. 14.
33. Michael Specter, "Occupation of a Nuclear Power Plant Signals Russian Labor's Anger," *New York Times,* December 7, 1996, pp. 1, 6.

34. Interview with Nikolai Bondarev, *PBS Front Line,* "Loose Nukes," November 20, 1996.
35. Interview with Yevgeniy Korolev in Yekaterinburg, September 10, 1994.
36. Interview with Nikolai Kukharin.
37. Bondarev, "Background Report," p. 13.
38. Interview with Aleksandr Emelyanenkov, *PBS Front Line,* "Loose Nukes," November 20, 1996.
39. William Potter, "Russia's Nuclear Entrepreneurs," *New York Times,* November 7, 1991; Vladimir Orlov, "Russian Nuclear Business: A Threat or a Bluff," *Moskovskiye Novost,* no. 19, May 10, 1992, p. 14.
40. "Protocol of Negotiations Between the Minister of the Russian Federation for Atomic Energy, Professor V. N. Mikhailov, and the Vice President of the Islamic Republic and President of the Organization for Atomic Energy of Iran, Dr. R. Amrollakhi" (Teheran), January 8, 1995, pp. 1-3 (see also Appendix); Stuart Goldman et al., "Russian Nuclear Reactor and Conventional Arms Transfers to Iran" (Washington, D.C.: Congressional Research Service [CRS] Report for Congress, May 23, 1995), pp. 5, 11.
41. "Atomic Energy Minister Holds News Conference About His Ministry's Activities," BBC Summary of World Broadcasts, June 25, 1997; Andrew Koch and Jeanette Wolf, "Iran's Nuclear Procurement Program: How Close to the Bomb?" *Non-Proliferation Review* 5, no. 1, (Fall 1997), pp. 124, 132. The authors mention a Swiss firm's 1993 sale of electrical discharge machinery, used to produce gas centrifuge components and to fabricate nuclear fuel, and a 1996 seizure by British Customs of 55 kilograms of maraging steel (the preferred material for making gas centrifuge rotors) bound for Iran from the United States.
42. Michael Gordon, "Russian Selling Atomic Plants to India; U.S. Protests Deal," *New York Times,* February 6, 1997, p. A3; Leonard Spector et al., *Tracking Nuclear Proliferation: A Guide in Maps and Charts, 1995* (Washington, D.C.: Carnegie Endowment for International Peace, 1995), p. 89; Shirley A. Kan, "China's Compliance with International Arms Control Agreements" (Washington, D.C.: CRS Report to Congress, September 16, 1997), pp. 6-7.
43. Nuclear reactors produce spent fuel that contains plutonium. The spent fuel from Bushehr reportedly could be reprocessed to produce as much as 180 kilograms of plutonium each year; unlike India, however, Iran does not have a large-scale reprocessing facility and is years away from building one. For example, see Koch and Wolf, "Iran's Nuclear Procurement Program," p. 128.
44. Kenneth Katzman, "Iran: Arms and Technology Acquisitions" (Washington, D.C.: CRS Report to Congress, October 31, 1997), pp. 3, 5. Katzman, however, later reports that China may already have supplied Iran with blueprints for the plan.
45. Koch and Wolf, "Iran's Nuclear Procurement Program," p. 132.

46. Interview with Yuriy Smirnov, *PBS Front Line*, "Loose Nukes," November 20, 1997.

47. Masland et al., "For Sale," *Newsweek*, p. 3.

48. Interview with Mark Hibbs, *PBS Front Line*, "Loose Nukes," November 20, 1996.

49. Josef Jaffe, "Bombs Bazaar Germany," *Suddeutsche Zeitung* (Munich), August 24, 1994, p. 4.

50. Mark Hibbs, "Agencies' Entrapment Justifies Mild Sentences in Munich Pu Case," *Nucleonics Week*, July 2, 1995, pp. 2-3.

51. Viktor Mikhailov, "Interviu Mesyatsa: Uchet i Kontrol Yadernykh Materialov: Vzglyad Glavy Minatoma," *Yaderny Kontrol'*, no. 2 (February 1995), pp. 9-10.

52. Interviews with Moscow investigative journalists, March 17-18, 1997.

CHAPTER 4

1. Center for Strategic and International Studies (CSIS), *Russian Organized Crime*, Task Force Report (Washington, D.C., 1997), p. 2.

2. Sam Nunn, "Introductory Remarks." In U.S. Senate Governmental Affairs Committee. *Organized Crime in the Former Soviet Union: Hearing before the Permanent Investigative Subcommittee*, Washington, D.C.: Federal Union Transcript Service, May 25, 1994, p. 3.

3. William Potter, "Nuclear Leakage from the Post-Soviet States." Written testimony prepared for the U.S. Senate Governmental Affairs Committee. *Global Proliferation of Weapons of Mass Destruction, Part II: Hearings before the Permanent Subcommittee on Investigations*, 104th Cong., 2nd sess., March 13, 20, and 22, p. 220.

4. Aleksandr Shvarev, "MVD RF Prinyalo Vyzov," *Nezavisimaya Gazeta*, September 1997, p. 1.

5. Vladimir Zimin, "International Cooperation of the Law Enforcement Bodies," Presentation at 14th European Policing Executive Conference, Stavanger, Norway, May 13, 1997, p. 1.

6. V. O. Ispravnikov and V. V. Kulikov, *Tenevaya Ekonomika u Rossii: Inoi Put' i Tret'ya Sila* (Moscow: Rossiiskiy Ekonomicheskii Zhurnal. Fond za Ekonomicheskuya Gramotnost', 1977), p. 37.

7. Ibid., p. 38; "Russia: Kulikov Discusses Measures to Fight Organized Crime," Moscow Interfax, 0818 GMT, June 13, 1997.

8. For example, British researcher Guy Dunn estimates that the Solntsevskaya gang has 3,500 to 4,000 members; however, a Russian source puts the number at only 250. See Guy Dunn, "Major Mafia Gangs in Russia," *Transnational Organized Crime* 2, nos. 2-3 (Summer-Autumn 1996), p. 68;

Maxim Glikin and Vakhtang Yakobidze, "The Red Wheel in Southern Moscow," *Obshchaya Gazeta*, no. 19, May 15-21, 1997, p. 7.

9. Dunn, "Major Mafia Gangs," p. 68.

10. CSIS, *Russian Organized Crime,* Task Force Report, p. 32.

11. Phil Williams, ed., *Russian Organized Crime: The New Threat?* (London: Frank Cass, 1997), p. 270; Yelena Dikun, "A Third of Income is Spent on Bribing Officials," *Daily Report. Central Asia,* FBIS-SOV-97-041-S, March 3, 1997, p. 21; U.S. Department of State, *International Narcotics Control Strategy Report* (Washington, D.C., March 1997), p. 579.

12. Ispravnikov and Kulikov, *Tenevaya Ekonomika,* pp. 28-43. The authors include in their estimate diverse illegal businesses such as narcotics, movement of contraband, underground distilling of alcohol, and banking and insurance fraud. Except for fraud, these businesses are categorized as forms of illegal trade. Most of the rest of the informal economy comprises unreported production and income. The authors cite evidence that as much as 50 percent of the receipts for small shops, stalls, coffeehouses, and restaurants are never put in cash registers and consequently are never counted for tax purposes. In addition, they note on page 43: "According to official statistics, 25 percent of Russian national income is paid out to the population in covert fashion."

13. Andrei Gilkin, "Interior Minister on Crime-Ridden Aluminum Industry" (Moscow: ITAR-TASS, 1926 GMT, February 21, 1997).

14. Interviews with representative of Atompromkompleks, a Yekaterinburg-based holding company, in Washington, D.C., mid-September, 1996.

15. Steve Liesman et al., "Without the Politburo Russia's Power Centers Are All Over the Map," *Wall Street Journal,* June 4, 1996, p. A6; *Russian Organized Crime,* pp. 38-39.

16. V. S. Ovchinskiiy, *Osnovy Bor'by, S Organizovannoi Prestupnostyu* (Moscow: INFRA-M, 1996), p. 186.

17. Simon Henderson, "Russia," *Financial Times Business Reports* 17, no. 15, July 18, 1997, pp. 15-19; Tom Hunter, "Russia's Mafiyas: The New Revolution," *Jane's Intelligence Review* 9, no. 6, June 1, 1997, p. 247; Alexander Golovenko, "Crime Rate Going Rampant," RUSSICA Information Inc. RusData Dialine *Russia Press Digest,* January 24, 1997.

18. Telephone interview with the U.S. Department of Commerce and the U.S.-China Business Council, June 10-11, 1997; *Russian Organized Crime,* pp. 38-39.

19. MVD, "Itogi Operativno-Sluzhebnoi Deyatel'nosti Organov Vnutrennykh Del i Sluzhebno-Boevoi Deyatel'nosti Vnutrennykh Voisk MVD Rossiiskoi Federatsii v 1996 Godu" (Moscow, 1997), p. 33; MVD, Itogi Operativno-Sluzhebnoi Deyatel'nosti Organov Vnutrennykh Del i Sluzhebno-Boevoi Deyatel'nosti Vnutrennykh Voisk MVD Rossii v 1995 Godu (Moscow, 1996), p. 27; Graham H. Turbiville, Jr., *Weapons Proliferation and Organized Crime: The Russian Military and Security Force Dimension,* INSS Occasional

Paper 10 (Colorado Springs, CO: USAF Institute for National Strategic Studies, June 1996), pp. 6-7; Sidney Zabludoff, "Colombian Narcotics Organization as Business Enterprises." U.S. State Department and Central Intelligence Agency Conference Report, *Economics of the Narcotics Industry* (Washington, D.C.: U.S. State Department, November 21-22, 1994), pp. 21-23.

20. Turbiville, *Weapons Proliferation and Organized Crime.*

21. Louise Shelley, "The Criminal-Political Nexus: Russian-Ukrainian Case Studies." Paper prepared for "Confronting the Security Challenges of the Political-Criminal Nexus," sponsored by the National Strategy Information Center, Georgetown University, Washington, D.C., October 30-31, 1997, p. 39.

22. Steve Liesman et al., "Without the Politburo Russia's Power Centers Are All over the Map," *Wall Street Journal,* June 4, 1996, p. A6; David Hoffman, "Banditag Threatens the New Russia," *Washington Post,* May 12, 1997, p. A16; MVD, "Itogi Operativno-Sluzhebnoi . . . v 1996 gody," p. 9; Williams, *Russian Organized Crime,* p.238.

23. James Meek, "Russian MP Shot by Contract Killer," *The Guardian,* April 28, 1994, p. 24; going rates for contract killings in Russia were published, perhaps unwisely, by the *Moscow News* in November 1995. According to the newspaper, an ordinary hit would cost $7,000, provided the victim did not have a bodyguard. Killing someone with a bodyguard would cost $12,000. Assassinating Boris Yeltsin would be a $180,000 job. "This sum embraces a 96 percent guarantee of success in the attempt, its technical preparation, expenditures for covering and organizing the escape of the killer from the crime scene, and even, if necessary, the elimination of the killer himself," the article claimed, citing MVD sources. Quoted in Williams, *Russian Organized Crime,* p. 232.

24. "Russia: Kulikov Discusses Measures to Fight Organized Crime." Most other bombings occurred in Krasnodar Krai and in the Caucasus republics of Dagestan and northern Ossetia.

25. "Russia: Crime, Terror Statistics Issued," Moscow Interfax, 0808 GMT, July 1, 1997.

26. Gennadiy Talalayev, "Boris Yeltsin Addresses All-Russia Conference on Problems of the Fight Against Organized Crime and Corruption: Full Text of Speech" (Moscow: ITAR-TASS, 1035 GMT, February 12, 1993), FBIS-SOV-93-028, February 12, 1993, pp. 24-25.

27. Cited in Center for Strategic and International Studies, Task Force Report (Washington, D.C.: CSIS, 1997), p. 66.

28. Stephen Handelman, *Comrade Criminal* (New Haven, CT: Yale University Press, 1995), pp. 58, 91.

29. V. B. Zhitenev, *Mafiya v Yekaterinburge* (Yekaterinburg: Yekaterinburg Institute of Social Research and Technology, 1990), p. 6.

30. Williams, *Russian Organized Crime,* p. 256.

31. Mark Deych, "Mafia Money Should Work for the State," *Moskovskiy Komsomolets,* November 10, 1996, p. 2. On Colombia's negotiations with the Medellin and Cali cartels, see Patrick Clawson and Rensselaer W. Lee III, *The Andean Cocaine Industry* (New York: St. Martin's Press, 1996), especially chapter 4. Such negotiations bought Medellin years of social peace, particularly in the period from 1989 to 1991, when severe narcoterrorist violence took place in Colombia, but the government paid a price in lost legitimacy.

32. *Russian Organized Crime,* pp. 2-3.

33. Clawson and Lee, *The Andean Cocaine Industry,* p. 87.

34. Douglas Farah, "Russian Mob, Drug Cartels Joining Forces," *Washington Post,* September 29, 1997, pp. A1, A16.

35. Vladimir Polyak, "The Russian Fathers in the Promised Land," *Moskovskiye Novosti,* no. 26, June 29-July 6, 1997, p. 25.

36. Pierre Lorraine, "Mafias Russes: Ebauche d'une Typologie," *Politique Etrangere* 61, no. 4 (Winter 1996-1997), p. 816.

37. Cited in *Russian Organized Crime,* p. 51.

38. "Intertwined with Criminals," *Der Spiegel,* October 6, 1997, pp. 34-35. A BND source interviewed by the author claims that the report was leaked by high German government officials, not by the BND itself. No doubt the objective was to derail the talks in Bonn; see also the response of SVR spokesman General Yuriy Kobaladze to the *Der Spiegel* article, "Mafiya i Razvedka: Antipody ili Siyamskiye Bliznetsy," *Izvestiya,* October 16, 1997, p. 3. Kobaladze argued that, absent clear proof of such a symbiosis, *Der Spiegel* could claim little right to publish the report at all.

39. Guy Dunn, "Major Mafia Gangs in Russia," *Transnational Organized Crime* 2, nos. 2-3 (Summer-Autumn 1996), pp. 63-68.

40. Ibid., pp. 64-69; Maksim Glikin and Vakhtang Yakobidze, "The Red Wheel in Southern Moscow," *Obshchaya Gazeta,* no. 19, May 15-21, 1997, p. 7; Victor Sokirko and Igor Moiseyev, "Chechen Assault Force Has Been Seizing Pieces of Russia Systematically and Without a Fight," *Komsomolskaya Pravda,* June 7, 1997, p. 2.

41. Remarks by James Woolsey in Center for Strategic and International Studies, *Global Organized Crime: The New Empire of Evil* (Washington, D.C., 1994), p. 14C.

42. "They Are Stealing," *Der Spiegel,* August 1, 1994, p. 61.

43. Kirill Belyaninov, "Istoriya, Shchastlivovo Priobreteniya Atomnoi Bomby," *Literaturnaya Gazeta,* August 24, 1994, p. 13.

44. One Far Eastern company known to the author issued a standing offer in late 1996 to purchase more than 80 different nuclear and radioactive commodities, among them plutonium, uranium, californium, iridium, and cesium and cobalt isotopes. The seller was asked to specify quality, weight, price terms, chemical analysis, purity, packing, and preferred means of payment.

45. François Gere, "In Search of a Missing Link: Nuclear Terrorism and Nuclear Smuggling." Unpublished manuscript (Como, Italy: Centro A. Volta, April 12-13, 1994).

46. Markets for radioactive isotopes are extremely thin. For example, total annual purchases in the West of cesium-137, one of the most commonly stolen radioactive materials, likely do not amount to more than 15 kilograms, obviously a minuscule amount. Telephone interview with representatives of Amersham Inc. of Arlington Heights, Illinois, mid-October 1994.

47. Bortosz Weglarazyk, "Atomic Smuggling cont'd: Nuclear Materials from Russia," *World Press Review* 43, no. 1 (January 1996), p. 28. Figure is attributed to British nuclear expert John Large.

48. Turbiville, *Weapons Proliferation and Organized Crime,* pp. 34-43.

49. Sergei Sokolov and Sergei Plushnikov, "How Arms Are Traded in Russia," *Novaya Gazeta,* no. 28, July 14, 1997, pp. 1-3.

50. See also remarks by Jonathan Tucker in U.S. Army War College Center for Strategic Leadership, *Report of the Executive Seminar on Special Material Smuggling* (Carlisle Barracks, PA: U.S. Army War College, September 1996), p. 31.

51. Turbiville, *Weapons Proliferation and Organized Crime,* pp. 12-13, 34, 42.

52. Ibid.; Aleksandr Kondrashov and Yuriy Smolin, "Pochemu voina v Chechnye nye konchaetsya?" *Argumenty i Fakty,* no. 15 (April 1996), p. 6.

53. Associated Press International News (Tokyo), "Witness: Russian Official Helped Japanese Cult Produce Nerve Gas," April 23, 1997; Associated Press Worldstream (Moscow), "Officials Release Japanese Cult Member," June 24, 1997; Leonid Krutakov and Ivan Kadulin, "Seko Asahara's Russian Trail," *Passport* (Moscow), no. 5, 1997, pp. 28-29.

54. D. W. Brackett, *Holy Terror: Armageddon in Tokyo* (New York: Weatherhill, 1996), p. 92. In March 1995 Aum released sarin in the Tokyo subway during rush hour, killing 12 people and injuring 5,000.

55. Tucker in U.S. Army War College, *Special Material Smuggling,* pp. 27-28; staff statement, "Global Proliferation of Weapons of Mass Destruction: A Case Study of the Aum Shinrikyo." In U.S. Senate Governmental Affairs Committee, *Global Proliferation of Weapons of Mass Destruction, Part II: Hearings before the Permament Subcommittee on Investigations,* October 31-November 1, 1995, p. 71.

56. Associated Press, "Russia for Sale, Plenty of Takers," *Chicago Tribune,* April 15, 1993, p. 18; Maksim Glikin, "Those Taking a Lot Are Giving Little—Tabulation of the Rankings, Bribes and Preventative Punishment," *Obshchaya Gazeta,* no. 46, 1996. *Foreign Broadcast Information Service.* J8V-97-022-S. *Daily Report Central Eurasia* (internet) February 3, 1997.

57. Interview with Moscow investigative journalists in Moscow, March 17-18, 1996.

58. Mikhail Kulik, "Guba Andreeva: Another Nuclear Theft Has Been Detected," *Yaderny Kontrol Digest,* no. 1 (Spring 1996), p. 20.

59. Ivan Ivanov, "International Narcotics Trafficking and the Former USSR" (Moscow: Feliks Research Group, February 1995), pp. 40, 49-50, 76.

60. "Nashu Pesnyu Nye Zadushish Nye Ubyesh," *Moskovskiy Komsomolets*, August 31, 1994, p. 1.

61. J. Mufelshulte and J. Marks, "Help From Uncle Sam," *Focus*, February 3, 1997, pp. 28-29.

62. Viktor Mikhailov, "Interviu Mesyatsa v Oblasti Ucheta, Kontrolya i Fizzashchity My Prikhodili Toi Skheme Kotoraya Effektivno Rabotala V Soyuze," *Yaderny Kontrol'*, no. 28 (April 1997), p. 10.

63. S. C. Gwynne and Larry Gurwin, "The Russia Connection," *Time*, July 8, 1995, p. 33; Tom Sawicki, "Sinned Against or Sinning," *The Jerusalem Report* (internet version), December 28, 1995.

64. Nunn, "Introductory Remarks."

CHAPTER 5

1. Interview at Interpol General Secretariat in Lyon, October 14-15, 1996; Robert Geher and Hannes Reichmann, "Rita and the Crossbows," *Wirtschaftswoche* (Vienna), April 16, 1992, pp. 40-43; "Radioactive Material Harmless," *Wiener Zeitung* (Vienna), July 11, 1992, p.5; Barrie Penrose and Oonagh Blackman, "Iraq A-bombs Plot Foiled," *London Sunday Express*, November 1, 1992, pp. 1, 2; Kirill Belyaninov, "Nuclear Nonsense, Black-Market Bombs and Fissile Flim-Flam," *Bulletin of Atomic Scientists* (March-April 1994), p.50.

2. Thomas B. Cochran, "Safeguarding Nuclear Weapons-Usable Materials in Russia." Paper presented at the International Forum "Illegal Traffic, Risks, Safeguards and Countermeasures," Como, Italy, June 12-13, 1997, p. 1; Leonard Spector et al., *Tracking Nuclear Proliferation* (Washington, D.C.: Carnegie Endowment for International Peace, 1995), p. M1.

3. Interview at Interpol General Secretariat in Lyon, October 14-15, 1996.

4. Phil Williams and Paul N. Woessner, *Nuclear Material Trafficking: An Interim Assessment*, Ridgway Viewpoints, no. 95-3 (Pittsburgh: Ridgway Center for International Security Studies, 1995), p. 9.

5. Interview with Peter Kroemer of the BKA in Wiesbaden, October 11, 1996; Bundeskriminalblatt (BKA), "Special Edition on Nuclear Criminality," vol. 45, no. 51, March 13, 1995; Reprinted in U.S. Senate Governmental Affairs Committee, *Global Proliferation of Weapons of Mass Destruction, Part II: Hearings before the Permament Subcommittee on Investigations*, 104th Cong., 2nd sess., March 13, 20, and 22, p. 765.

6. Interview with Gustav Illich, *PBS Frontline*, "Loose Nukes," November 20, 1996.

7. Ibid.

8. Paolo Biondani, "Uranium Hunting," *Literaturnaya Gazeta,* March 11, 1992, p. 15.

9. See, for example, "TV Reporter Offered East European Plutonium," *Hamburg DPA* (in German), 1347 GMT, December 27, 1992; J. Jachowicz and Katorzyna Kesicka, "Uranium Notebooks," *Gazeta Wyborcza* (Warsaw), January 21, 1993, p. 1.

10. Claire Sterling, *Thieves' World* (New York: Simon and Schuster, 1994), pp. 217-218.

11. Interviews in Lyon on October 14-15, 1996.

12. Eric Nadler, PBS *Front Line* reporter, account of interview with Romano Dulce in Como, Italy, April, 1996, personal communication, undated, p. 2.

13. Ibid.; "Italian Judge Wants Laws Against Smuggling of Nuclear Materials," *Reuter Newsweek,* January 10, 1992; "Following the Arrest of Romano Dolce, Swiss Authorities Deceived: Canton of Zurich Wants to Take Action," Bern ASTA/SDAA Database (in French), 1443 GMT, May 23, 1994.

14. Leonid L. Fituni, *CIS Organized Crime and Its International Activities* (Wilbad Kreuth, Germany: Russian Academy of Sciences. Center for Strategic and Global Studies, 1993), pp. 10-11; R. James Woolsey, "Global Organized Crime: Threats to U.S. and International Security," in Center for Strategic and International Studies, *Global Organized Crime: The New Empire of Evil* (Washington, D.C., 1994), p. 136.

15. House Republican Research Committee, Task Force on Terrorism and Unconventional Warfare, *The New Nuclear Smuggling System* (Washington, D.C., June 7, 1993), pp. 1-9.

16. Maria Novella de Luca, "How I Captured Uranium Pirates." *La Repubblica* (Rome), internet version, March 31, 1998; Alfio Sciacca, "U.S.-Manufactured Material Came from Africa." *Corriere della Sera* (Milan), internet version, March 21, 1998.

17. Interview with Major Francesco Bruzzese at the Carabinieri headquarters in Rome, March 28, 1997; Environmental Crime Prevention Program, *Criminal Policies for the Environment and Related Technologies* (Naples: Istituto Poligrafico e Zecca dello Stato, March 1997), p. 142; John Hooper, "Gangsters Clean Up by Polluting Paradise," *The Observer* (London), March 22, 1998, p. 18.

18. Charles Richards and Harvey Mann, "The Hunt for Red Mercury," *Independent* (London), April 13, 1992, p. 10; *Thieves' World,* pp. 216-217; Aleksei Khazov, "Nuclear Alarm in Rome. Not only Baghdad and Tripoli, but mafia terrorists from any country in the world could now own nuclear components from the former USSR," *Moscovskiye Novosti,* February 10, 1992, p. 12.

19. Richards and Mann, "The Hunt for Red Mercury"; Biondani, "Uranium Hunting"; Sterling, *Thieves' World,* op. cit., pp. 216-217.

20. Sterling, *Thieves' World,* pp. 217-218; Richards and Mann,"The Hunt for Red Mercury."

21. "Interior Ministry Comments on Plutonium Seizure," Sofia BTA (in English), 2035 GMT, November 2, 1992; Penrose and Blackman, "Iraq A-bomb Plot Foiled," pp. 1-2.

22. E. Gors et al., "Smuggling of Nuclear Materials Dangerous Locker at Railway Station," *Bild am Sonntag* (Hamburg), October 11, 1992, p. 4; Sterling, *Thieves' World*, p. 223.

23. Interview with Kroemer; "Anyone Will Give In," *Der Spiegel*, February 7, 1994, pp. 76-79; BKA, "Nuclear Criminality," p. 763; Peter Kroemer, "The Threat of Nuclear Crime," *International Criminal Police Review*, nos. 458-459 (1996), pp. 7-10.

24. Indeed, at least four European governments treat nuclear smuggling administratively as a crime against the environment. In Italy, nuclear offenses fall under the jurisdiction of the Nucleo Operativo Ecologico, which is dually subordinate to the Defense and Environment ministries. In Germany, the BKA Environmental Crimes Division handles nuclear contraband cases inside the country.

25. Interview with Interpol General Secretariat in Lyon, October 14-15, 1996.

26. Mark Hibbs, "Plutonium, Politics, and Panic," *Bulletin of the Atomic Scientists* 50, no. 6 (November-December 1994), pp. 25-27.

27. Eric Nadler, personal communication, July 7, 1997.

28. Ibid; "Find-13. Red Alert," *Der Spiegel*, July 18, 1994, pp. 18-22; "Hungry Wolves," *Der Spiegel*, August 1, 1994, pp. 61-61; Thomas Scheuer, "Disastrous Chain Reaction," *Focus*, July 25, 1994, pp. 30-31.

29. William Potter, "Nuclear Smuggling from the Former Soviet Union," Testimony prepared for the Permanent Subcommittee on Government Affairs, August 13, 1996, p. 6.

30. See, for example, Williams and Woessner, *Nuclear Material Trafficking*, pp. 8-9; Hibbs, "Plutonium, Politics, and Panic," p. 20; "Death and Terror from the Laboratory," *Der Spiegel*, August 22, 1994, pp. 18-25.

31. Hibbs, "Plutonium, Politics, and Panic," p. 26; A. L. (not identified), "Come to Moscow. Here You Will Get Everything," *Welt am Sonntag*, August 7, 1994, p. 6; Aleksandr Kondrashov, "Atomic Bombs from Stolen Uranium," *Argumenty i Fakty*, no. 16 (April 1996), p. 7.

32. Potter, "Nuclear Smuggling," p. 7; interviews with Interpol.

33. Williams and Woessner, "Nuclear Trafficking," p. 12.

34. Ibid.; "Staff Statement," in U.S. Senate Governmental Affairs Committee, *Global Proliferation of Weapons of Mass Destruction, Part II: Hearings before the Permament Subcommittee on Investigations*, 104th Cong., 2nd sess., March 13, 20, and 22, pp. 393-398; "El Hombre Nuclear," *Semana*, (Bogotá), August 23-30, 1994, p. 30; "Panic Made in Pullach," *Der Spiegel*, April 10, 1995, pp. 36-57.

35. "Panic Made in Pullach."

36. "Report by Bavarian Criminal Investigation Office," in U.S. Senate, *Hearings on Global Proliferation*, p. 805.

37. Ibid.; U.S. Senate, "Staff Statement."

38. "Panic Made in Pullach"; U.S. Senate, "Staff Statement"; Interpol, "Project Nuclear;" p. 64; S. Carcar and F. Mercado, "Civil Guardsmen Decorated Several Times is Key Man in Smuggling Plutonium to Germany," *El País* (Madrid), May 12, 1995, p. 6.

39. FSK, "Letter to German Ministry of Justice," October 24, 1995; personal communication from Igor Matveenko of the IPPE, late March 1996. Matveenko found a copy of the letter as published in an issue of the local newspaper *Vechernyy Obninsk*. The date of the issue could not be identified.

40. Mark Hibbs, "Smuggler Names Obninsk as Source of Plutonium Flown to Germany," *Nucleonics Week,* November 9, 1995, p. 1; Interview with Gennadiy Pshakin in Moscow, October 28, 1996.

41. Hibbs, "Plutonium, Politics, and Panic," p. 27.

42. "Panic Made in Pullach."

43. Mark Hibbs, "Schmidbauer, Agencies to be Probed in Bonn Plutonium Sting Operation," *Nuclear Fuel,* April 24, 1995, p. 2.

44. Adam Tanner, "Plutonium Find Sparks German Visit," *Moscow Times* (International Weekly Edition), August 21, 1994, p. 9; Rich Atkinson, "Officials Say Contraband Not a Threat," *Washington Post,* August 29, 1994, p. 20; Hibbs, "Plutonium, Politics, and Panic"; "Nuclear Materials: Germany Urges EU Response on Illegal Nuclear Trade," Europe Information Series, *European Report,* no. 1972, September 3, 1994; "Kohl Views Election, Uranium Smuggling," Mainz ZDK Television Network, 1710 GMT, August 14, 1994.

45. Bruce Nelan, "Formula for Terror," *Time,* August 29, 1994, p. 47.

46. "Bavarian Minister Cited on Plutonium Smuggling," Berlin DDP/AND, 1402 GMT, August 31, 1994. The MINATOM line at the time was that the plutonium, obtained from a German nuclear plant, was put on a Lufthansa flight in Germany, flown to Russia, somehow kept on the plane, and then flown back to Munich. See interview with Mark Hibbs, *PBS Front Line,* "Loose Nukes," November 20, 1996; Mark Hibbs, "Europeans Term 'Worthless' MINATOM Claim That No HEU or Pu Is Missing," *Nuclear Fuel,* March 27, 1995, p. 12. Cited in Jessica Stern, "U.S. Assistance Program for Improving MPC&A in the Former Soviet Union," *Non-Proliferation Review* 3, no. 2 (Winter 1996), p. 28.

47. "Who Stands to Gain from the Uproar over Plutonium," *Rossiiskaya Gazeta,* August 18, 1994, p. 6.

48. "Counterintelligence Chief Heads Nuclear Monitoring Body," Moscow Ostankino Television Channel One Network (in Russian), 1700 GMT, August 23, 1994; Williams and Woessner, *Nuclear Trafficking,* pp. 16-23; Olga Semenova, "Russia: Leadership Said to Approve of Nuclear Smuggling Memo," Moscow, ITAR-TASS (in Russian), 0845 GMT, August 24, 1994.

49. U.S. Senate, "Staff Statement."

50. Ibid.

51. Maggie Ledford Lawson and Jan Stojaspal, "Suspects Charged in 1994 Uranium Smuggling Case," *Prague Post,* October 9-15, 1996, p. 1; U.S. Senate, "Staff Statement"; interviews with Sustav Illich and Vaclav Havlik; Detective Rathansky's investigation, "Loose Nukes."

52. Interviews with Gustav Illich and Vaclav Havlik, "Loose Nukes."

53. Maggie Ledford Lawson and Jan Stojaspal, "Uranium Trade Secrets Unveiled," *Prague Post,* December 4, 1996, p. 1; Nadler, personal communication, July 7, 1997; U.S. Senate, "Staff Statement," pp. 1-2; Detective Rathanasky's investigation, "Loose Nukes"; Lawson and Stojaspal, "Uranium Trade Secrets."

54. A confidential police report, "Loose Nukes"; U.S. Senate, "Staff Statement," p. 3.

55. Ondrej Benda and Ross Larsen, "Uranium Smuggling Case Botched, Judge Tells Cops," *Prague Post,* September 23, 1997, p. 1.

56. IAEA, "Second Quarter 1997—Summary Listing of Trafficking Incidents" (Vienna), May 12, 1997, p. 5.

57. According to U.S. Senate investigators, Czech officials claim that the material seized in Prague was part of a larger theft of 10 kilograms and that the "Russians seized the other 7 kilograms." Theft of such a quantity would confirm the horrendous security conditions at Russian nuclear enterprises. See U.S. Senate, "Staff Statement," p. 1.

58. Roland Eggelston, "Russia: Were Intelligence Officers Involved in Plutonium Smuggling?" Radio Free Europe/Radio Liberty Report, February 14, 1997, pp. 1-3.

59. Juergen Marks, "Alarm in Bogotá," *Focus,* June 30, 1997, pp. 42-44.

CHAPTER 6

1. Aleksandr Golubyev and Maksim Varybdin, "GUOP Utverzhdayet: Khishcheniya Ne Opasny Dlya Nashevo Zdorovya," *Kommersant Daily,* July 22, 1994, p.14.

2. Hard statistical evidence for these claims is lacking. Interview with Yuriy Volodin of Gosatomnadzor in Moscow, December 17, 1997.

3. Center for Strategic Leadership, U.S. Army War College, *Report of the Executive Seminar on Nuclear Smuggling* (Carlisle Barracks, PA: U.S. Army War College, September 13, 1996), p. 26.

4. Interview with Major Jan Rathausky, PBS Front Line, "Loose Nukes," November 20, 1996.

5. In both the 1988 and 1996 versions of the code, penalties are increased to up to ten years if trafficking results in loss of life.

6. Interview with Colonel Dmitriy Medvedev of the MVD Organized Crime Division in Moscow, July 19, 1994; MVD, "Press Release. Theft of Radioactive Materials. Reality and Conjecture," October 10, 1995, p. 1.

7. See, for example, Nadezhda Popova, "A VCR for 9 Kilograms of Uranium," *Rosiiskie Vesti,* August 26, 1994, p. 20; *Current Digest of the Soviet Press* 46, no. 34, 1994; Vladimir Otyashin, "The Incredible Uranium Adventure. They Carried Radioactive 'Death' Out of the Plant in Their Pants Pockets," *Trud,* June 11, 1993, p. 2; Victor Litovkin, "Podorvalis' Na Kradenom Uranye," *Izvestiya,* July 27, 1994, p. 4; MVD, "Press Release"; Interview with Yuriy Smirnov, *PBS Front Line,* "Loose Nukes."

8. Kirill Belyaninov, "Nuclear Nonsense, Black-Market Bombs and Fissile Flim-Flam," p. 48; interview with Kiril Belyaninov, Moscow, August 11, 1994; Andrei Ishchenko, "Uranium Transported in a Passenger Rail Car and Stored in a Cool Place—Details About the Exposed Affairs of the Misappropriation of Uranium-235," *Novaya Yezhednevnaya Gazeta,* June 16, 1994, p. 1; Foreign Broadcast Information Service(FBIS)-SOV-94-118, June 20, 1994, p. 41.

9. Kirill Belyaninov, "Two Bags Full of Money," *Stern* (Hamburg), August 18, 1994, pp. 20-21; FBIS-SOV-94-162, August 22, 1994, pp. 11-12; interviews with Kirill Belyaninov, mid and late August, 1994.

10. Center for Strategic and International Studies, *The Nuclear Black Market,* Task Force Report (Washington, D.C., 1996), p. 14.

11. Interviews with Kirill Belyaninov in Moscow, mid-March, 1996.

12. Interview with Moscow investigative journalists in Moscow, August 12-13, 1994.

13. Kirill Belyaninov, "Utechka," *Literaturnaya Gazeta,* January 20, 1993, p. 13; "In Russia One Can Acquire a Nuclear Bomb for Personal Possession," *Novaya Yezhednevnaya Gazeta,* July 21, 1993, p. 3; Joint Publications Research Service-TND-93-026, August 10, 1993, p. 18; Belyaninov, "Nuclear Nonsense," *Bulletin of the Atomic Scientists* 50, no. 2 (March-April 1994), pp. 44, 50.

14. Interviews with officials of the MVD Organized Crime Division in Moscow, July 13-14, 1994; interview with officials of the MVD Main Administrator for Combating Narcotics, September 15, 1994.

15. Remarks by Mikhail Yegorov, U.S. Senate Permanent Subcommittee on Investigations Committee on Governmental Affairs hearing, "Organized Crime in the Former Soviet Union," Reuters Federal News Transcript Service, May 25, 1994, p. 24.

16. "Krast' Uran ne nuzhno, on togo ne stoit," *Segodnya,* March 10, 1993, p. 7. Cited in Monterey Institute of International Studies and Carnegie Endowment for International Peace, *Nuclear Successor States of the Former Soviet Union* (Washington, D.C.), no. 1, May 1994, p. 39.

17. Monterey Institute, *Nuclear Successor States,* p. 38.

18. William Potter, "Nuclear Leakage from the Post-Soviet States." Written testimony prepared for the U.S. Senate Governmental Affairs Committee, *Global Proliferation of Weapons of Mass Destruction, Part II: Hearings before the Permament Subcommittee on Investigations,* 104th Cong., 2nd sess., March 13, 20, and 22, pp. 208, 209.

19. Interview at Elektrostal' Machine Building Plant, September 5, 1994.

20. Interview with Smirnov, "Loose Nukes."

21. On this episode, see: Potter testimony, p. 3; Viktor Litovkin, "Kapitan 3 ranga i yevo prokuratura," *Izvestiya,* January 31, 1996, p. 5 (Litovkin's article suggests that the case against Bakshanskiy was motivated in part by Russian religious bigotry.); and Mikhail Kulik, "Guba Andreeva. Another Nuclear Theft Has Been Detected," *Yaderny Kontrol Digest,* no. 1 (Spring 1996), pp. 16-21.

22. Andrew Cockburn and Leslie Cockburn, *One Point Safe* (New York: Anchor Books, 1997), p. 76. The authors provide a detailed account of the Sevnorput theft on pp. 66-77; Victor Litovkin, "Breakdown: Trial of Three Northern Fleet Officers," *Izvestiya,* May 12, 1995, p. 5.

23. William Potter and Oleg Bukharin, "Potatoes Are Guarded Better," *Bulletin of the Atomic Scientists* (May-June 1995), pp. 46-47; Potter testimony, p. 4; Kulik, "Guba Andreeva"; Viktor Litovkin, "Podorvalis' na Kradenom Uranye," *Izvestiya;* Cockburn and Cockburn, *One Point Safe,* p. 74.

24. Leonid Krutkov, "Uranium Up for Grabs," *Moscow News,* March 3, 1995, p. 9; Litovkin, "Breakdown."

25. Mikhail Kulik, "Nekotorye Problemy Khraneniya Yadernykh Materialov na Severnom Flotye," *Yaderny Kontrol',* no. 2 (February 1995), p. 13.

26. Interviews with Russian investigative journalists in Moscow, March 17-18, 1996. The information reputedly comes from Federal Security Service and military intelligence sources.

27. The 34 members in the group, as of early 1997, were obliged to ensure that nuclear exports are made only under appropriate safeguards, physical protection, and nonproliferation conditions. The NSG's export guidelines include 65 dual-use materials with nuclear applications. See Monterey Institute of International Studies Center for Nonproliferation Studies, Inventory of International Non-Proliferation Organizations and Regimes, 1996-1997 edition (Monterey, CA, May 1997), p. 21; Potter testimony, p. 11.

28. U.S. Senate, "Staff Statement"; U.S. Senate Governmental Affairs Committee, *Global Proliferation of Weapons of Mass Destruction, Part II: Hearings before the Permament Subcommittee on Investigations,* 104th Cong., 2nd sess., March 13, 20, and 22, Appendix 2, p. 420; Potter testimony, p. 208.

29. William C. Potter, "Nuclear Exports from the Former Soviet Union: What's New, What's True," *Arms Control Today* (January-February 1993), p. 3.

30. Aleksandr Kondrashev, "Atomic Bombs from Stolen Warheads," *Argumenty i Fakty,* no. 16 (April 1996), p. 7; Igor Petrov, "Chechen Drug Transit Traces Lead to Kremlin," *Zavtra,* no. 23 (June 1996), p. 5.

31. Interview with Russian State Customs Administration in Moscow, October 23, 1996.

32. Alexei Tarasov, "Krasnoyarsk Physicists Sold Neither Atomic Bomb Nor Their Country," Russica Information, Inc. RusData Dialine, *Russian Press Digest*, May 11, 1996.

33. Cockburn and Cockburn, *One Point Safe,* pp. 161, 175; in November 1994, approximately 600 kilograms of weapons-grade HEU were flown out of Ulba and were transported to the United States. The HEU had been stored under highly insecure conditions, and there were reports that Iran also was interested in purchasing the material. According to a Kazakh government source, the United States paid $25 million, or approximately $42,000 per kilogram, mostly in the form of nuclear-related equipment.

34. Tim Zimmerman and Alan Cooperman, "The Russian Connection," *U.S. News & World Report*, October 23, 1995, p. 56.

35. Ibid., pp. 58-60.

36. Ibid., pp. 60-61.

37. Interview with Yuriy Alekseyev in Moscow, December 16, 1996.

38. Zimmerman and Cooperman, "The Russian Connection," pp. 64-65.

39. Ibid., p. 64; law faculty, St. Petersburg State University, *Ugolovny Kodeks Rossiiskoi Federatsii* (St. Petersburg: Severo-Zapad, 1994), p. 67.

40. Zimmerman and Cooperman, "The Russian Connection," p. 65.

41. "Ukraine Refutes Sale of Warheads to PLO," *Uryadovyy Kuryer* (Kiev), June 15, 1993, p. 2; Joint Publications Research Service-TND-93-019, June 22, 1993, pp. 22-23; "Atomic Bombs for Sale," *Pravda*, January 6, 1992, p. 5; Joint Publications Research Service-TND-002, January 31, 1992, pp. 47-48; "Kazakhstan Denies Nuclear Agreements with Iran," Moscow TASS International Service, 1809 GMT, January 14, 1992.

42. Jim Morris, "Loose Cannon on Target," *Soldier of Fortune*, no. 3 (March 1995), p. 35. One such weapon could devastate 80 Manhattan city blocks, according to the magazine.

43. Yevgeniy Maslin, "Interviu Mesyatsa, poka chtoni odin yaderniy Boyepripas v Rossil ne propadal i ne byl pokhishchen," *Yaderny Kontrol',* no. 5, May 1995, p. 5.

44. "Nuclear Security: The Defense Ministry's Viewpoint," *Yaderny Kontrol Digest*, no. 1 (Spring 1995), pp. 2-3.

45. Andre Khalip, "Russia Denies Nuclear Warheads Theft," Reuters, North American Wire, April 21, 1997.

46. Vladimir Orlov, "Accounting, Control and Physical Protection of Fissile Materials and Nuclear Weapons in the Russian Federation: Current Situation and Main Concerns." Paper presented at the International Seminar on MPC&A in Russia and NIS, Bonn, Germany, April 7-8, 1997, p.18; interviews with Valeriy Davydov of the Russian-American Information Press Center in Moscow, May 13-14, 1997; Cockburn and Cockburn, *One Point Safe,* pp. 78-79; Scott Parrish, "Are Suitcase Nukes on the Loose? The Story

Behind the Controversy," Monterey Institute of International Studies, Center for Nonproliferation Studies, November 1997, p. 1.

47. Interview with Moscow investigative journalist in Moscow, March 18, 1996.

48. Parish, "Suitcase Nukes."

49. Yuriy Shchekochikin, "Podrobnosti Znamenity Ucheny Utverzhdaet Vozmozhno. My Vsye Sidim na Chemodanakh Yadernykh. Sensatsionnoe Pis'mo Akademika Yablokov v Novuyu Gazetu," *Novaya Gazeta,* September 22, 1997, p. 1; "Alexander Lebed's Claim that Russia Has Lost More than 100 Nuclear Bombs Receives the Inattention It Deserves," *Rossiiskaya Gazeta,* September 6, 1997.

50. BBC Summary of World Broadcasts, "Former Security Official Thinks Low-Yield Nuclear Arms May Exist," September 15, 1997; David Hoffman, "Suitcase Nuclear Weapons Safety Kept, Russian Says," *The Washington Post,* September 14, 1997, p. A23.

51. Interview with Valeriy N. Spektor of the Russian Academy of Sciences in Moscow, October 14, 1997.

52. Parish, "Suitcase Nukes," pp. 6-7.

53. On Lebed's statements, see R. Jeffrey Smith and David Hoffman, "No Support Found for Report of Lost Russian Suitcase-Sized Nuclear Weapons," *Washington Post,* September 5, 1997, p. 19; CBS, interview with Alexander Lebed, *60 Minutes,* September 8, 1997.

54. Nikolai Kravchenko, "Interviu Mesyatsa: Lish' 25 protsentov punktov propuska na granitse oborudovany spetsial' nymi priborami dlya presecheniya yadernoi Kontrabandy," *Yaderny Kontrol'* (August-September 1996), p. 8.

55. Phil Williams and Paul N. Woessner, *Nuclear Materials Trafficking: An Interim Assessment,* Ridgway Viewpoints, no. 95-3 (Pittsburgh, PA: Ridgway Center for International Security Studies, 1995), p. 17.

56. Interview with Major Jon Rathausky, *PBS Frontline,* "Loose Nukes."

57. "Panic Made in Pullach," *Der Spiegel,* April 10, 1995, pp. 36-57.

58. Interview with Gennadiy Pshakin in Moscow, October 28, 1996.

59. Interview with John Large of Large and Associates in London, February 20, 1997; "Nuclear Officials Allegedly Offered Plutonium Sale to Britain," *The Times* (London), August 18, 1994, p. 1.

60. Akira Oseki, "UK Engineer—An Offer to Sell Him Plutonium," *Asahi Shimbun* (Tokyo), August 20, 1994, p. 27.

61. Igor Korolkov, "Atomic Racket," *Izvestiya,* March 28, 1995, p. 5; Aleksandr Pashkov, "A Case that Is Hard for Even the Court to Get Its Teeth Into: The Case of the Theft of Nuclear Materials from a Super-Secret Nuclear Center," *Izvestiya,* December 23, 1995, p. 5.

62. Interview with Nikolai Kravchenko of the Russian State Customs Committee in Moscow, October 16, 1997. "Mecheniye Izotopy," *Chelyabinskiy Rabochiy,* June 26, 1997, p. 2; Kravchenko interview.

63. Kravchenko, "Interviu Mesyatsa," p.8

64. Alexi Ivanov, "An Overview of the General Structure Regarding Illegal Proliferation of Fissionable Materials from Russia in the Area of National Security." Unpublished manuscript, Russian Academy of Sciences, January 20, 1997, pp. 4-5.

65. Interviews at the Russian Academy of Sciences, December 21, 1996; February 17, 1997; and May 12, 1997. Note that the implied black-market price of weapons-grade HEU is $125,000 to $200,000 per kilogram, according to the scientist's account.

66. "An Overview . . . Regarding Illegal Proliferation," p. 7.

67. For an excellent discussion of this issue, see Jacques Sapir, "State Weakening and Proliferation: The Russian Case." Paper prepared for the Fissile Material Workshop no. 5, Livermore, CA, February 3-4, 1998, pp. 3-4.

68. Monterey Institute of International Studies and Carnegie Endowment for International Peace, *Nuclear Successor States of the Former Soviet Union,* no. 4 (Washington, D.C., May 1996), p. 87; Center for Strategic Leadership, U.S. Army War College, *Report of the Executive Seminar on Nuclear Materials Smuggling* (Carlisle Barracks, PA: U.S. Army War College, September 13, 1996), p. 25.

69. William Potter, "Less Well-Known Cases of Nuclear Terrorism and Nuclear Diversion in the Former Soviet Union," Monterey Institute, Center for Nonproliferation Studies (August 1997), p. 1.

70. Center for Strategic Leadership, "Report of the Executive Seminar"; Oleg Bukharin, "Upgrading Security at Nuclear Power Plants in the Newly Independent States," *The Non-Proliferation Review* 4, no. 2 (Winter 1997), p. 29.

71. Many experts doubt that such weapons can contaminate an area much larger than that affected by the explosion itself. A device that effectively vaporized the radioactive material, however, would have catastrophic effects.

72. Nikolai Bondarev, "Background Report: Incidents in Russia of the Attempts for Illegal Transport of Special Nuclear Material and their Classification for RRC KI" (Moscow: The Kurchatov Institute, November 1994), p. 6. "Expelled Swede Sought to Obtain Nuclear Warhead Components," *Unian* (Kiev), 2005 GMT, April 15, 1994. Joint Publication Research Service, TND-94-010, May 5, 1994, p. 37.

73. Olivia Ward, "Deadly Dose of Radiation Is Murder . . . Russian-Style, Fears on Rise About Nuclear Terrorism," *Toronto Star,* January 25, 1994, p. 1.

CHAPTER 7

1. Russian nuclear scientist Oleg Bukharin observed in a July 1994 paper, "The instrumentation base of safeguards is shrinking and becoming obsolete"; in

the attempt to cut corners production facilities eliminate material-control related positions: see Oleg Bukharin, "U.S.-Russian Cooperation in the Area of Nuclear Safeguards." Paper presented to the meeting of the Export Control, Physical Security, and Safeguards Working Group of the CIS Non-Proliferation Project, Center for Non-Proliferation Studies, Monterey Institute of International Affairs, Minsk, June 9, 1994, p.3.

2. Written testimony of Thomas MacNamara for U.S. Senate Governmental Affairs Committee, *Global Proliferation of Weapons of Mass Destruction, Part II: Hearings before the Permament Subcommittee on Investigations,* 104th Cong., 2nd sess., March 13, 20, and 22, p. 430.

3. Guy R. Roberts, *Five Minutes Past Midnight: The Clear and Present Danger of Nuclear Weapons Grade Fissile Materials,* INSS Occasional Paper 8 (Colorado Springs, CO: USAF Institute for National Security Studies, February 1996), p. 2; Graham Allison, et al., *Avoiding Nuclear Anarchy,* (Cambridge, MA: MIT Press, 1996), p. 12.

4. For a discussion of nuclear deployment decisions and factors affecting them, see William H. Kincaid, *Nuclear Proliferation: Diminishing Threat?* INSS Occasional Paper 6 (Colorado Springs, CO: USAF Institute for National Security Studies, December 1995), pp. ix, x, 21-28.

5. On this point, see "It's Time to Reconsider the Shunning of Iran," *Washington Post,* July 20, 1997, pp. CA, C6.

6. On these points, see Henry Sokolski, "Curbing Proliferation's Legitimization." Paper presented at the Conference on Non-Governmental Security Threats, "The 'Gray Area' Challenge," sponsored by the Standing Committee on the Law and National Security and the Center for National Security Law, Washington, D.C., December 2, 1994, pp. 1-6.

7. Statement of Harold Johnson, "Nuclear Non-Proliferation. U.S. Efforts to Help Newly-Independent States Improve Their Nuclear Material Controls." Written testimony before the U.S. Senate Governmental Affairs Committee, *Global Proliferation of Weapons of Mass Destruction, Part II: Hearings before the Permament Subcommittee on Investigations,* 104th Cong., 2nd sess., March 13, 20, and 22, p.192.

8. National Research Council, *Proliferation Concerns* (Washington, D.C.: National Academy Press, 1997), p. 69.

9. Jessica Stern, "Teaching Nuclear Custodians to Fish." Unpublished mss., September 11, 1996, p. 8.

10. National Research Council, *Proliferation Concerns,* p. 13.

11. Nikolai Filonov, "O Deyatelnosti Gosatomnadzora v Oblasti Yadernoi i Radiyatsionnoi Bezopasnosti' Rossii v 1995 Godu," *Yaderny Kontrol',* no. 20-21 (August-September 1996), p. 31; GAN, *Otchet o Deyatelnosti Federal'nogo Nadzora Rossii po Yadernoi i Radiyatsionnoi Bezopasnost'* (Moscow, 1996), pp. 149-150.

12. Mikhail Kulik, "Guba Andreeva: Another Nuclear Theft Has Been Detected," *Yaderny Kontrol Digest,* no. 1 (Spring 1996), p. 21.

13. Author's estimate of the total cost of this equipment is $750,000 to $1 million. This would be a remarkably cheap and useful investment for the United States. See interview with Russian State Customs Committee in Moscow, October 23, 1996; interviews with delegation of Russian State Customs Committee in Washington, D.C., June 14, 1996.

14. Telephone interview with Rick Galbraith, U.S. Customs, Washington, D.C., October 13, 1999.

15. Non-Proliferation Experts Group, "Programme for Preventing and Combatting Illicit Trafficking in Nuclear Material" (Moscow), May 30, 1996, pp. 1-2.

16. Barry Kellman and David S. Gualtieri, "Barricading the Nuclear Window— A Legal Regime to Control Nuclear Smuggling," *University of Illinois Law Review*, 1996, no. 3 (1996), pp. 719-723; interviews with Interpol officials in Lyon, October 21, 1997. One observable effect of such limitations is to diminish the effectiveness of the International Criminal Police Organization (Interpol), which relies entirely on information that member countries are willing to provide to track illegal nuclear transactions and nuclear supplier networks.

17. See, for example, Phil Williams and Paul Woessner, *Nuclear Material Trafficking: An Interim Assessment*, Ridgway Viewpoints, no. 95-3 (Pittsburgh, PA: Ridgway Center for International Security Studies 1995), p. 17.

18. R. Jeffrey Smith, "CIA to Enlarge Non-Proliferation Center: Low-Level Attempt to Decrease Its Power Prompts Tenet to Beef Up Staff," *Washington Post*, November 14, 1997, p. A15.

19. Allison, et al., *Avoiding Nuclear Anarchy*, pp. 90, 150-151.

20. The International Science and Technology Center, *Annual Report January-December 1996* (Moscow, 1997), p. 6.

21. Allison, et al., *Avoiding Nuclear Anarchy*, p. 91.

22. Other problems mentioned by Russian applicants include a lengthy approval process for ISTC grants (which usually require a Western sponsor) and long delays in receiving funding for approved proposals.

23. Allison et al., *Avoiding Nuclear Anarchy*, p. 151; Holdren, "Reducing the Threat of Nuclear Theft in the Former Soviet Union," *Arms Control Today* (March 1996), pp. 19-20.

24. John C. Baker, "Non-Proliferation Incentives for Emerging Technology Providers in the Newly Independent States," Paper presented at the Conference on Non-Proliferation and Safeguards of Nuclear Materials in Russia, Kurchatov Institute, Moscow, May 17, 1996, p. 4.

25. For example, David Kay agrees by noting "The spread of nuclear power programs provides very legitimate cover for almost all of the purely nuclear technology and training that cannot otherwise be acquired." See David Kay, "Iraq and Beyond: Understanding the Threat of Weapons Proliferation," in: U.S. Senate Governmental Affairs Committee, *Global Proliferation of Weapons of Mass Destruction, Part II: Hearings before the Permanent Subcommittee on Investigations*, 104th Cong., 2nd sess., March 13, 20, and 22, p. 332.

26. Richard Falkenrath, "The HEU Deal," in Allison, et al., *Avoiding Nuclear Anarchy,* p. 235.

EPILOGUE

1. Richard G. Lugar, "Viewpoint: The Threat of Weapons of Mass Destruction: A U.S. Response," *The Non-Proliferation Review* 6, no. 2, Spring-Summer 1999, p. 5.
2. On DOE programs, see General Accounting Office (GAO), *Nuclear Nonproliferation: Concerns with DOE's Efforts to Reduce the Risks Posed by Russia's Unemployed Weapons Scientists* (Washington, DC: GAO, February 1999); and National Research Council, *Protecting Nuclear Weapons Material in Russia* (Washington, DC: National Academy Press, 1999). DOE's program to reemploy displaced weapons scientists is knows as the "Initiatives for Proliferation Prevention." A related initiative, the International Science and Technology Center, funds scientific research for peaceful purposes in the NIS; the State Department oversees the U.S. portion of the Center.
3. Author interview with DOE official, March 25, 1999.
4. Author interview with staff member of the Institute of Physics and Power Engineering, Obninsk, Russia, December 21, 1996.
5. Steve Goldstein, "The Black Market in Weapons Components," *The Philadelphia Inquirer,* January 10, 1999. Nikolai Kravchenko, "Interview of the Month," *Yaderny Kontrol,* August-September 1996, p. 8. More sensitive U.S.-made equipment is only beginning to be deployed at customs posts.
6. *Statement by Director of Central Intelligence George J. Tenet before the Senate Armed Services Committee Hearing on Current and Projected National Security Threats,* Washington, DC: Federal Document Clearing House, February 2, 1999.

Selected Bibliography

BOOKS AND PAMPHLETS

Allison, Graham T., et al. *Avoiding Nuclear Anarchy*. Cambridge, MA: MIT Press, 1996.

Brackett, D. W. *Holy Terror: Armageddon in Tokyo*. New York: Weatherhill, 1996.

Center for Strategic and International Studies. *Global Organized Crime: The New Empire of Evil*. Washington, D.C., 1994.

———. *The Nuclear Black Market*. Task Force Report. Washington, D.C., 1996.

———. *Russian Organized Crime*. Task Force Report. Washington, D.C., 1997.

Clawson, Patrick L., and Rensselaer W. Lee III. *The Andean Cocaine Industry*. New York: St. Martin's Press, 1996.

Cochran, Thomas, et al. *Making the Russian Bomb: From Stalin to Yeltsin*. Boulder, CO: Westview Press, 1995.

Cockburn, Andrew, and Leslie Cockburn. *One Point Safe*. New York: Anchor Books, 1997.

Counterproliferation Program Review Committee. Report on Activities and Programs for Countering Proliferation. Washington, D.C., May 1995.

Fituni, Leonid L. *CIS Organized Crime and Its International Activities*. Wilbad Kreuth, Germany: Russian Academy of Sciences Center for Strategic and Global Studies, 1993.

Ford, James L., and C. Richard Schuller. *Controlling Threats to Nuclear Security: A Holistic Model*. Washington, D.C.: National Defense University Press, June 1997.

Gurov, Aleksandr. *Organozovannoye Prestupnost'-Ne Mif a Realnost'*. Moscow: Znaniye, 1992.

Handelman, Stephen. *Comrade Criminal*. New Haven, CT: Yale University Press, 1995.

Holloway, David. *Stalin and the Bomb*. New Haven, CT: Yale University Press, 1994.

Ignatov, A. N., and Krasikov Yu. *Ugolovniy Kodeks Rossiiskoi Federatsii*. Moscow: Infra M-Norma, 1996.

Institute of National Strategic Studies, National Defense University. *1997 Strategic Assessment.* Washington, D.C.: U.S. Government Printing Office, 1997.

Ispravnikov, V. O., and V. V. Kulikov. *Tenevaya Ekonomika v Rossii: Inoi Put' i Tret'ya Sila.* Moscow: Rossiiskiy Ekonomicheskii Zhurnal. Fond za Ekonomicheskuyu Gramotnost', 1997.

Kincaid, William H. *Nuclear Proliferation: Diminishing Threat?* INSS Occasional Paper 6. Colorado Springs, CO: Institute for National Security Studies, December 1995.

Kokoski, Richard. *Technology and the Proliferation of Nuclear Weapons.* New York: Oxford University Press, 1995.

Kuznetsov, Vladimir M. *"Gosudarstvennaya" Radiyatsiya.* Moscow, 1994.

Larsen, Jeffrey A., and Gregory J. Rattray. *Arms Control: Toward the 21st Century.* Boulder, CO: Lynne Rienner, 1996.

Law Faculty, St. Petersburg State University. *Ugolovniy Kodeks Rossiiskoi Federatsii.* Vol. 1. St. Petersburg: Severo-Zapad, 1994.

Lewis, William E., and Stuart E. Johnson, eds. *Weapons of Mass Destruction: New Perspectives on Counterproliferation.* Washington, D.C.: National Defense University Press, April 1995.

Monterey Institute of International Studies and the Carnegie Endowment for International Peace. *Nuclear Successor States of the Former Soviet Union.* No. 4. Washington, D.C., May 1996.

———. *Nuclear Successor States of the Former Soviet Union.* No. 1. Washington, D.C., May 1994.

Monterey Institute of International Studies and the Center for Non-Proliferation Studies (CNS). *Inventory of International Non-Proliferation Organizations and Regimes.* 1996-1997 edition. Monterey, CA, May 1997.

National Research Council. *Proliferation Concerns.* Washington, D.C.: National Academy Press, 1997.

Nilsen, Thomas, and Nils Bohmer. *Sources to Radioactive Contamination in Murmansk and Arkhangelsk Counties.* Bellona Report, vol. 1. Oslo: The Bellona Foundation, 1994.

Ovchinnikov, V. S., et al. *Osnovy Bor'by s Organizovannoi Prestupnostyu.* Moscow: Infra-m, 1996.

Roberts, Guy R. *Five Minutes Past Midnight: The Clear and Present Danger of Nuclear Weapons Grade Fissile Materials.* INSS Occasional Paper 8. Colorado Springs, CO: USAF Institute for National Security Studies, February 1996.

Spector, Leonard S., et al. *Tracking Nuclear Proliferation: A Guide in Maps and Charts, 1995.* Washington, D.C.: Carnegie Endowment for International Peace, 1995.

Sterling, Claire. *Thieves' World: The Threat of the New Global Network of Organized Crime.* New York: Simon and Schuster, 1994.

Turbiville, Graham. *Weapons Proliferation and Organized Crime: The Russian Security Force Dimensions.* INSS Occasional Paper 10. Colorado Springs, CO: USAF Institute for National Security Studies, June 1996.

United States Department of Energy. *Nuclear Terms Handbook 1993.* Washington, D.C., 1993.

———. *Nuclear Terms Handbook 1996.* Washington, D.C., 1996.

Williams, Phil, and Paul N. Woessner. *Nuclear Material Trafficking: An Interim Assessment.* Ridgway Viewpoints, no. 95-3. Pittsburgh: Ridgway Center for International Security Studies, 1995.

Williams, Phil, et al. *Organized Crime: The New Threat.* London: Frank Cass, 1997.

Zhitenev, V. B., ed. *Mafiya v Yekaterinburge.* Yekaterinburg: Yekaterinburg Institute of Social Research and Technology, 1990.

GOVERNMENT DOCUMENTS

Center for Strategic Leadership, U.S. Army War College. *Report of the Executive Seminar on Special Materials Smuggling.* Carlisle Barracks, PA: U.S. Army War College, September 13, 1996.

Goldman, Stuart, et al. "Russian Nuclear Reactor and Conventional Arms Transfers to Iran." Washington, D.C.: Congressional Research Service, Report for Congress, May 23, 1995.

Gosatomnadzor. *Otchet o Deyatel'nosti Federal'nogo Nadzora Rossii po Yadernoi Bezopasnosti.* Moscow, 1996.

House Republican Research Committee, Task Force on Terrorism and Unconventional Warfare. *The New Nuclear Smuggling System.* Washington, D.C., June 7, 1993.

International Atomic Energy Agency. "Measures Against Illicit Trafficking in Nuclear Material and Other Radioactive Sources." Report by the Director General to the General Conference. Vienna, Austria, August 20, 1996.

———. "Second Quarter 1997—Summary Listing of Illicit Trafficking Incidents." Vienna, Austria, May 12, 1997.

The International Science and Technology Center. *Annual Report January-December 1996.* Moscow, 1997.

Kan, Shirley A. "China's Compliance with International Arms Control Agreements." Washington, D.C., Congressional Research Service Report to Congress, September 16, 1997.

Katzman, Kenneth. "Iran: Arms and Technology Acquisition." Washington, D.C.: Congressional Research Service Report to Congress, October 31, 1997.

Kurchatov Institute. *Godovoi Otchet 1995*. Moscow, 1995.

————. *Proceedings of International Conference on Non-Proliferation and Safeguards of Nuclear Materials in Russia*. Moscow: Nuclear Society of Russia, May 14-17, 1996.

Mayak Proizvodstennoye Ob'yedineniye. *45 Let*. Yekaterinburg: Ural'skiy Rabochiy, June 12, 1993.

Ministerio dell'Ambiente Nucleo Operativo Ecologico dei Carabinieri. *Attivita Operativa*. January 1-December 31, 1995. Rome, 1996.

Ministerstvo Vnutrennykh Del. *Itogi Operativno-Sluzhebnoi Deyatel'nosti Organov Vnutrennykh Del i Sluzhebno-Boevoi Deyatel'nosti Vnutrennykh Voisk MVD Rossiiskoi Federatsii v 1996 godu*. Moscow, 1997.

————. *Itogi Operativno-Sluzhebnoi Deyatel'nosti Organov Vnutrennykh Del i Sluzhebno-Boevoi Deyatel'nosti Vnutrennykh Voisk MVD Rossii v 1995 godu*. Moscow, 1996.

————. "Press-Relis. Khishcheniye Radioaktivnykh Materialov. Realnost' i Domysly." Moscow, October 10, 1995.

Moscow Nuclear Safety and Security Summit. Moscow: International Life, 1996.

New York State Organized Crime Task Force, et al., *An Analysis of Russian Emigre Crime in the Tri-State Region*. New Brunswick, NJ: Rutgers State University, June 1996.

President of the United States. *Comprehensive Readiness Program for Countering Proliferation of Weapons of Mass Destruction*. 15th Congress, 1st Session. House Document 105-79. Washington, D.C.: U.S. Government Printing Office, 1997.

Sterlinski, Slawomir, and Tadeusz Hodys. "Polish Prevention System Against Illicit Trafficking of Radioactive Substances and Nuclear Materials." Warsaw, Central Laboratory for Radiological Protection and Border Movement Control. Department of the Border Guard Headquarters, 1997.

United States Agency for International Development. "Monitoring Country Progress in Central and Eastern Europe and the Newly Independent States." Washington, D.C., September 1997.

United States Department of Energy. *Isotope Production and Distribution*. Washington, D.C., April 1992.

————. *MPC&A Program Strategic Plan*. Washington, D.C., January 1998.

————. *Partnership for Nuclear Material Security*. Washington, D.C., January 1997.

————. *United States/Former Soviet Union.* Progress of Cooperation in Nuclear Materials Protection. Control and Accounting. Washington, D.C., December 1996.

United States Department of State. *International Narcotics Control Strategy Report.* Washington, D.C., March 1997.

United States General Accounting Office. *Nuclear Non-Proliferation: Status of U.S. Efforts to Improve Nuclear Material Control in Newly Independent States.* Washington, D.C., March 1991.

U.S. Senate Committee on Governmental Affairs. *Global Proliferation of Weapons of Mass Destruction: Hearings before the Permanent Subcommittee on Investigations, Part II.* 104th Cong., 2nd sess., March 13, 20, and 22, 1996.

Willrich, Mason, and Theodore B. Taylor. *Nuclear Theft: Risks and Safeguards.* Cambridge, MA: Ballinger, 1974.

ARTICLES, REPORTS, AND TESTIMONY

Bertsch, Gary. "Prepared Statement." In Permanent Subcommittee on Investigations, U.S. Senate Committee on Governmental Affairs. *Hearings on Global Proliferation of Weapons of Mass Destruction.* Part II. Washington, D.C.: U.S. Government Printing Office, 1996, pp. 253-269. (Hereafter cited as *Hearings on Global Proliferation.*)

Baker, John. "Non-Proliferation Incentives for Emerging Technology Providers in the Newly Independent States." Paper presented at the Conference on Non-Proliferation and Safeguards of Nuclear Materials in Russia. Kurchatov Institute, Moscow, May 17, 1996.

Belyaninov, Kirill. "Nuclear Nonsense, Black-Market Bombs, and Fissile Flim-Flam." *Bulletin of the Atomic Scientists* 50, no. 2 (March-April 1994), pp. 34-50.

Bondarev, Nikolai. "Background Report: Incidents in Russia of the Attempts for Illegal Transport of Special Nuclear Material and Their Classification for RRC KI." Moscow: The Kurchatov Institute, November 1994.

Bukharin, Oleg. "Upgrading Security at Nuclear Power Plants in the Newly Independent States." *Non-Proliferation Review* 4, no. 2 (Winter 1997), pp. 28-40.

————. "U.S.-Russian Cooperation in the Area of Nuclear Safeguards." Paper presented to the meeting of the Export Control, Physical Security, and Safeguards Working Group of the CIS Non-Proliferation Project. Center for Non-Proliferation Studies. Monterey Institute of International Studies, Minsk, June 9-10, 1994.

Bukharin, Oleg, and William Potter. "Potatoes Were Guarded Better." *Bulletin of the Atomic Scientists* 51, no. 3 (May-June 1995), pp. 46-50.

Cherepanov, Nikolai. "The Lack of Control Over Radioactive Materials at Customs." *Yaderny Kontrol Digest,* no. 4 (Spring-Summer 1994), pp. 13-14.

Cochran, Thomas. "Safeguarding Nuclear Weapons-Usable Material in Russia." Paper presented at International Forum, "Illegal Nuclear Traffic: Risks, Safeguards, and Countermeasures." Como, Italy, June 13-14, 1997.

Dunn, Guy. "Major Mafia Gangs in Russia." *Transnational Organized Crime* 2, nos. 2-3 (Summer-Autumn 1996), pp. 63-80.

Ewell, Emily. "Trip Report. Uzbekistan, Kazakhstan, Ukraine." Monterey Institute of International Studies, Center for Nonproliferation Studies (May 1996).

Filonov, Nikolai. "O Deyatel'nosti Gosatomnadzora v Oblasti Yadernoi i Radiatsionnoi Bezopasnosti Rossii v 1995 godu." *Yaderny Kontrol',* nos. 20-21 (August-September 1996), pp. 31-34.

Ford, James. "Nuclear Smuggling: How Serious a Threat?" Strategic Forum, no. 59. Washington, D.C.: National Defense University, January 1996, pp. 1-4.

Gere, François. "In Search of a Missing Link. Nuclear Terrorism and Nuclear Smuggling." Como, Italy: Centro A. Volta, April 13-14, 1994.

Hersh, Seymour M. "The Wild East." *The Atlantic Monthly* 273, no. 6 (June 1994), pp. 61-89.

Hibbs, Mark. "Plutonium, Politics, and Panic." *Bulletin of the Atomic Scientists* 50, no. 6 (November-December 1994), pp. 24-31.

Holdren, John. "Reducing the Threat of Nuclear Theft in the Former Soviet Union." *Arms Control Today,* no. 3 (March 1996), pp. 14-20.

Hunter, Tom, "Russia's Mafiyas: The New Revolution." *James Intelligence Review* 9, no. 6 (June 1, 1997), p. 247.

Kay, David. "Iraq and Beyond: Understanding the Threat of Weapons Proliferation," in *Hearings on Global Proliferation,* pp. 324-332.

Kellman, Barry, and David S. Gualtieri. "Barricading the Nuclear Window—A Legal Regime to Curtail Nuclear Smuggling." *University of Illinois Law Review* 1996, no. 3 (1996), pp. 667-741.

Koch, Andrew, and Jeanette Wolf. "Iran's Nuclear Procurement Program: How Close the Bomb?" *Non-Proliferation Review* 4, no. 1 (Fall 1997), pp. 123-135.

Kravchenko, Nikolai. "Interviu Mesyatsa: Lish 25 Protsentov Punktov Propuska na Granitse Oborudovany Spetsialnymi Priborini dlya Presecheniya Yadernoi Kontrabandy." *Yaderny Kontrol',* nos. 20-21 (August-September 1996), p. 8-10.

Kroemer, Peter. "The Threat of Nuclear Crime." *International Criminal Police Review,* nos. 458-459 (1996), pp. 7-11.

Kulik, Mikhail. "Guba Andreeva. Another Nuclear Theft Has Been Detected." *Yaderny Kontrol Digest,* no. 1 (Spring 1996), pp. 16-21.

———. "Nekotoriye Problemy Khraneniya Yadernykh Materialov na Severnom Flotye," *Yaderny Kontrol',* no. 2 (February 1996), pp. 12-15.

Lee, Rensselaer W. "Drugs in Communist States and Former Communist States." *Transnational Organized Crime* 1, no. 2 (Summer 1995), pp. 193-205.

———. "Post-Soviet Nuclear Trafficking: Myths, Half-Truths, and the Reality." *Current History* (October 1995), pp. 343-348.

———. "Smuggling Update." *Bulletin of the Atomic Scientists* 53, no. 3 (May-June 1997), pp. 52-56.

Lorraine, Pierre. "Mafias Russes: Ebauche d'une Typologie." *Politiques Etrangere* 61, no. 4 (Winter 1996-1997), pp. 813-821.

Maslin, Yevgeniy. "Interviu Mesyatsa: Poka Chto Ni Odin Yaderny Boyepripas v Rossii ne Propodal i ne Byl Pokhishchen." *Yaderny Kontrol',* no. 5 (May 1995), pp. 9-14.

———. "Nuclear Security: The Defense Ministry's Viewpoint." *Yaderny Kontrol Digest,* no. 1 (Spring 1996), pp. 2-3.

Mikhailov, Viktor. "Demontazh Odnogo Yadernogo Boyezaryad Obkhoditsya Rossii v 10-15 Tysych Dollarov." *Yaderny Kontrol',* no. 17, May 1996, pp. 2-5.

———. "Interviu Mesyatsa: Uchet i Kontrol Yadernykh Materialov: Vzglyad Glavy Minatoma." *Yaderny Kontrol',* no. 2, February 1995, pp. 9-11.

———. "Interviu Mesyatsa: V Oblasti Ucheta, Kontrolya i Fizzashchity My Prikhodili k Toi Skheme Kotoraya Effektivno Rabotale u Soyuzke." *Yaderny Kontrol',* no. 28 (April 1997) pp. 14-17.

———. "Nuclear Trade: Special Agencies Were Both Buyers and Sellers." *Yaderny Kontrol Digest,* no. 4, Summer 1997, pp. 2-5.

Morris, Jim. "Loose Cannon on Target." *Soldier of Fortune,* no. 3 (March 1995), pp. 32-35, 69.

Orlov, Vladimir. "Accounting, Control, and Physical Protection of Fissile Materials and Nuclear Weapons in the Russian Federation: Current Situation and Main Concerns." Paper presented at the International Seminar on MPC&A in Russia and NIS, Bonn, April 7-8, 1997.

———. "Moscow Nuclear Safety and Security Summit: Summing Up the Results." *Yaderny Kontrol Digest,* no. 2, Summer 1996, pp. 1-8.

———. "The Temptation to Export." *Yaderny Kontrol Digest,* no. 3 (Winter 1996-1997), p. 1.

Parish, Scott. "Are Suitcase Nukes on the Loose? The Story Behind the Controversy." Monterey Institute of International Studies, Center for Non-Proliferation Studies, November 1997.

Potter, William C. "Less Well-Known Cases of Nuclear Terrorism and Nuclear Diversions in the Former Soviet Union." Monterey Institute, Center for Nonproliferation Studies, August 1997.

———. "Nuclear Exports from the Former Soviet Union: What's New, What's True." *Arms Control Today* (January-February 1993), pp. 3-10.

———."Nuclear Leakage from the Post-Soviet States." Written testimony prepared for the U.S. Senate Permanent Subcommittee on Investigations, Committee on Governmental Affairs, *Global Proliferation of Weapons of Mass Destruction,* Part II, March 13, 20, and 22, 1996 (Washington, D.C.: U.S. Government Printing Office, 1996.

———. "The Post-Soviet Nuclear Proliferation Challenge." Paper presented for the Aspen Strategy Group meeting. Aspen, Colorado, August 10-15, 1996.

———. "The Post-Soviet Nuclear Proliferation Challenge." Testimony prepared for the hearing on Proliferation: Russian Case Studies, U.S. Senate Governmental Affairs Subcommittee on International Security Proliferation and Federal Service. Washington, D.C., June 5, 1997.

Sapir, Jacques. "State Weakening and Proliferation: The Russian Case." Paper prepared for the Fissile Material Workshop no. 5, Livermore CA, February 3-4, 1998.

Schaper, Annette. "Nuclear Smuggling in Europe—Real Dangers and Enigmatic Deception." Paper presented at the forum "Illegal Nuclear Traffic: Risks, Safeguards, and Countermeasures," Como, Italy, June 11-13, 1997.

Shelley, Louise. "The Criminal Political Nexus: Russian-Ukranian Case Studies." Paper prepared for "Confronting the Security Challenge of the Political-Criminal Nexus." Sponsored by the National Strategy Information Center, Georgetown University, Washington, D.C., October 30-31, 1997.

Sokolski, Henry. "Curbing Proliferation's Legitimation." Paper presented at the Conference on Non-Governmental Security Threats: "The 'Grey Area' Challenge," sponsored by the American Bar Association Standing Committee on Law and National Security and the Center for National Security Law, Washington, D.C., December 2, 1994.

Spector, Leonard S. "Consequences of China's Military Sales to Iran." Testimony before the Committee on International Relations, U.S. House of Representatives, September 12, 1996.

Stern, Jessica E. "Teaching Nuclear Custodians to Fish." Unpublished mss., September 11, 1996.

————. "U.S. Assistance Programs for Improving MPC&A in the Former Soviet Union." *Non-Proliferation Review* 3, no. 1 (Winter 1996), pp. 17-32.

Weglarazyk, Bortosz. "Atomic Smuggling cont'd: Nuclear Materials from Russia." *World Press Review* 43, no. 1 (January 1996).

Williams, Phil, and Paul Woessner. "The Real Threat of Nuclear Smuggling." *Scientific American* 274, no. 1 (January 1996), pp. 40-44.

Zabludoff, Sidney. "Colombian Narcotics Organizations as Business Enterprises." U.S. State Department and Central Intelligence Agency Conference Report. *Economics of the Narcotics Industry,* Washington, D.C., November 21-22, 1994.

Zimmerman, Tim, and Cooperman, Alan, "The Russian Connection." *U.S. News and World Report* 119, no. 16, (October 23, 1995), pp. 56-67.

Index

(italicized page numbers indicate figure/table)